AFTERWORKS

for
Dan
Lee

robert kondo

kevin o'brien

louis gonzales

simon dunsdon

nathan stanton

sanjay patel

max brace

cover by
jay shuster

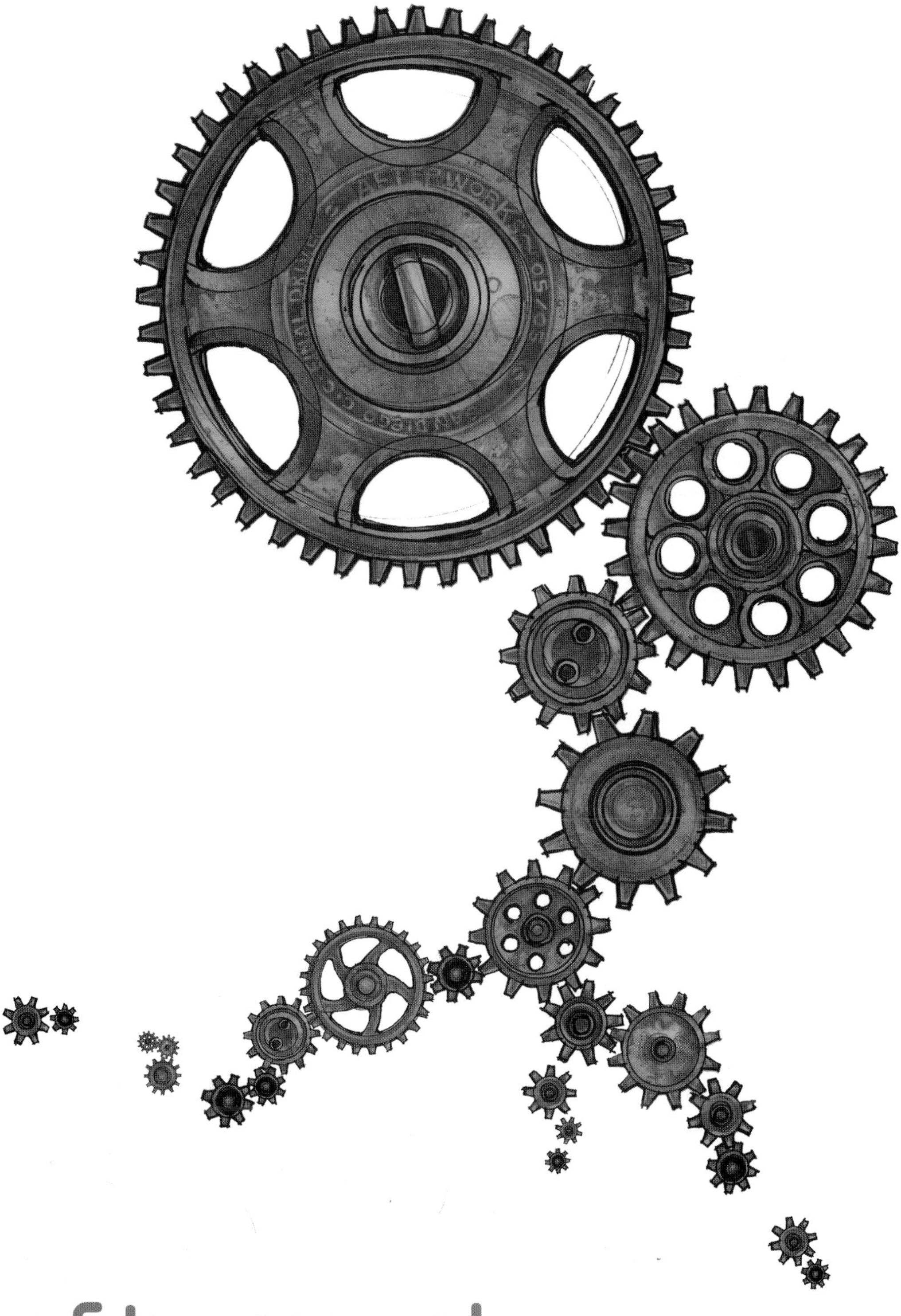

afterworks

AFTERWORKS, vol 1. 2006. Published by Image Comics, Inc., Office of publication: 1942
University Avenue, Suite 305, Berkeley, California 94704. Copyright © 2006 E-Ville Press. All
rights reserved. AFTERWORKS and all characters contained herein copyright 2006 respective
artists. Image Comics® is a trademark of Image Comics, Inc. All rights reserved. No part of
this publication may be reproduced or transmitted, in any form or by any means (except for
short excerpts for review purposes) without the express written permission of Image Comics,
Inc. All names, characters, events and locales in this publication are entirely fictional. Any
resemblance to actual persons (living or dead), events or places, without satiric intent, is
coincidental. PRINTED IN CANADA.

robert kondo

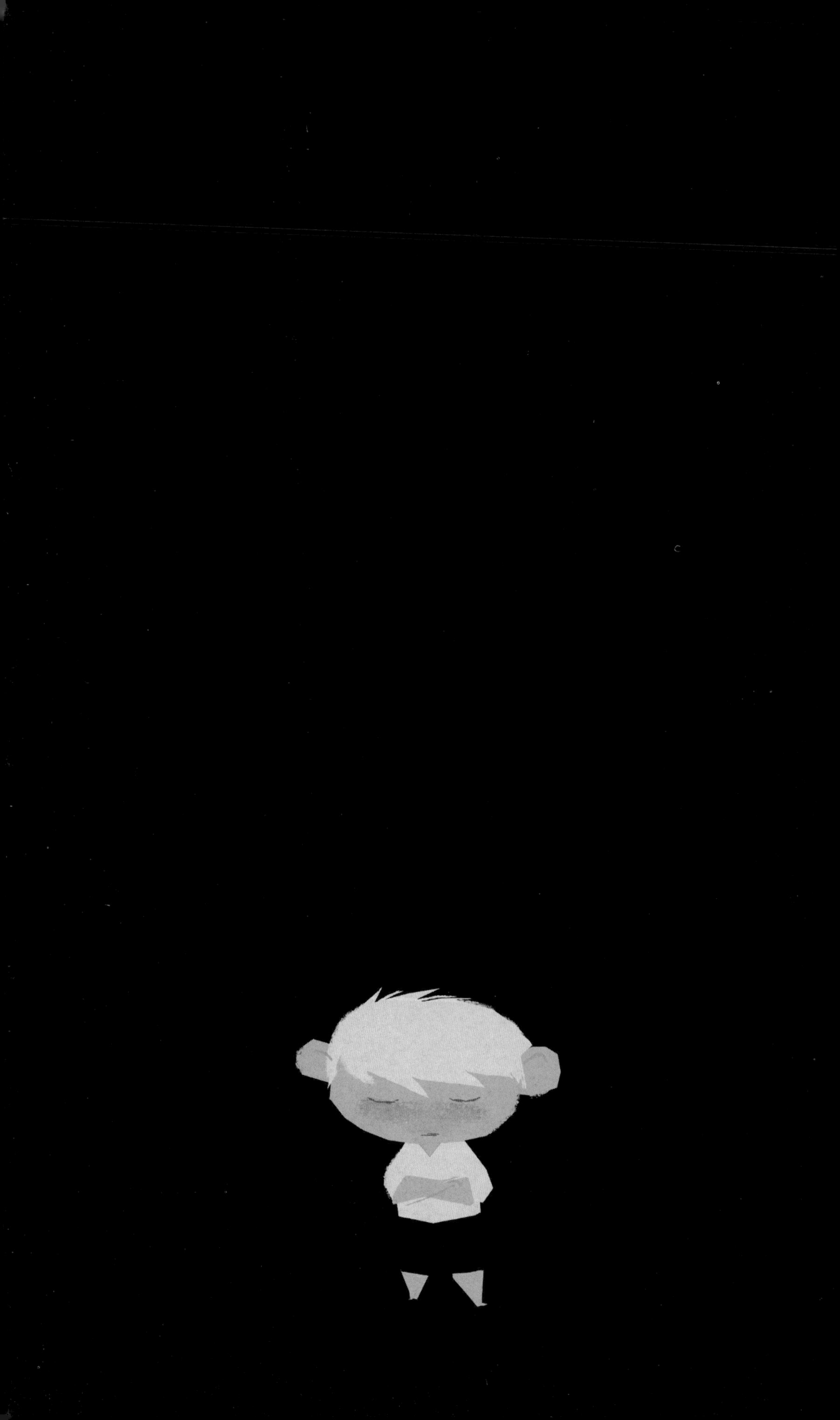

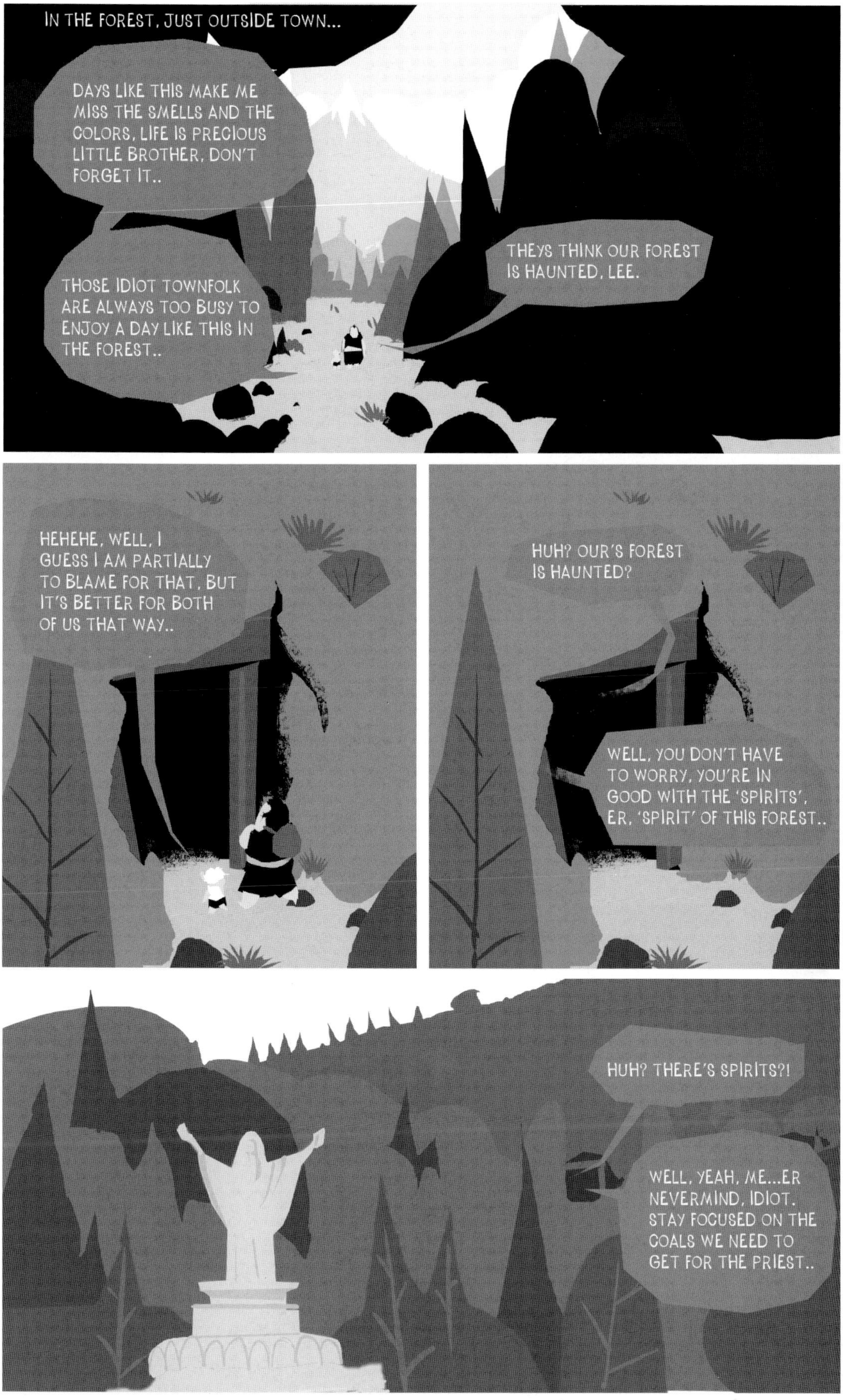
IN THE FOREST, JUST OUTSIDE TOWN...
DAYS LIKE THIS MAKE ME MISS THE SMELLS AND THE COLORS, LIFE IS PRECIOUS LITTLE BROTHER, DON'T FORGET IT..
THOSE IDIOT TOWNFOLK ARE ALWAYS TOO BUSY TO ENJOY A DAY LIKE THIS IN THE FOREST..
THEYS THINK OUR FOREST IS HAUNTED, LEE.
HEHEHE, WELL, I GUESS I AM PARTIALLY TO BLAME FOR THAT, BUT IT'S BETTER FOR BOTH OF US THAT WAY..
HUH? OUR'S FOREST IS HAUNTED?
WELL, YOU DON'T HAVE TO WORRY, YOU'RE IN GOOD WITH THE 'SPIRITS', ER, 'SPIRIT' OF THIS FOREST..
HUH? THERE'S SPIRITS?!
WELL, YEAH, ME...ER NEVERMIND, IDIOT. STAY FOCUSED ON THE COALS WE NEED TO GET FOR THE PRIEST..

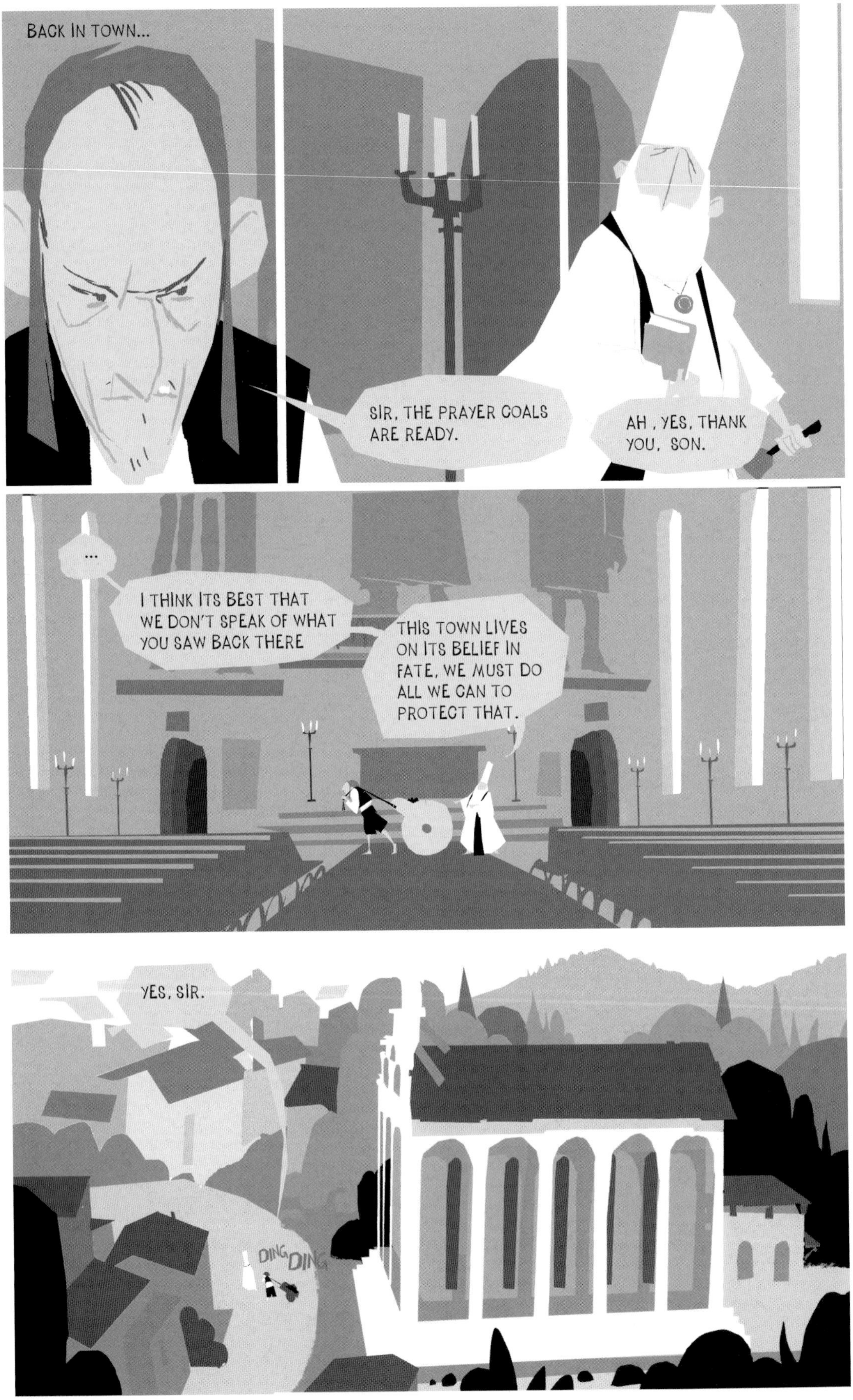
BACK IN TOWN...
SIR, THE PRAYER COALS ARE READY.
AH , YES, THANK YOU, SON.
...
I THINK ITS BEST THAT WE DON'T SPEAK OF WHAT YOU SAW BACK THERE
THIS TOWN LIVES ON ITS BELIEF IN FATE, WE MUST DO ALL WE CAN TO PROTECT THAT.
YES, SIR.
DING DING

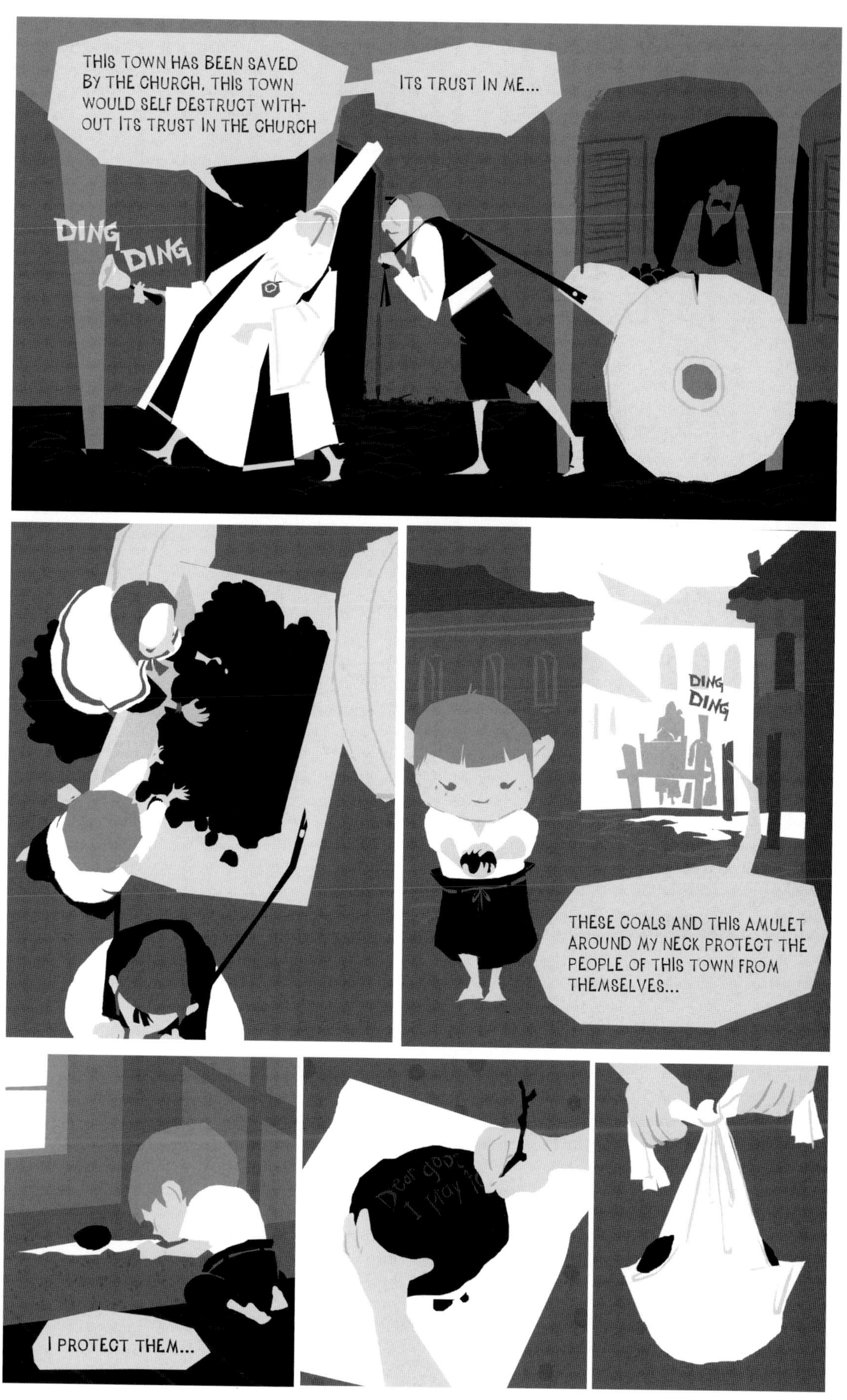
THIS TOWN HAS BEEN SAVED BY THE CHURCH, THIS TOWN WOULD SELF DESTRUCT WITH-OUT ITS TRUST IN THE CHURCH
ITS TRUST IN ME...
DING DING
DING DING
THESE COALS AND THIS AMULET AROUND MY NECK PROTECT THE PEOPLE OF THIS TOWN FROM THEMSELVES...
I PROTECT THEM...

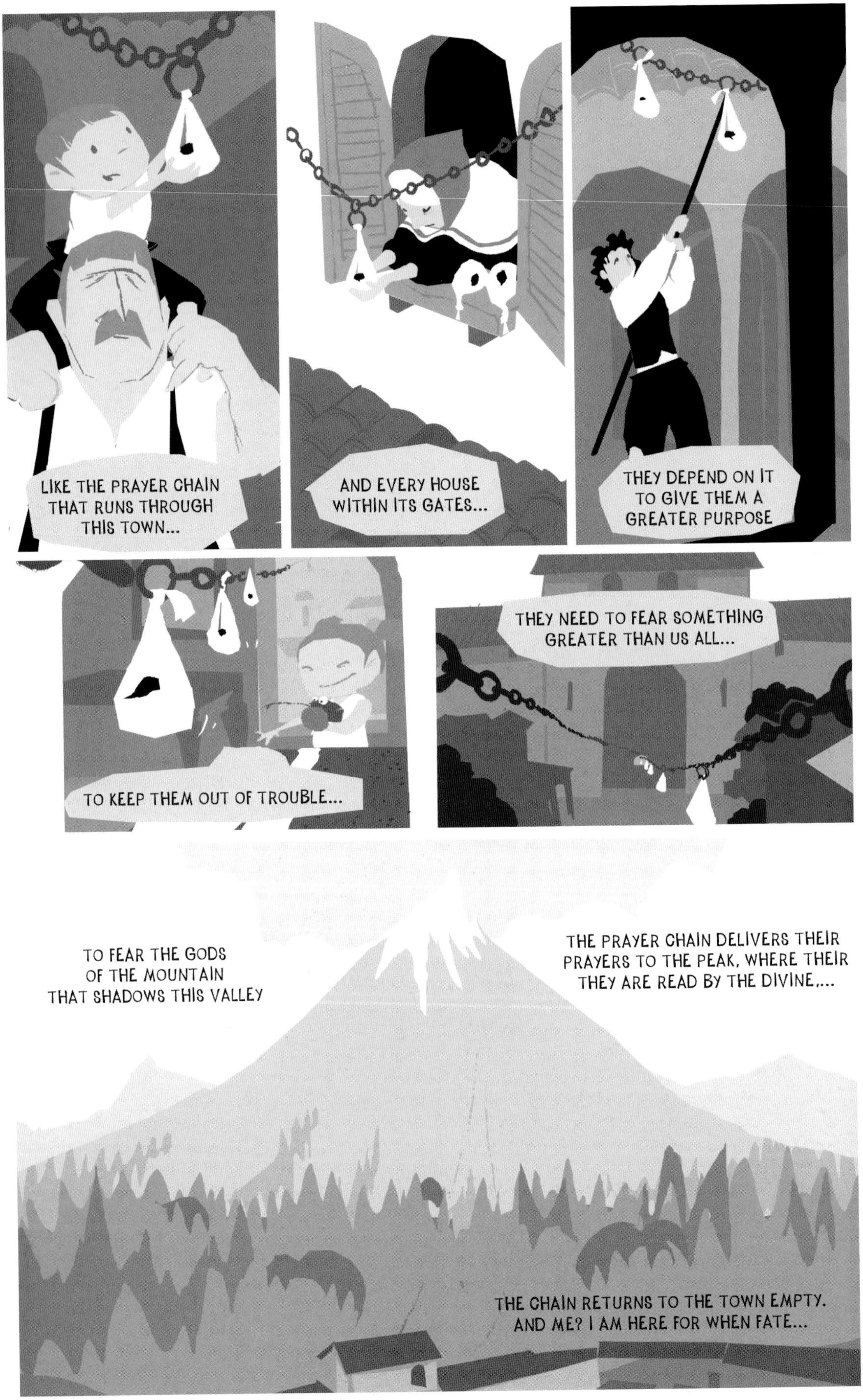
LIKE THE PRAYER CHAIN THAT RUNS THROUGH THIS TOWN...
AND EVERY HOUSE WITHIN ITS GATES...
THEY DEPEND ON IT TO GIVE THEM A GREATER PURPOSE
TO KEEP THEM OUT OF TROUBLE...
THEY NEED TO FEAR SOMETHING GREATER THAN US ALL...
TO FEAR THE GODS OF THE MOUNTAIN THAT SHADOWS THIS VALLEY
THE PRAYER CHAIN DELIVERS THEIR PRAYERS TO THE PEAK, WHERE THEIR THEY ARE READ BY THE DIVINE,...
THE CHAIN RETURNS TO THE TOWN EMPTY. AND ME? I AM HERE FOR WHEN FATE...

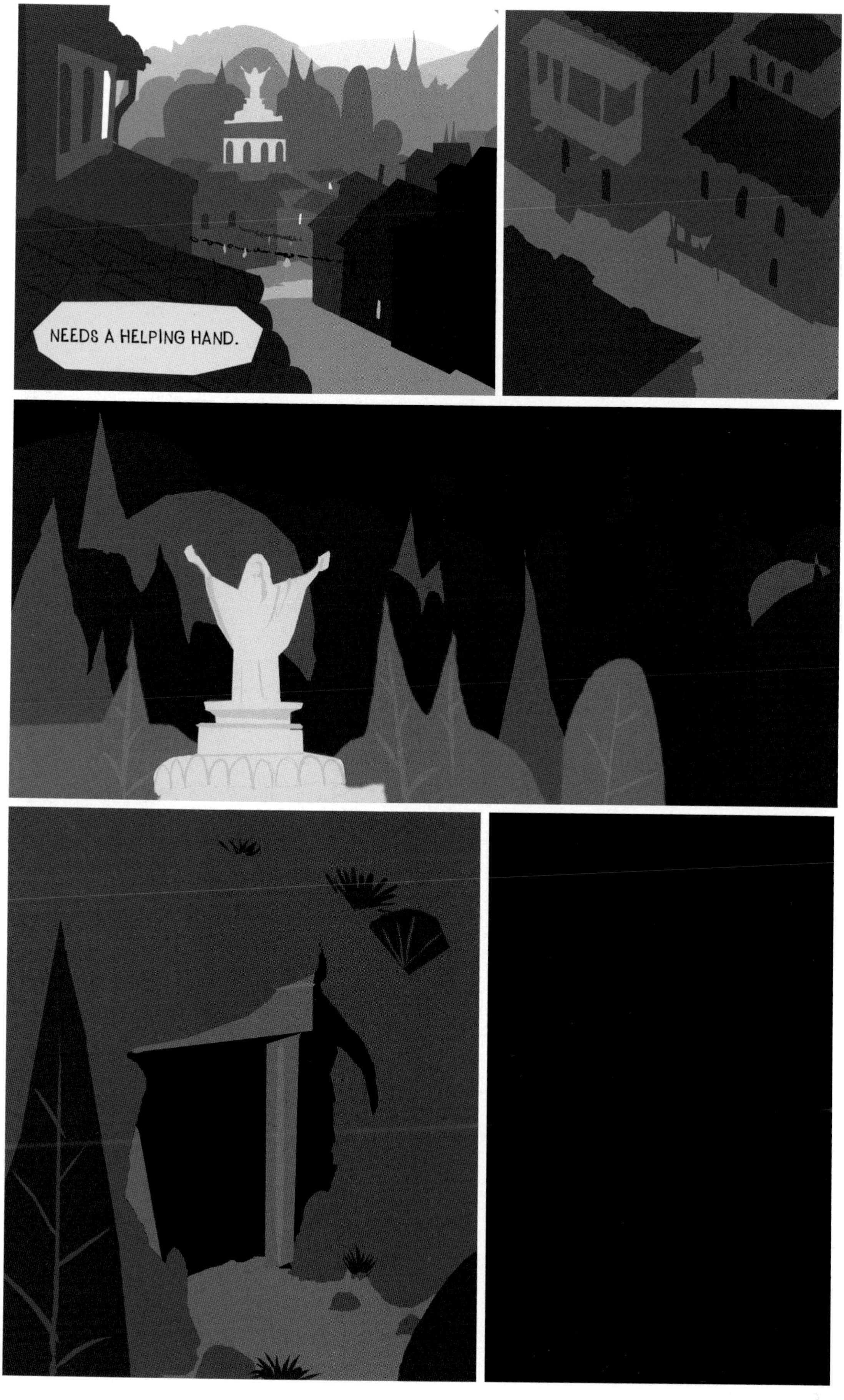
NEEDS A HELPING HAND.

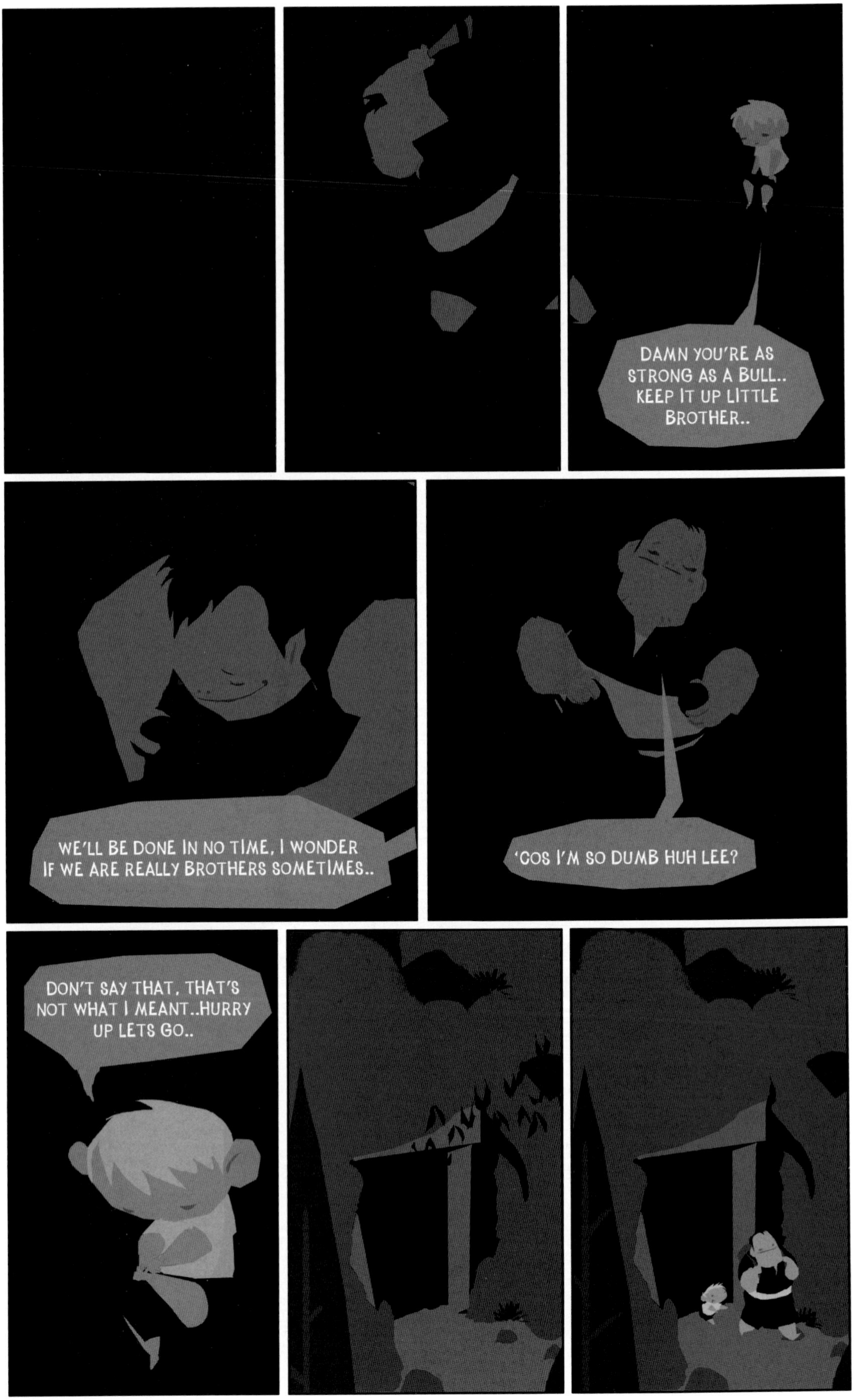
DAMN YOU'RE AS STRONG AS A BULL.. KEEP IT UP LITTLE BROTHER..
WE'LL BE DONE IN NO TIME. I WONDER IF WE ARE REALLY BROTHERS SOMETIMES..
'COS I'M SO DUMB HUH LEE?
DON'T SAY THAT. THAT'S NOT WHAT I MEANT..HURRY UP LETS GO..

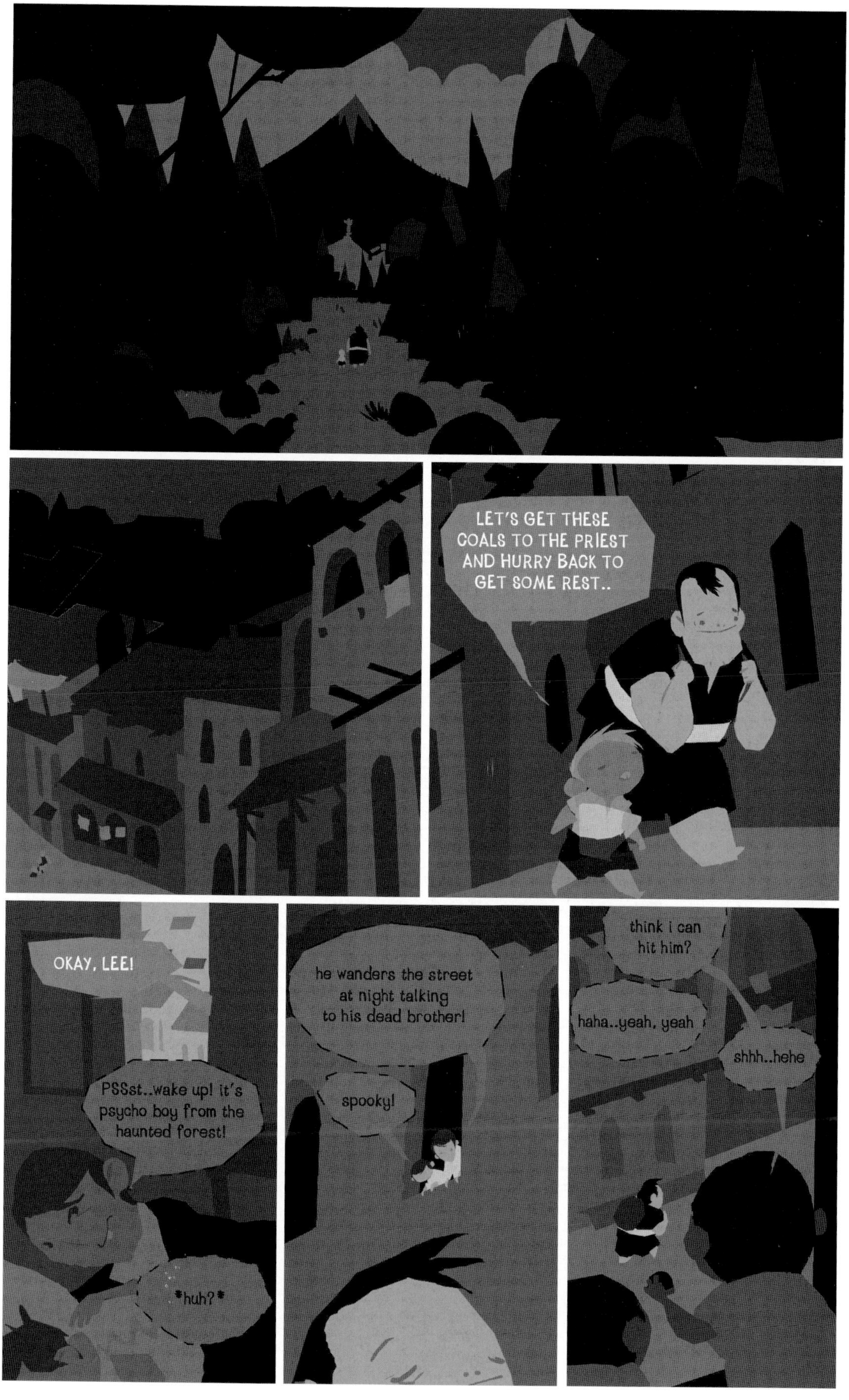
LET'S GET THESE COALS TO THE PRIEST AND HURRY BACK TO GET SOME REST..
OKAY, LEE!
PSSst..wake up! it's psycho boy from the haunted forest!
huh?
he wanders the street at night talking to his dead brother!
spooky!
think i can hit him?
haha..yeah, yeah
shhh..hehe

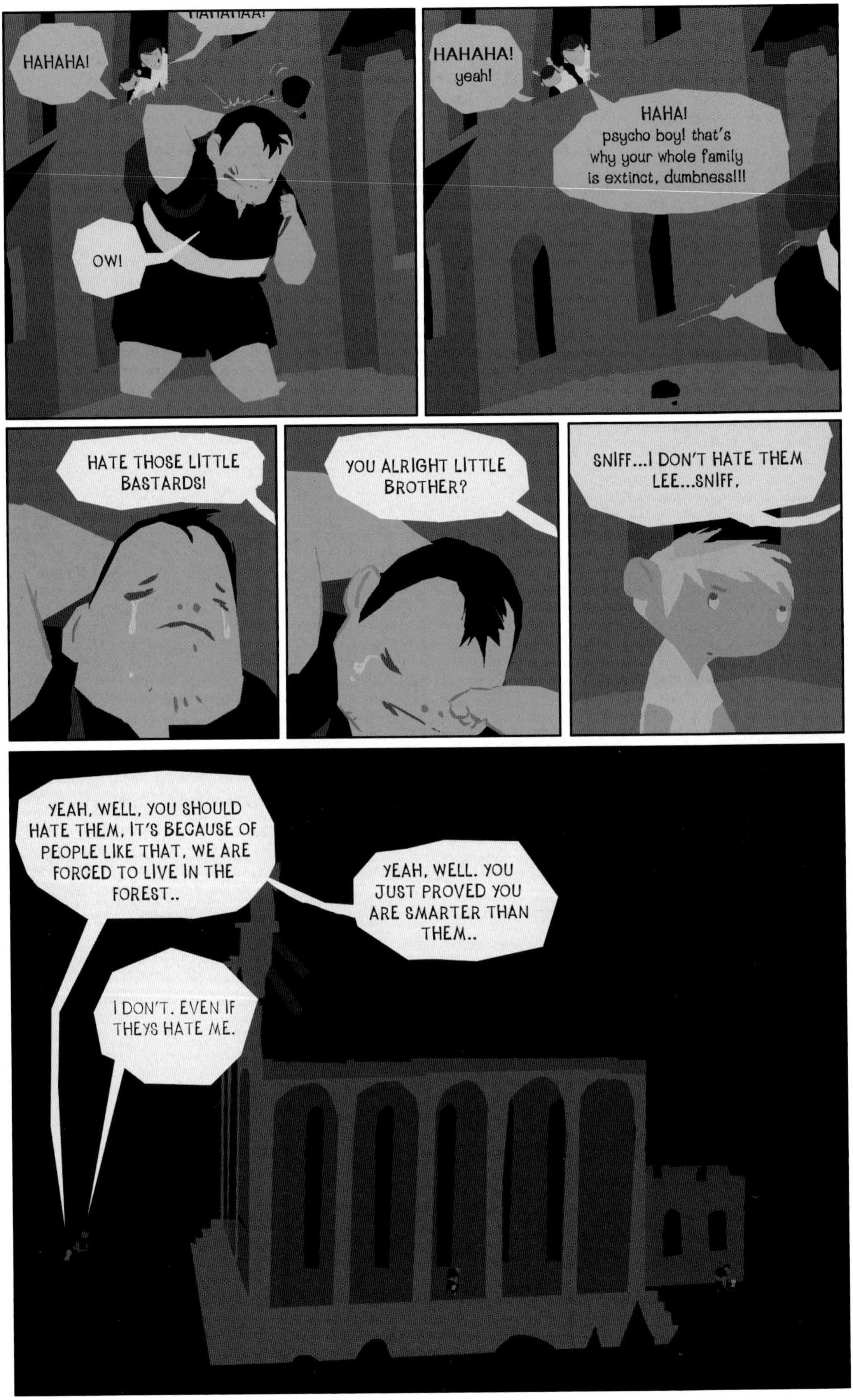
HAHAHA!
HAHAHAA!
OW!
HAHAHA! yeah!
HAHA! psycho boy! that's why your whole family is extinct, dumbness!!!
HATE THOSE LITTLE BASTARDS!
YOU ALRIGHT LITTLE BROTHER?
SNIFF...I DON'T HATE THEM LEE...SNIFF.
YEAH, WELL, YOU SHOULD HATE THEM, IT'S BECAUSE OF PEOPLE LIKE THAT, WE ARE FORCED TO LIVE IN THE FOREST..
I DON'T. EVEN IF THEYS HATE ME.
YEAH, WELL. YOU JUST PROVED YOU ARE SMARTER THAN THEM..

DAMN ASSISTANT,
I'LL HAVE TO TAKE CARE
OF HIM IF HE SAYS ANYTHING...

IF THE TOWN KNEW
THE AMULET WAS FIXED
THERE WOULD BE CHAOS!

KNOCK!
KNOCK!
KNOCK!
KNOCK!

KNOCK!
KNOCK!
KNOCK!
KNOCK!

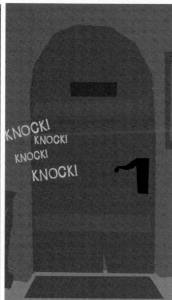

KNOCK!
KNOCK!
KNOCK!
KNOCK!

WE'RE HERE,
MR. PRIEST!

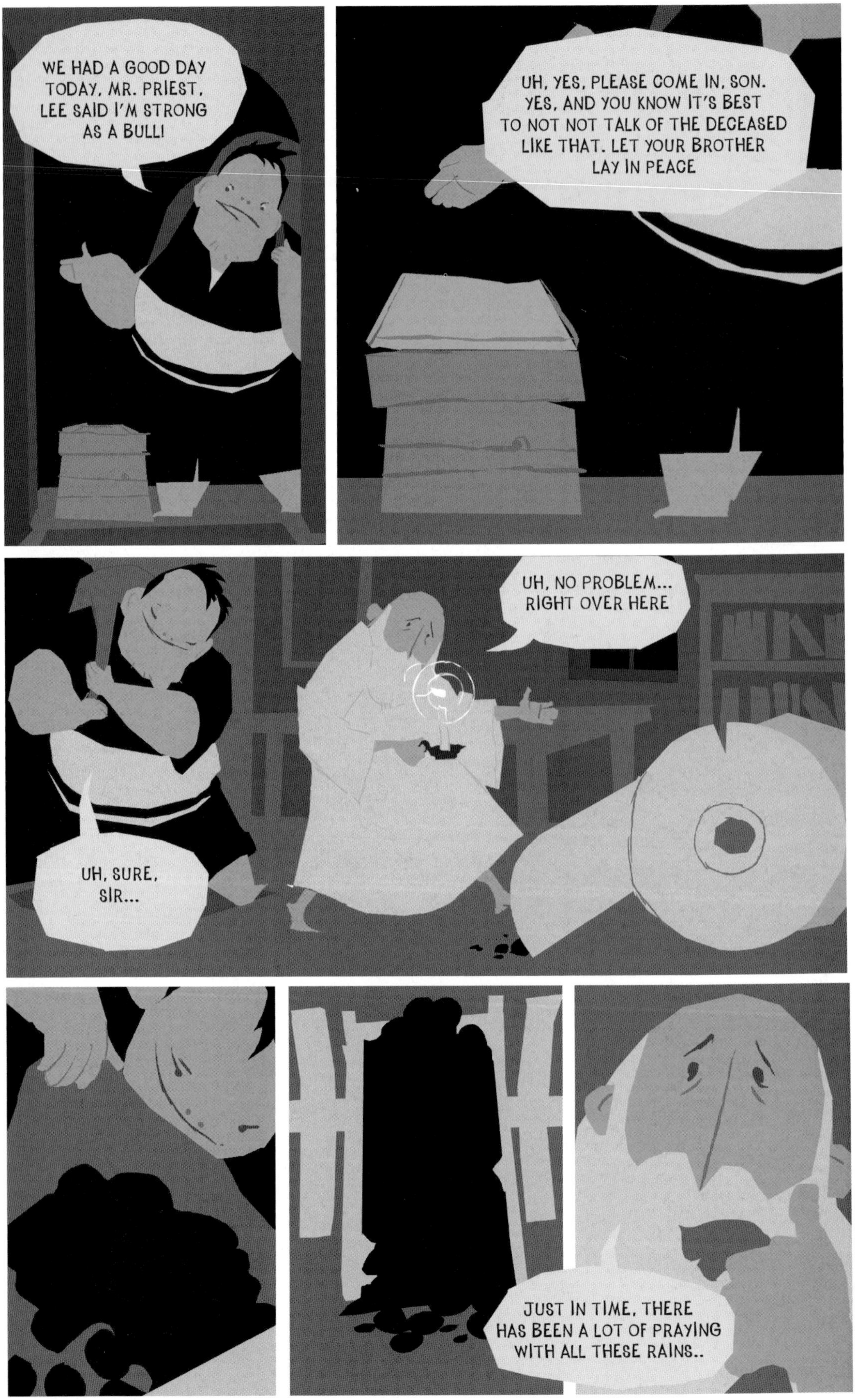
WE HAD A GOOD DAY TODAY, MR. PRIEST, LEE SAID I'M STRONG AS A BULL!
UH, YES, PLEASE COME IN, SON. YES, AND YOU KNOW IT'S BEST TO NOT NOT TALK OF THE DECEASED LIKE THAT. LET YOUR BROTHER LAY IN PEACE
UH, SURE, SIR...
UH, NO PROBLEM... RIGHT OVER HERE
JUST IN TIME, THERE HAS BEEN A LOT OF PRAYING WITH ALL THESE RAINS..

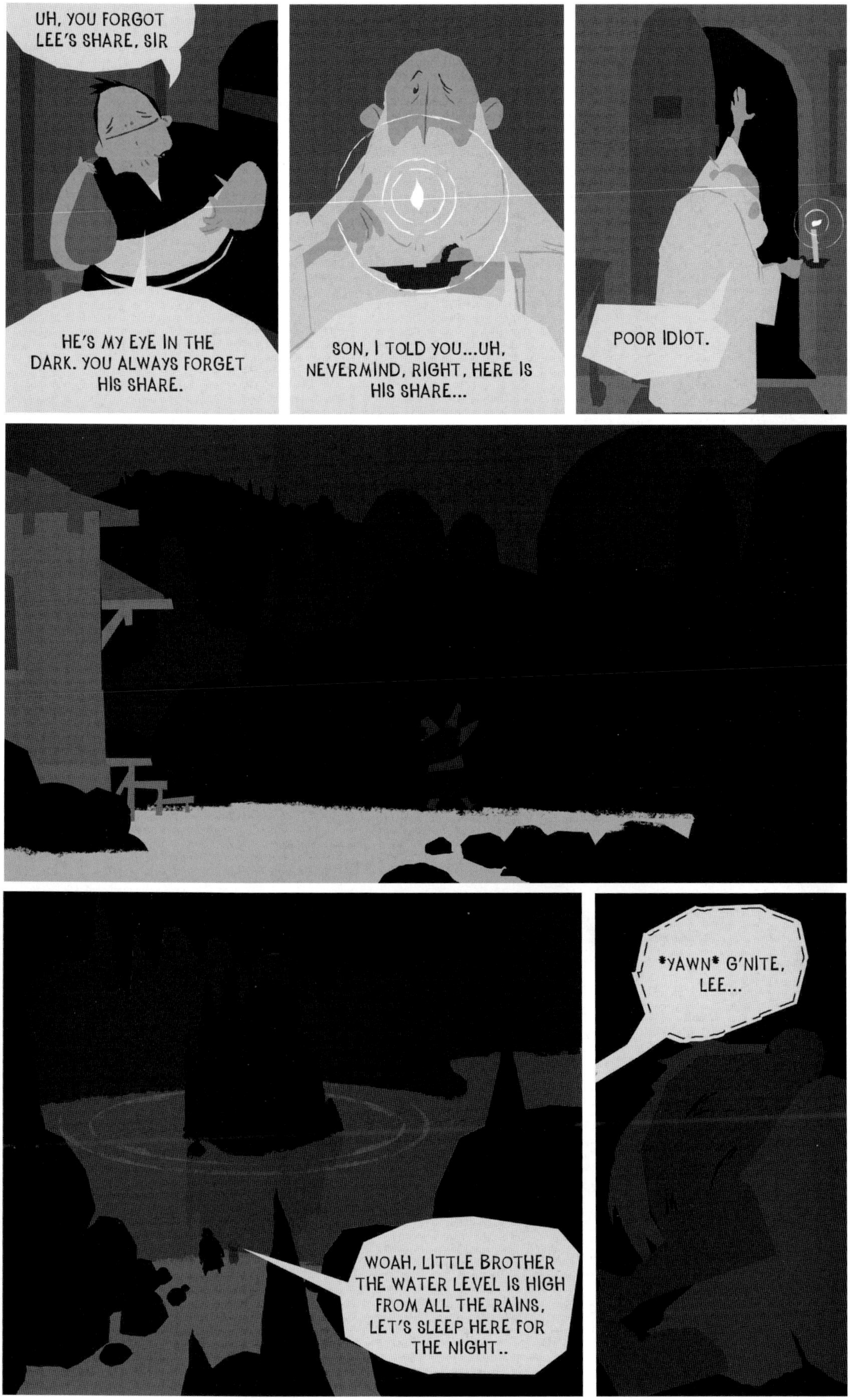
UH, YOU FORGOT LEE'S SHARE, SIR
HE'S MY EYE IN THE DARK. YOU ALWAYS FORGET HIS SHARE.
SON, I TOLD YOU...UH, NEVERMIND, RIGHT, HERE IS HIS SHARE...
POOR IDIOT.
WOAH, LITTLE BROTHER THE WATER LEVEL IS HIGH FROM ALL THE RAINS, LET'S SLEEP HERE FOR THE NIGHT..
YAWN G'NITE, LEE...

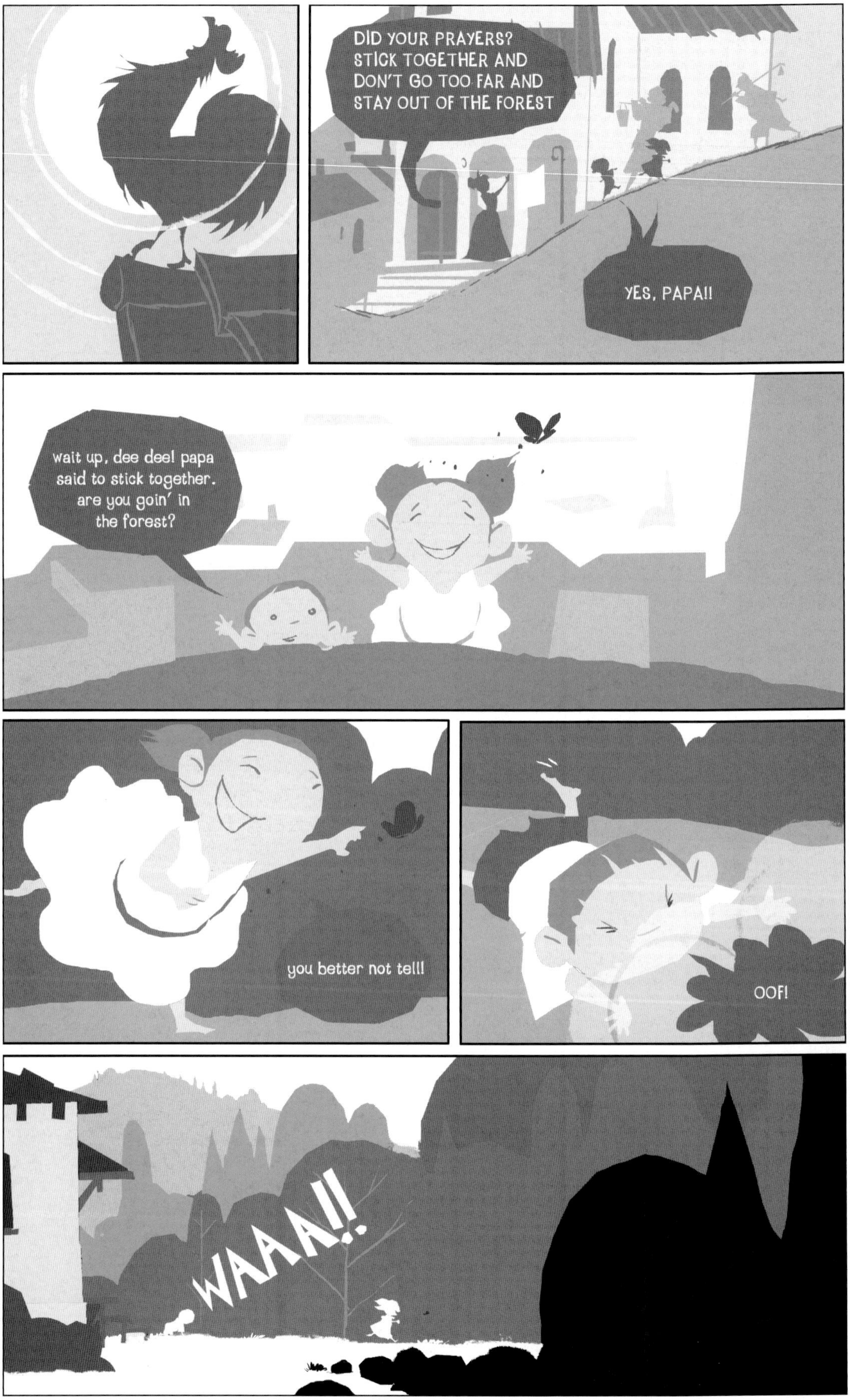

DID YOUR PRAYERS? STICK TOGETHER AND DON'T GO TOO FAR AND STAY OUT OF THE FOREST
YES, PAPA!!
wait up, dee dee! papa said to stick together. are you goin' in the forest?
you better not tell!
OOF!
WAAA!!

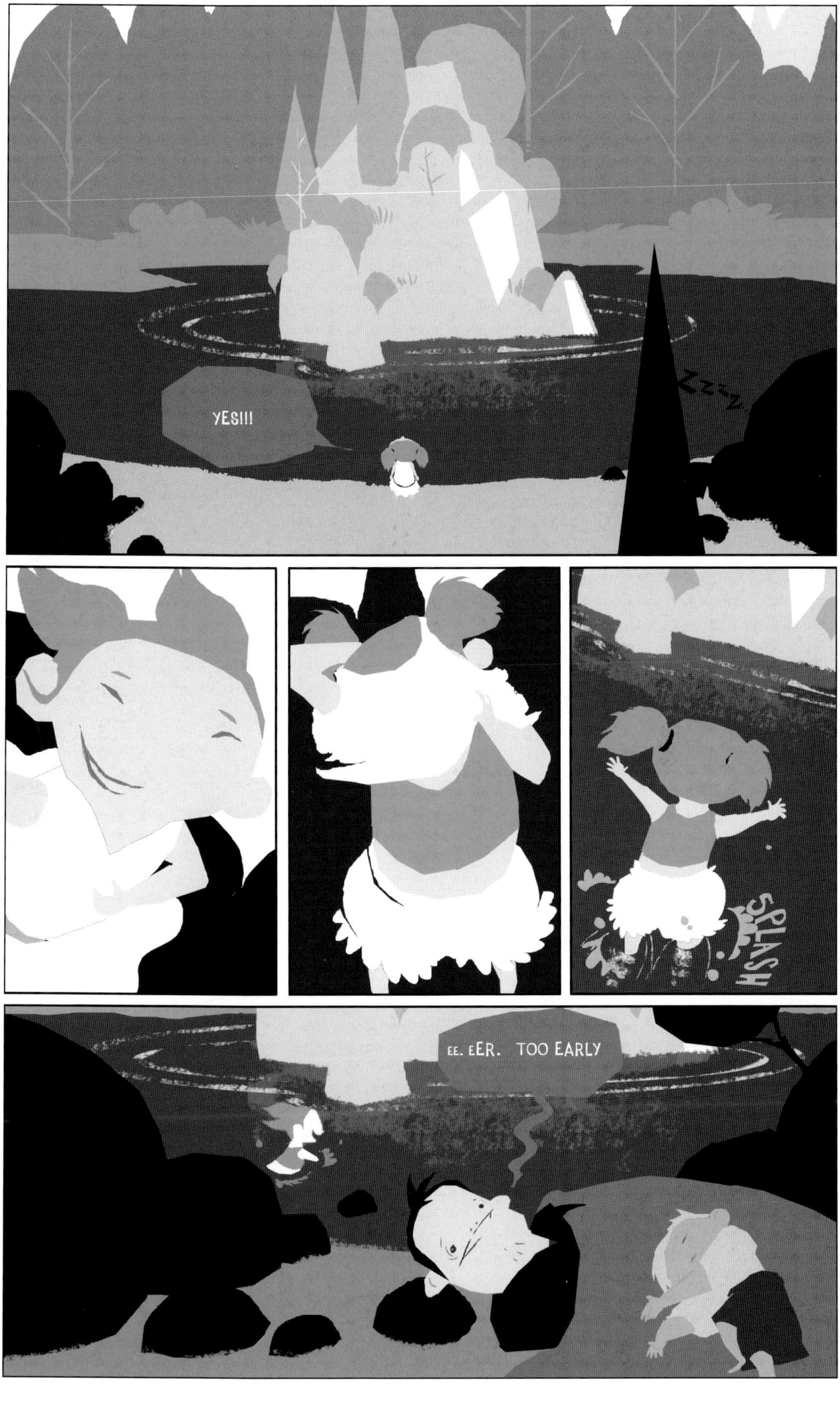
YES!!!
Zzzz
SPLASH
EE. EER. TOO EARLY

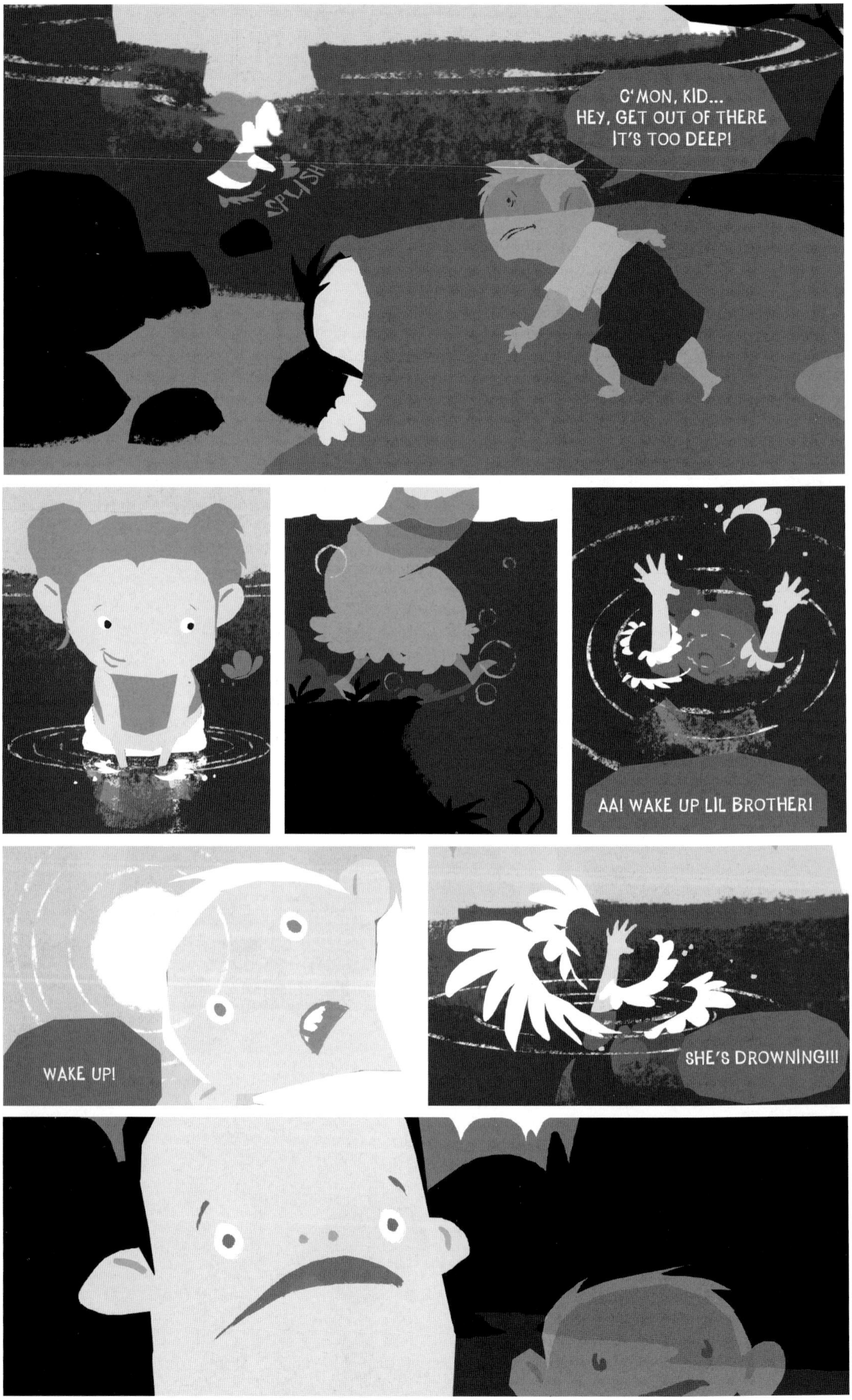
C'MON, KID...
HEY, GET OUT OF THERE
IT'S TOO DEEP!
SPLISH
AA! WAKE UP LIL BROTHER!
WAKE UP!
SHE'S DROWNING!!!

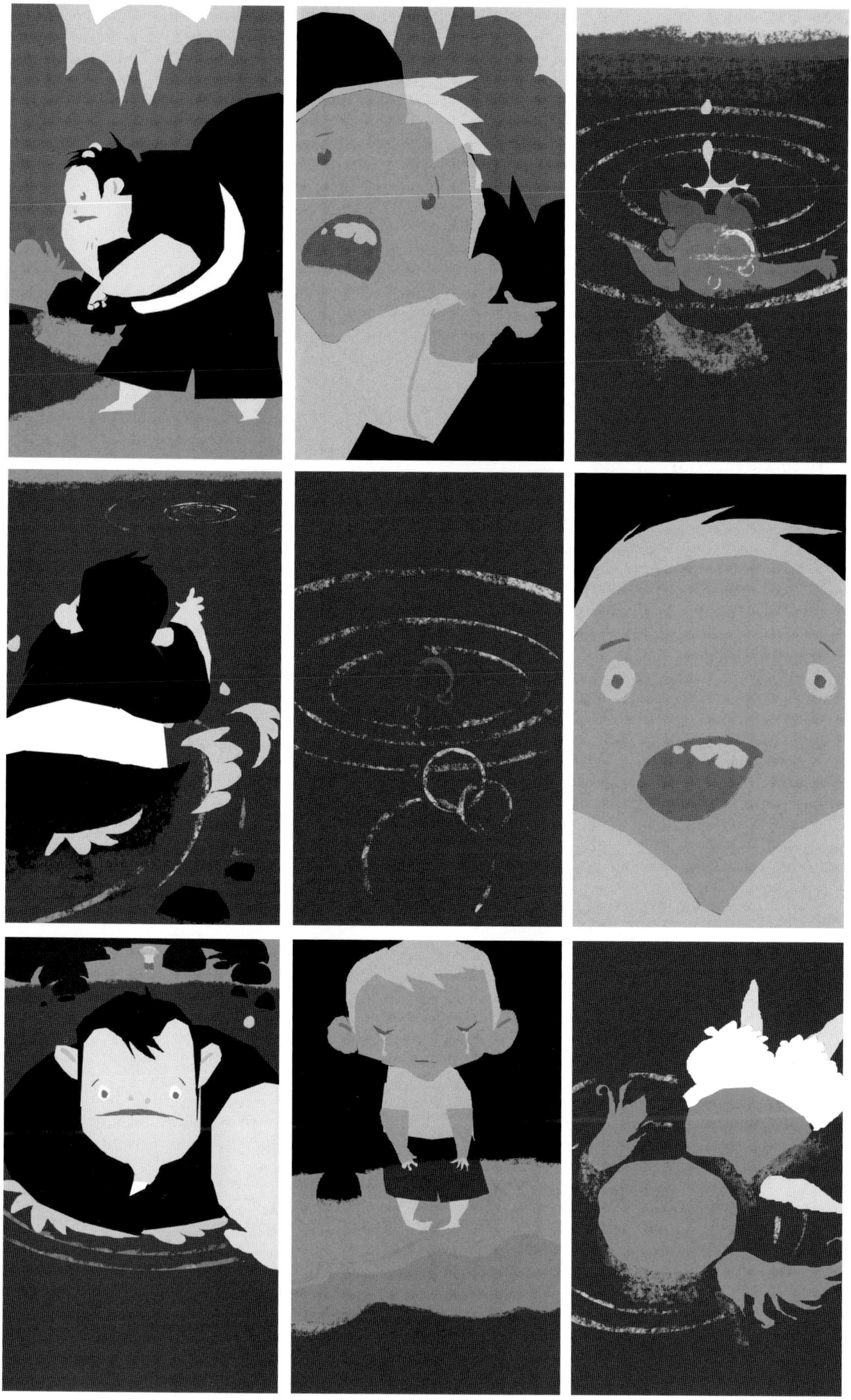

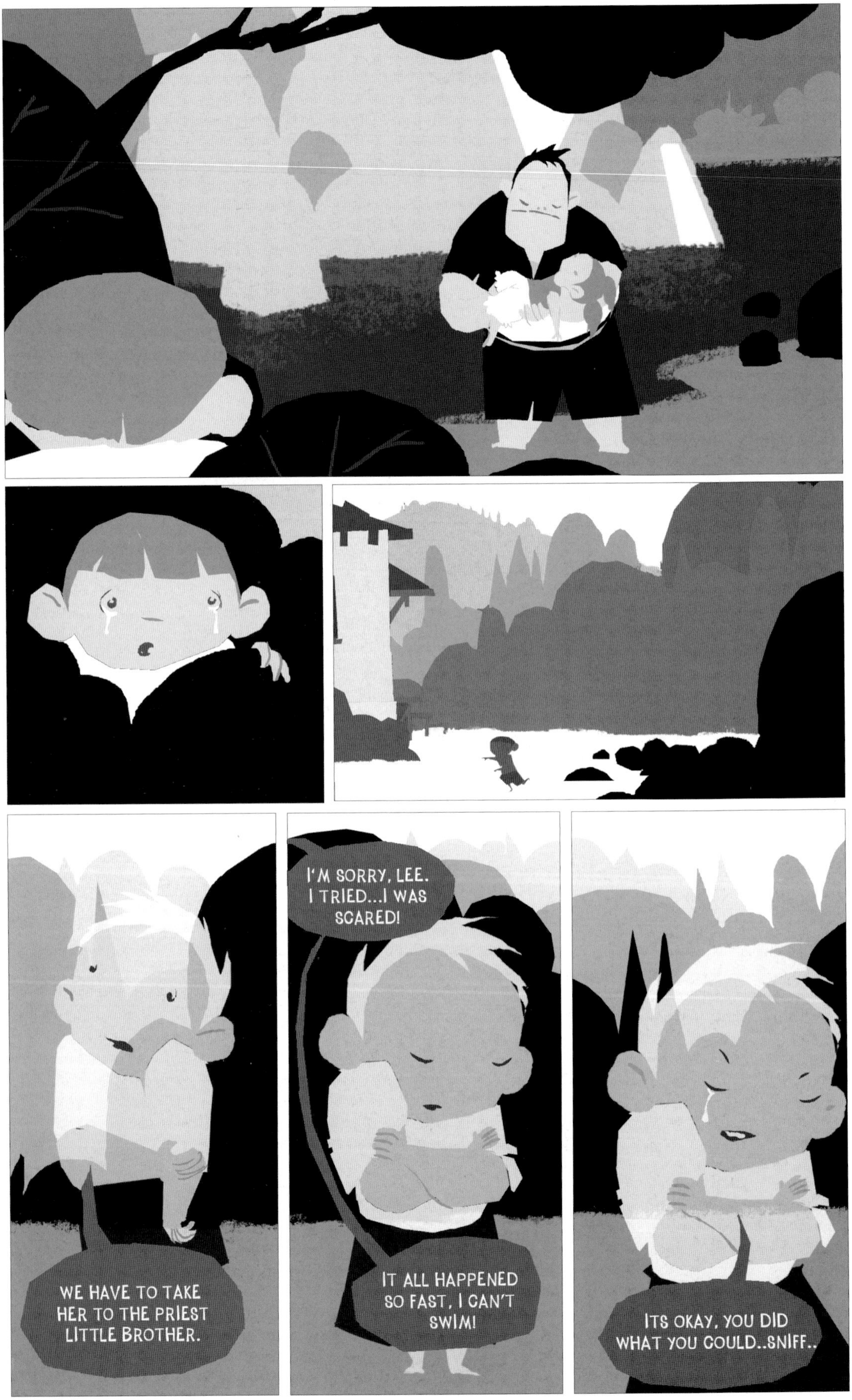
WE HAVE TO TAKE HER TO THE PRIEST LITTLE BROTHER.
I'M SORRY, LEE. I TRIED...I WAS SCARED!
IT ALL HAPPENED SO FAST, I CAN'T SWIM!
ITS OKAY, YOU DID WHAT YOU COULD..SNIFF..

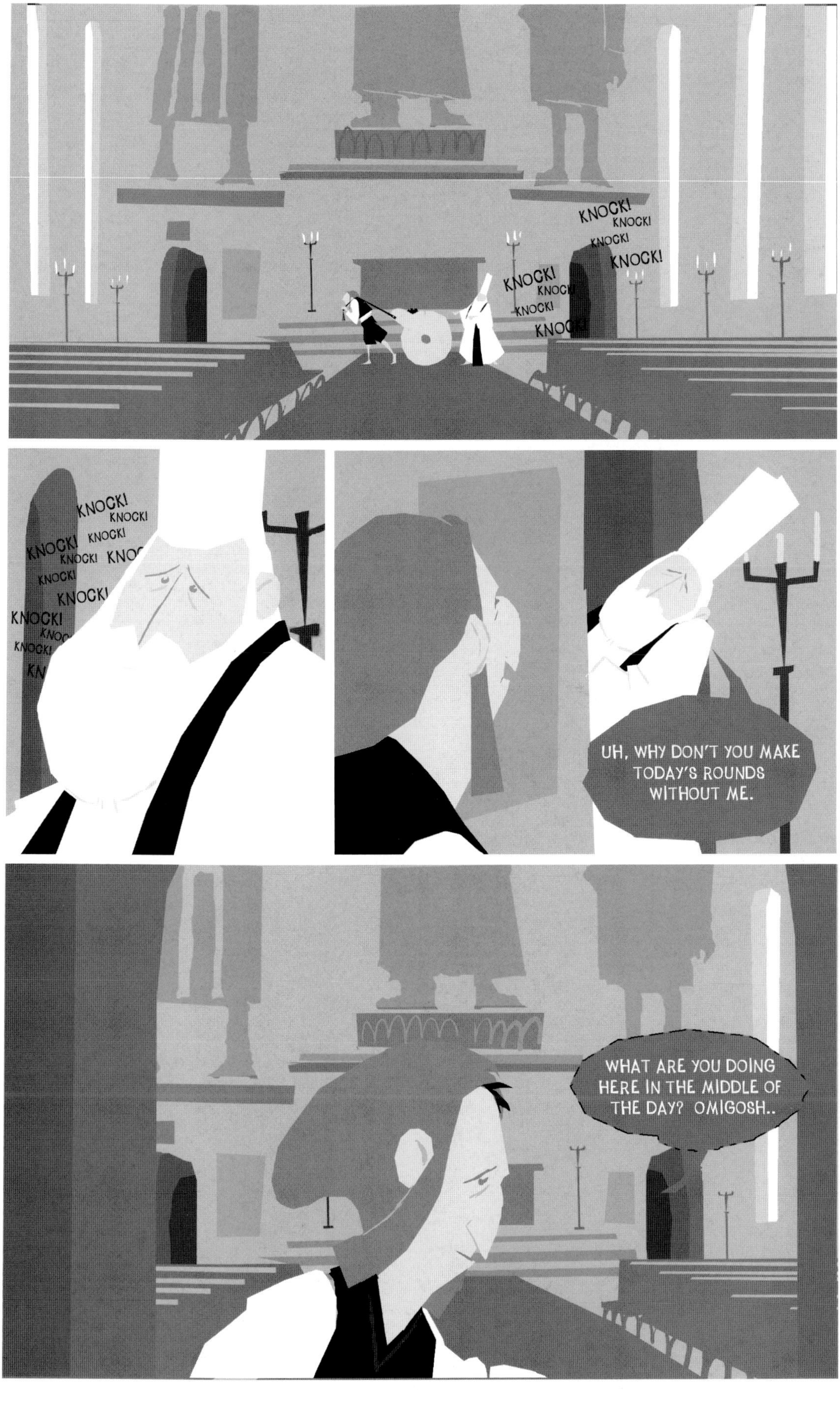

KNOCK! KNOCK! KNOCK! KNOCK!
KNOCK! KNOCK! KNOCK! KNOCK!
KNOCK! KNOCK! KNOCK! KNOCK! KNOCK! KNOCK! KNOCK!
UH, WHY DON'T YOU MAKE TODAY'S ROUNDS WITHOUT ME.
WHAT ARE YOU DOING HERE IN THE MIDDLE OF THE DAY? OMIGOSH..

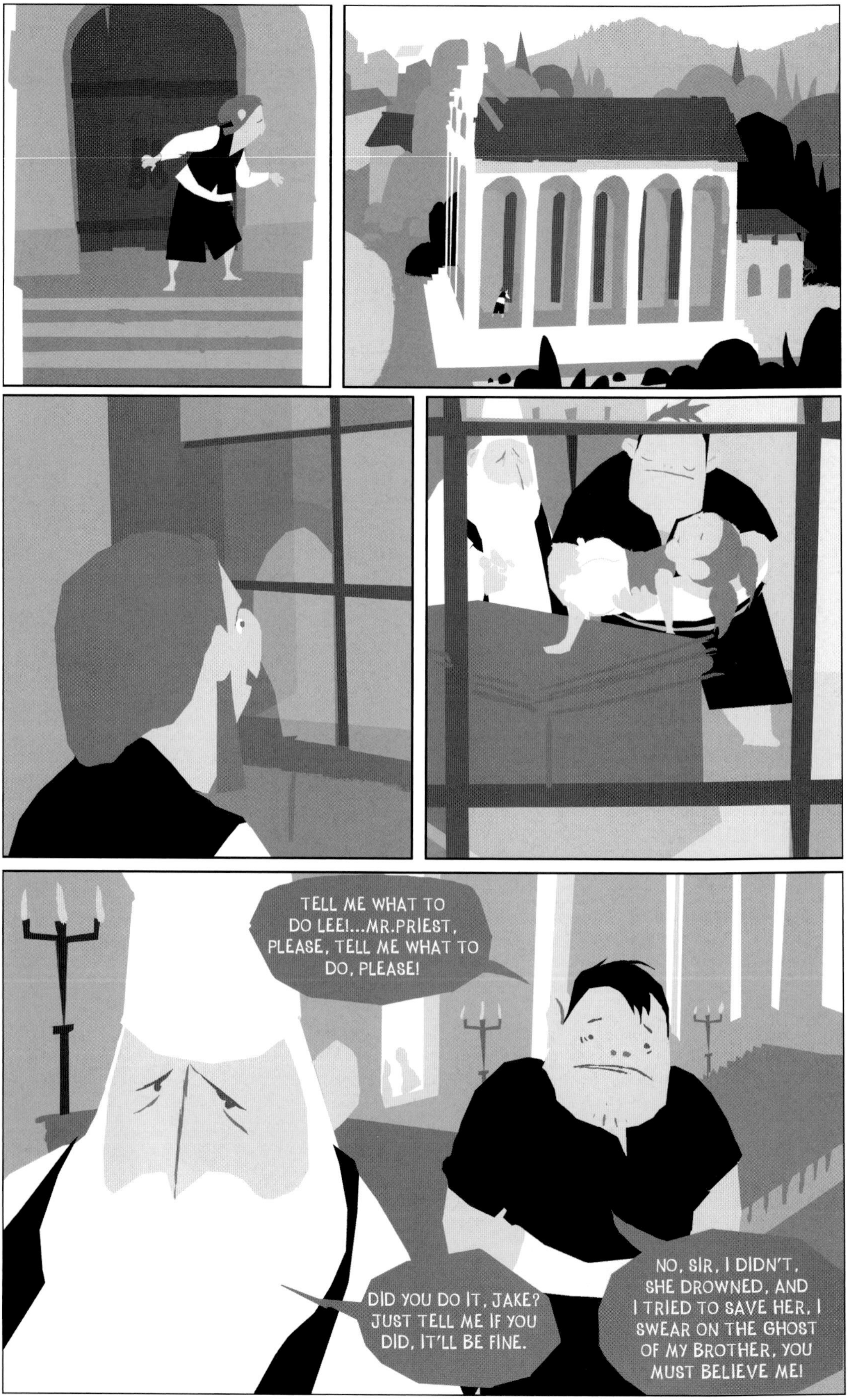
TELL ME WHAT TO DO LEE!...MR.PRIEST, PLEASE, TELL ME WHAT TO DO, PLEASE!
DID YOU DO IT, JAKE? JUST TELL ME IF YOU DID, IT'LL BE FINE.
NO, SIR, I DIDN'T, SHE DROWNED, AND I TRIED TO SAVE HER, I SWEAR ON THE GHOST OF MY BROTHER, YOU MUST BELIEVE ME!

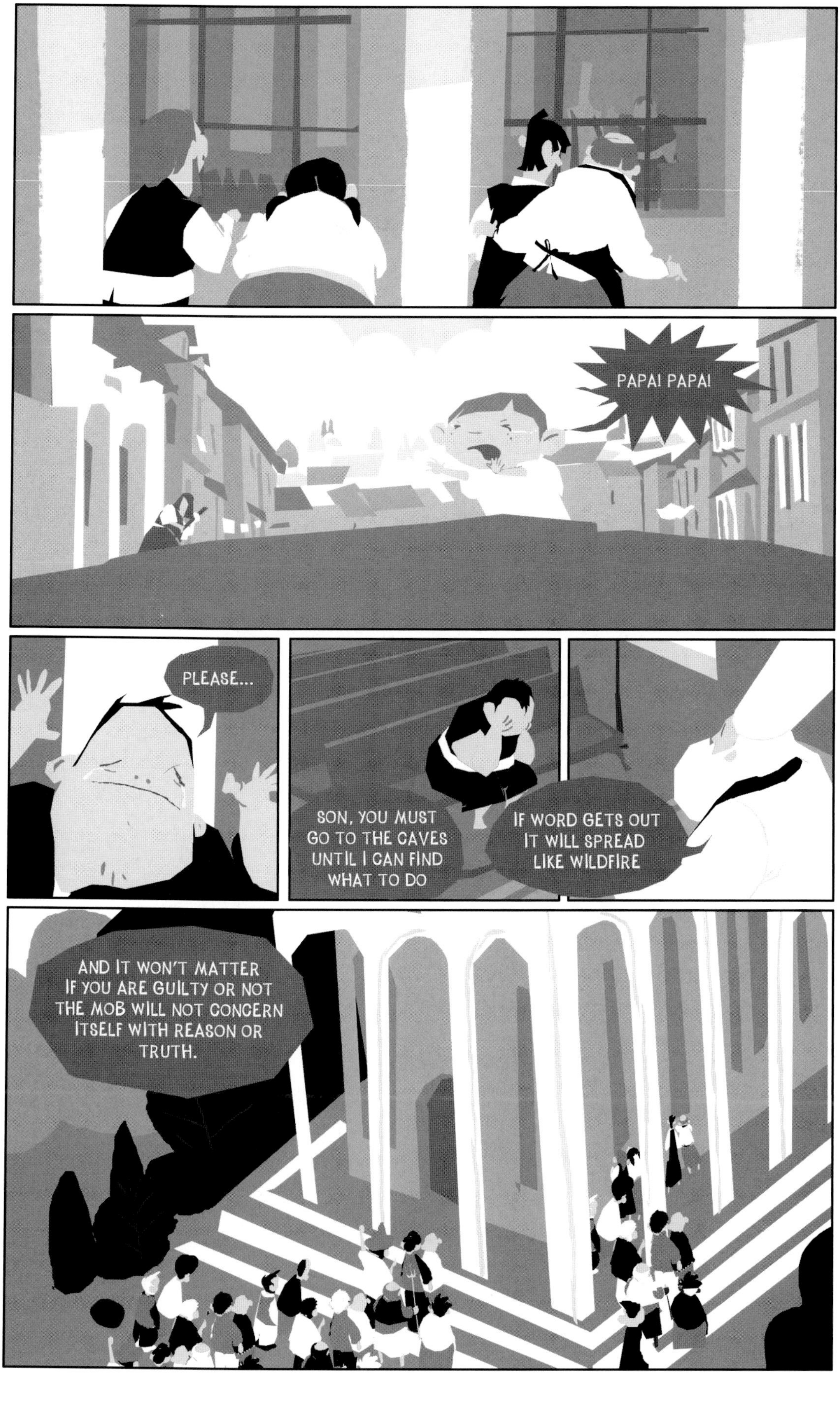
PAPA! PAPA!
PLEASE...
SON, YOU MUST GO TO THE CAVES UNTIL I CAN FIND WHAT TO DO
IF WORD GETS OUT IT WILL SPREAD LIKE WILDFIRE
AND IT WON'T MATTER IF YOU ARE GUILTY OR NOT THE MOB WILL NOT CONCERN ITSELF WITH REASON OR TRUTH.

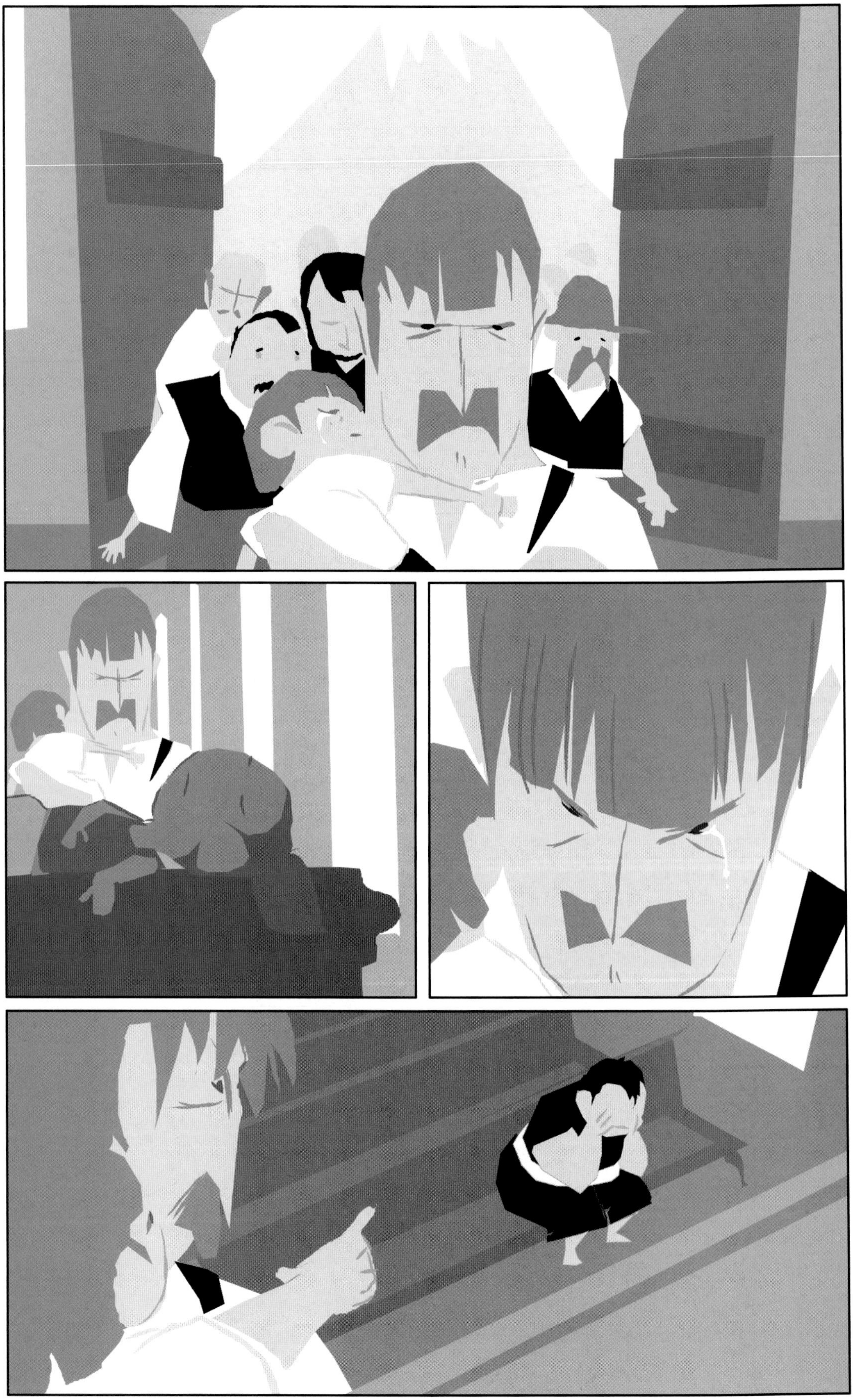

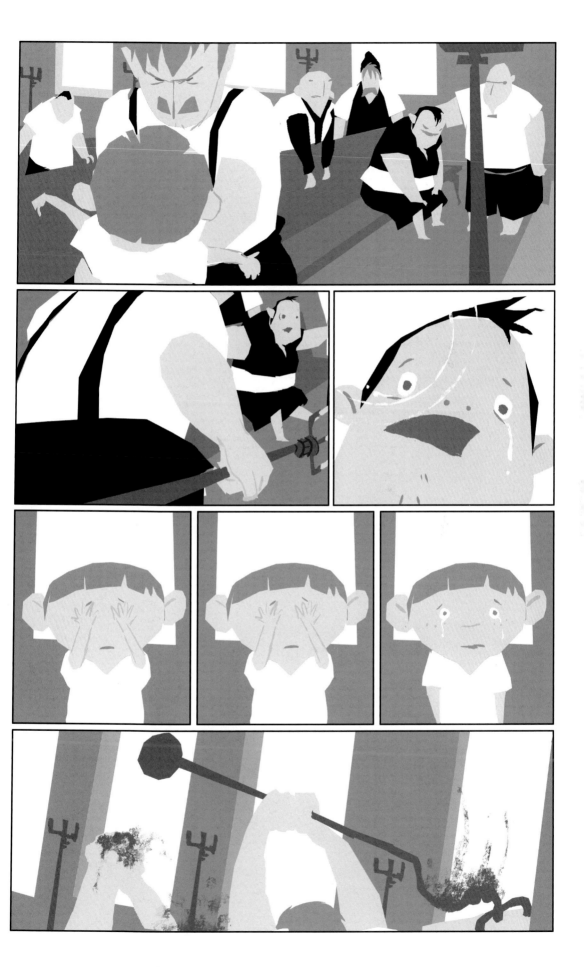

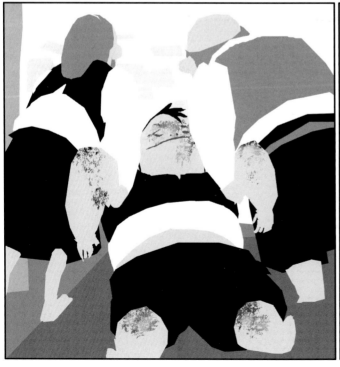

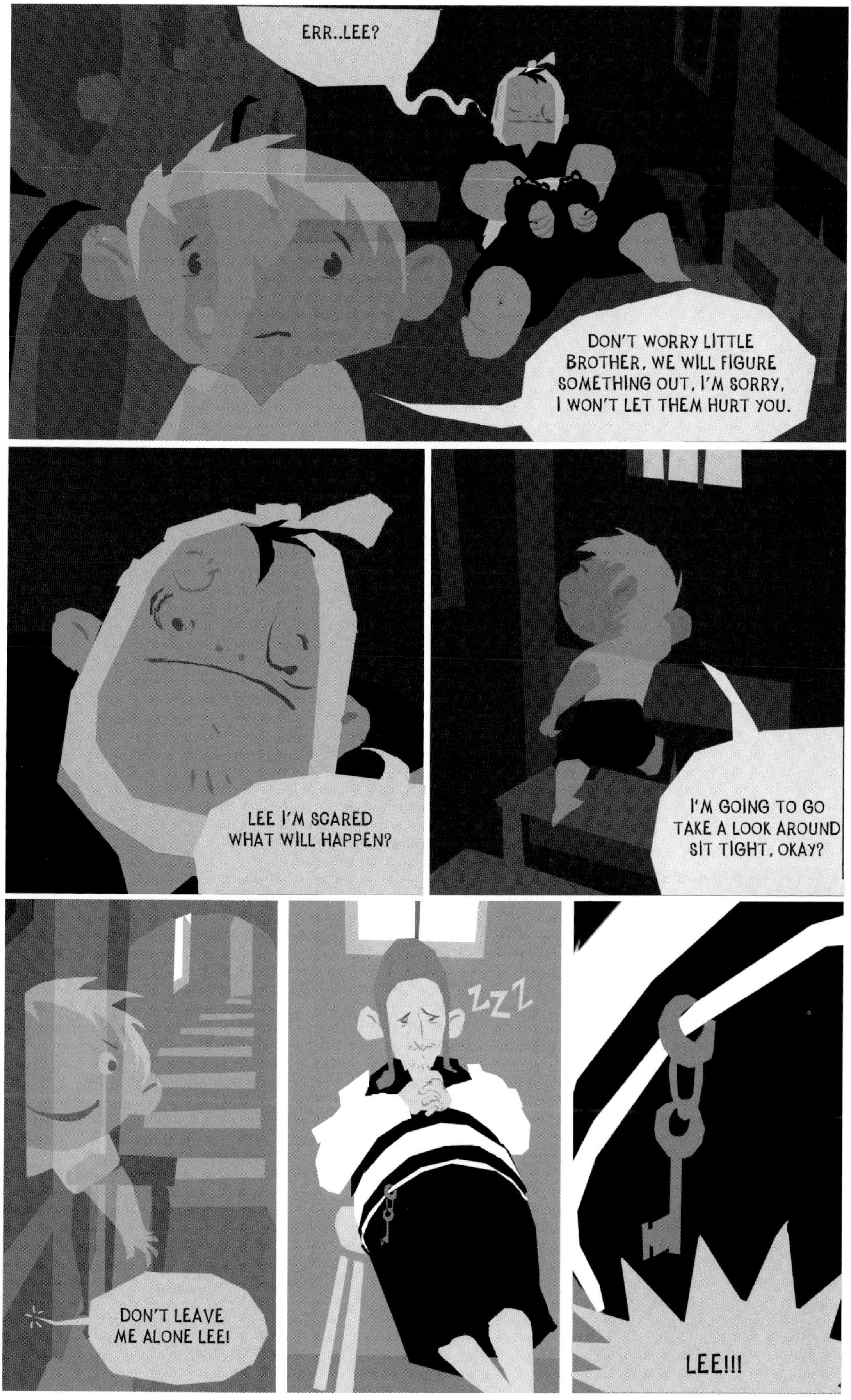
ERR..LEE?
DON'T WORRY LITTLE BROTHER, WE WILL FIGURE SOMETHING OUT, I'M SORRY, I WON'T LET THEM HURT YOU.
LEE I'M SCARED WHAT WILL HAPPEN?
I'M GOING TO GO TAKE A LOOK AROUND SIT TIGHT, OKAY?
DON'T LEAVE ME ALONE LEE!
ZZZ
LEE!!!

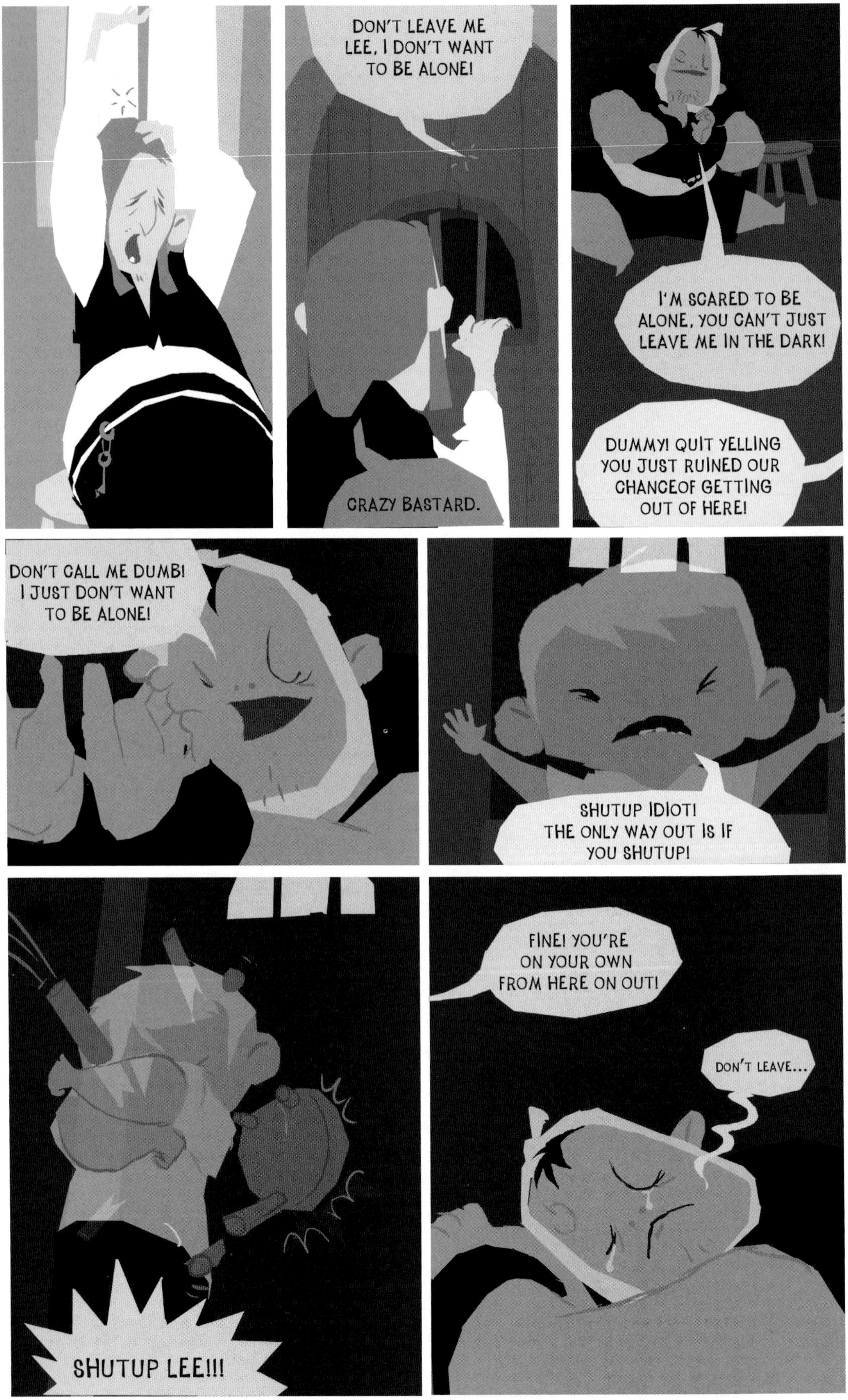
DON'T LEAVE ME LEE, I DON'T WANT TO BE ALONE!
CRAZY BASTARD.
I'M SCARED TO BE ALONE, YOU CAN'T JUST LEAVE ME IN THE DARK!
DUMMY! QUIT YELLING YOU JUST RUINED OUR CHANCEOF GETTING OUT OF HERE!
DON'T CALL ME DUMB! I JUST DON'T WANT TO BE ALONE!
SHUTUP IDIOT! THE ONLY WAY OUT IS IF YOU SHUTUP!
SHUTUP LEE!!!
FINE! YOU'RE ON YOUR OWN FROM HERE ON OUT!
DON'T LEAVE...

LEE?...

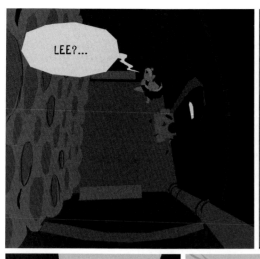

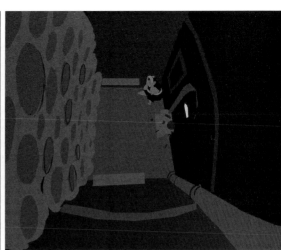

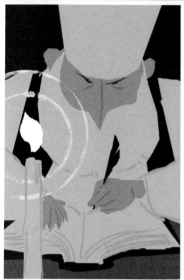

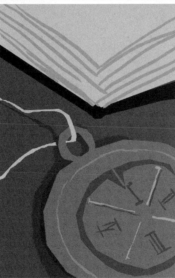

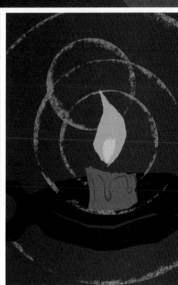

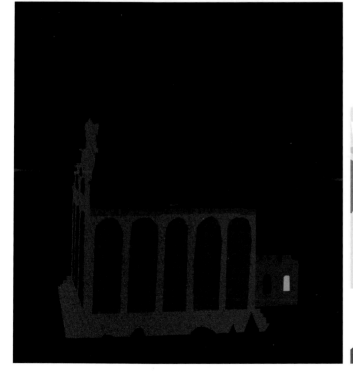

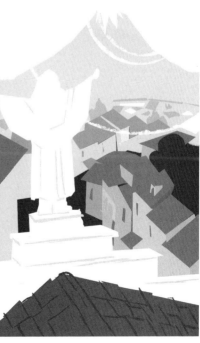

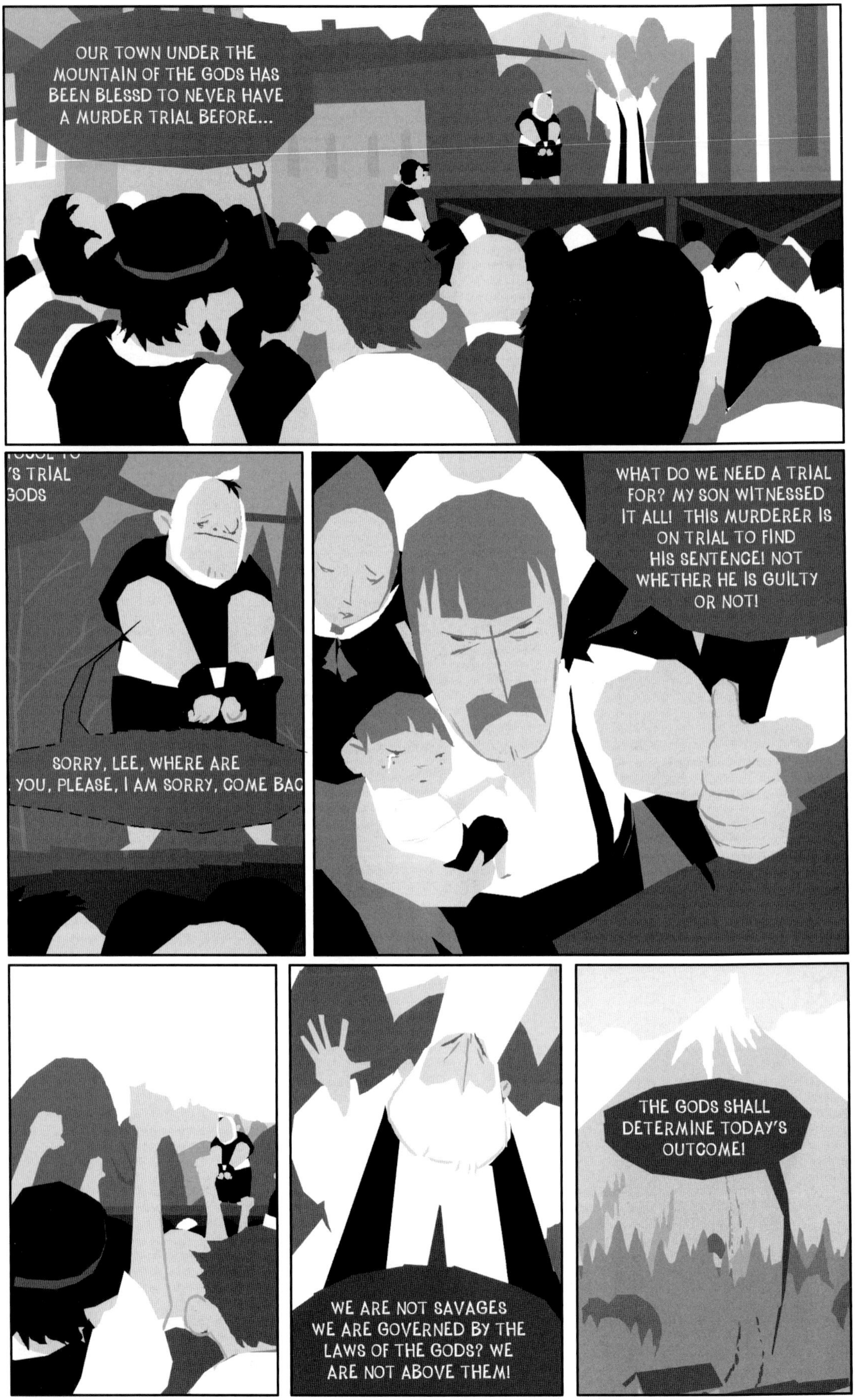
OUR TOWN UNDER THE MOUNTAIN OF THE GODS HAS BEEN BLESSD TO NEVER HAVE A MURDER TRIAL BEFORE...
'S TRIAL
GODS
SORRY, LEE, WHERE ARE
YOU, PLEASE, I AM SORRY, COME BAC
WHAT DO WE NEED A TRIAL FOR? MY SON WITNESSED IT ALL! THIS MURDERER IS ON TRIAL TO FIND HIS SENTENCE! NOT WHETHER HE IS GUILTY OR NOT!
WE ARE NOT SAVAGES WE ARE GOVERNED BY THE LAWS OF THE GODS? WE ARE NOT ABOVE THEM!
THE GODS SHALL DETERMINE TODAY'S OUTCOME!

THE GODS HAVE GRANTED US THE POWER TO DETERMINE A MAN'S FATE THROUGH THIS RELIC

THE GODS CONTROL THIS AMULET, NO MAN CAN CHANGE ITS OUTCOME

WELL, SURELY IF NO MAN CAN CONTROL IT'S OUTCOME, PERHAPS, THE FATHER OF THE DECEASED WOULD LIKE TO SPIN ITS FATE.

. . .

UH, CERTAINLY

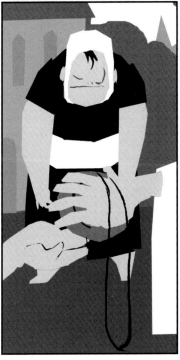

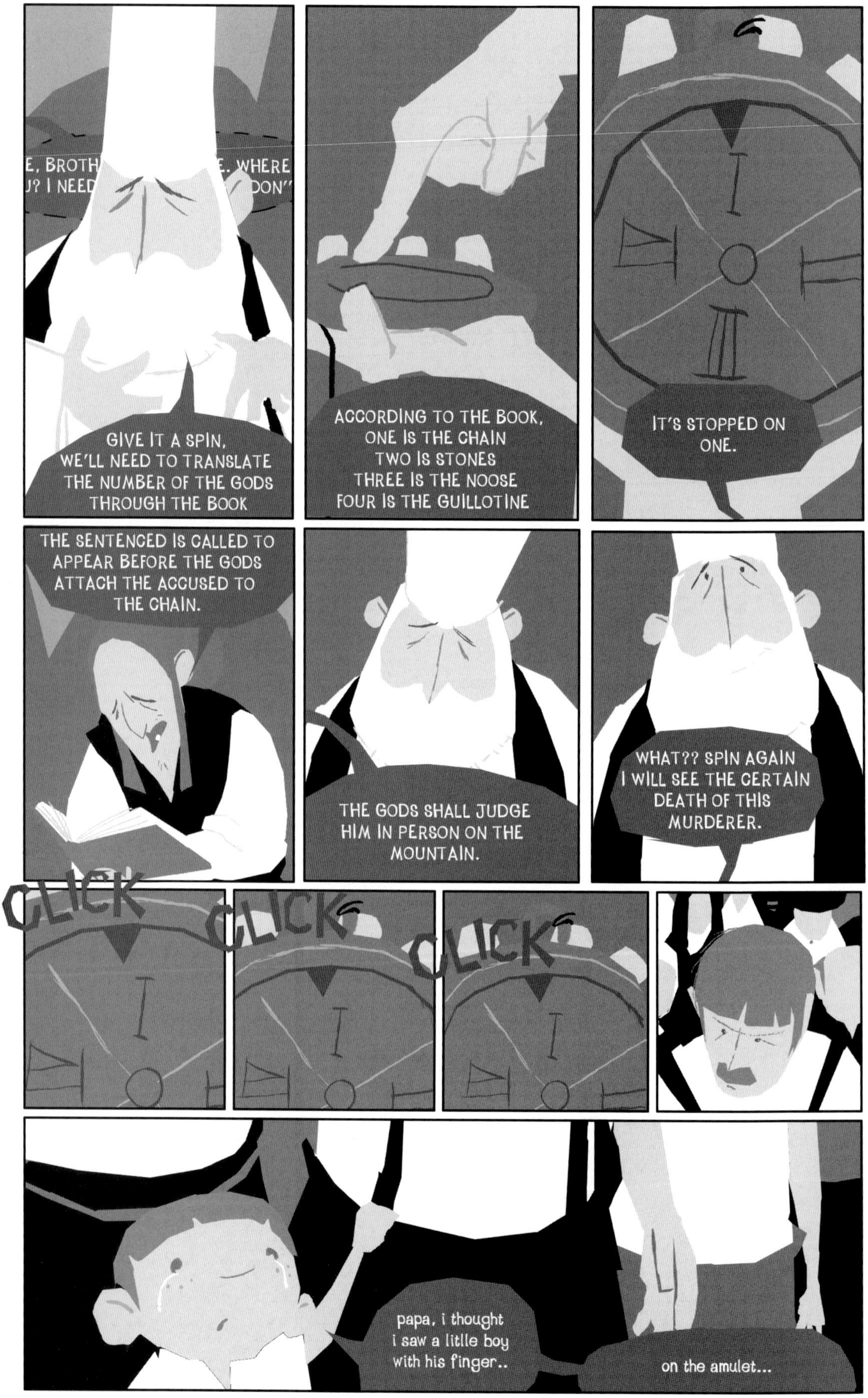
GIVE IT A SPIN, WE'LL NEED TO TRANSLATE THE NUMBER OF THE GODS THROUGH THE BOOK
ACCORDING TO THE BOOK, ONE IS THE CHAIN TWO IS STONES THREE IS THE NOOSE FOUR IS THE GUILLOTINE
IT'S STOPPED ON ONE.
THE SENTENCED IS CALLED TO APPEAR BEFORE THE GODS ATTACH THE ACCUSED TO THE CHAIN.
THE GODS SHALL JUDGE HIM IN PERSON ON THE MOUNTAIN.
WHAT?? SPIN AGAIN I WILL SEE THE CERTAIN DEATH OF THIS MURDERER.
CLICK
CLICK
CLICK
papa, i thought i saw a little boy with his finger..
on the amulet...

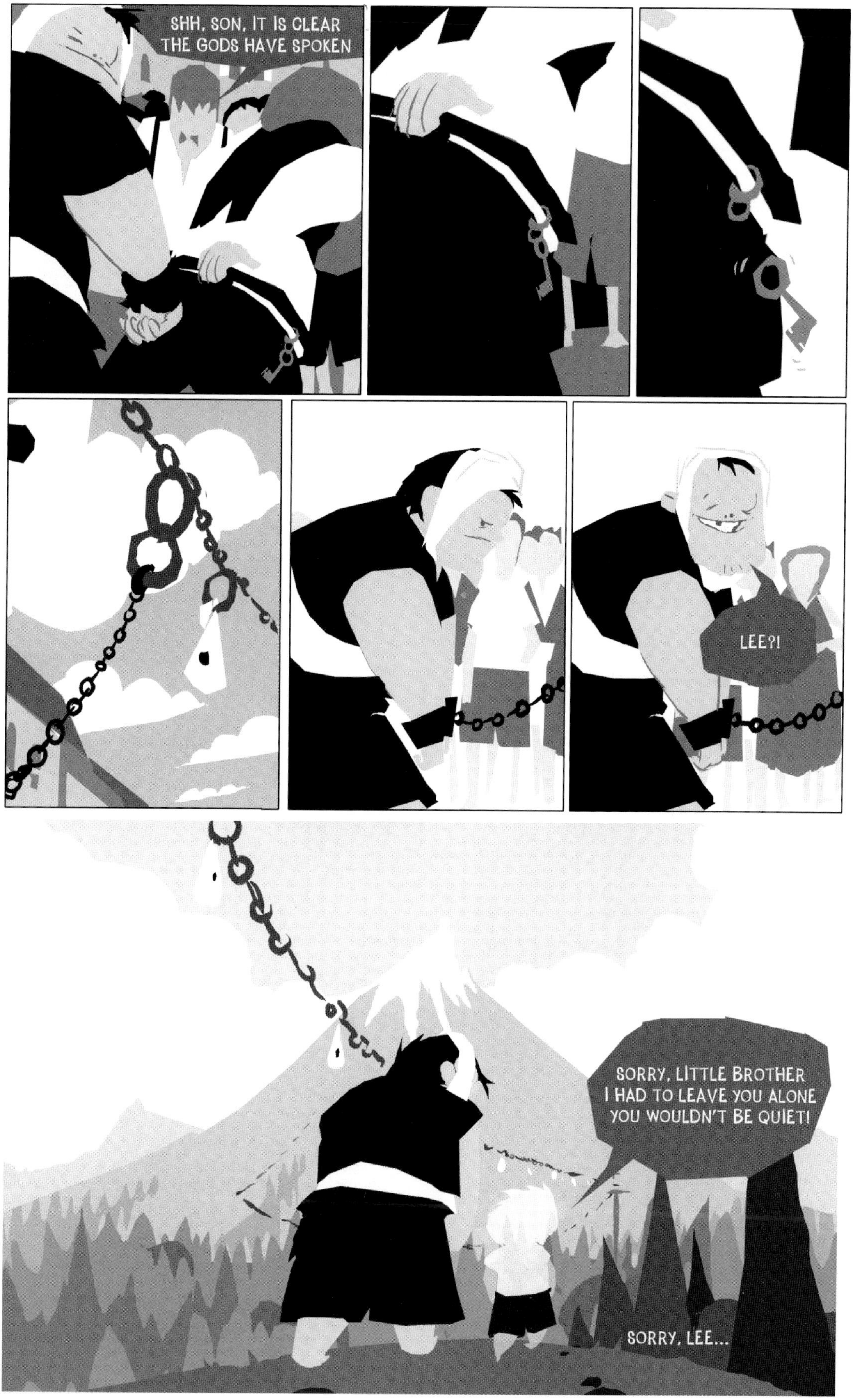
SHH, SON, IT IS CLEAR THE GODS HAVE SPOKEN
LEE?!
SORRY, LITTLE BROTHER I HAD TO LEAVE YOU ALONE YOU WOULDN'T BE QUIET!
SORRY, LEE...

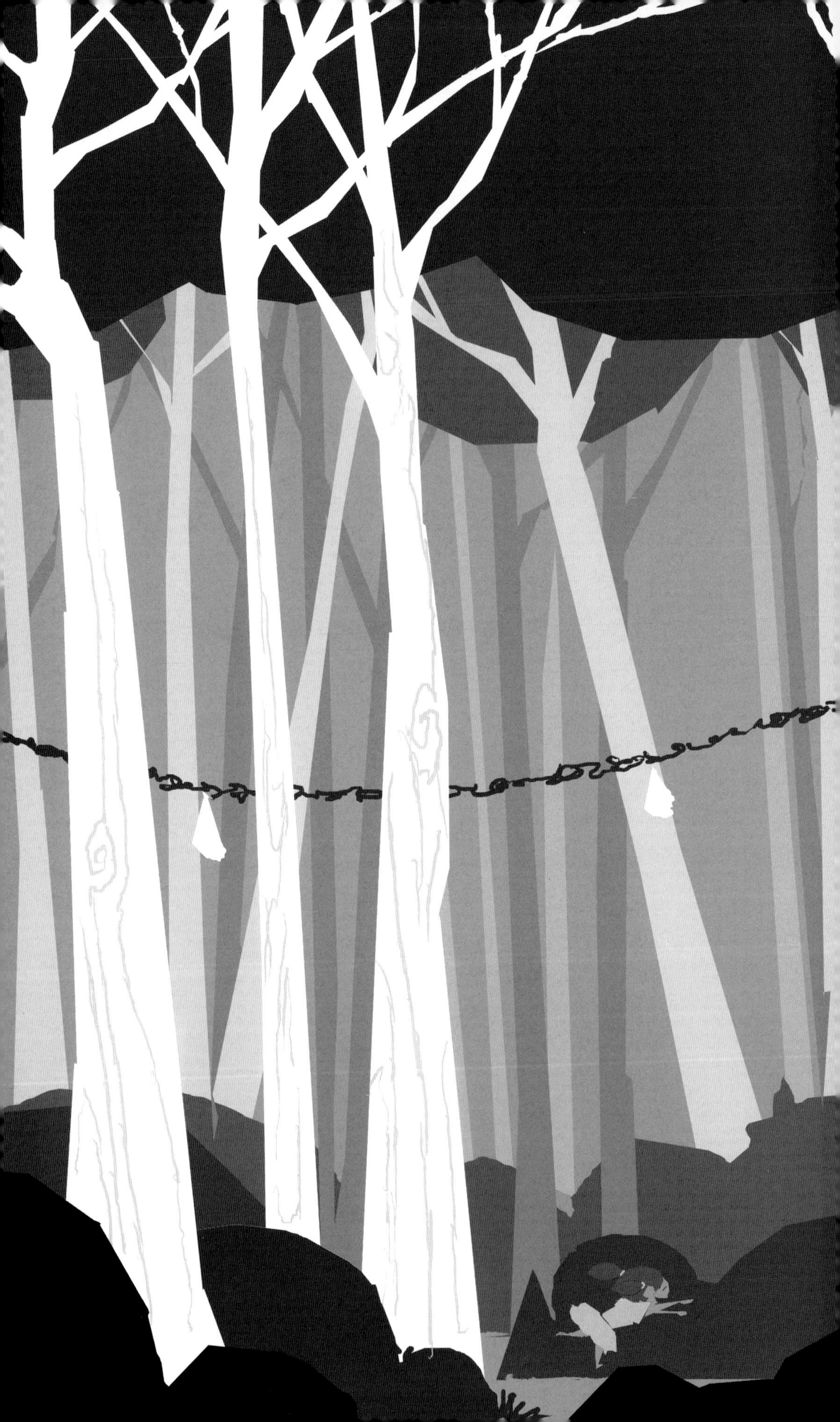

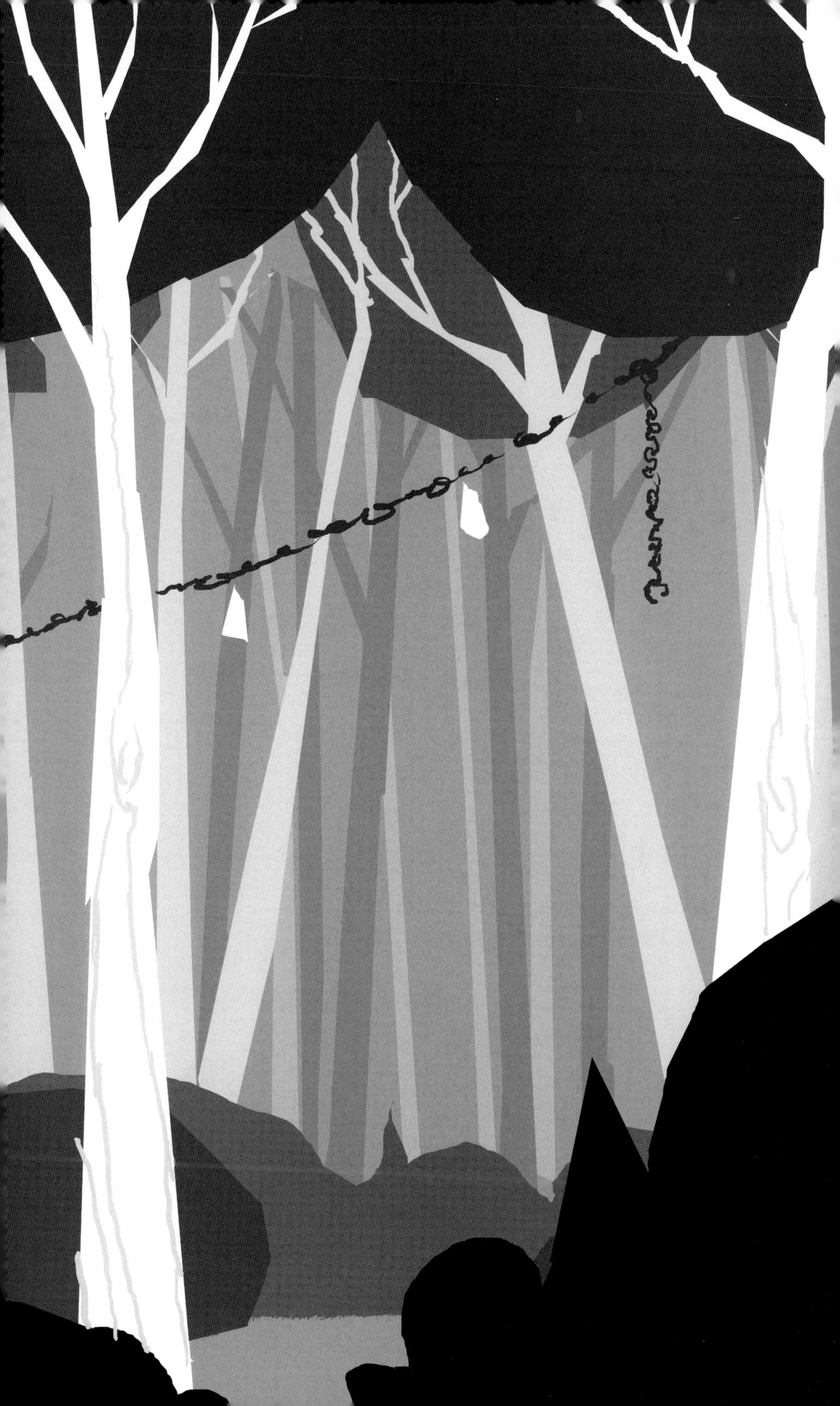

kevin o'brien

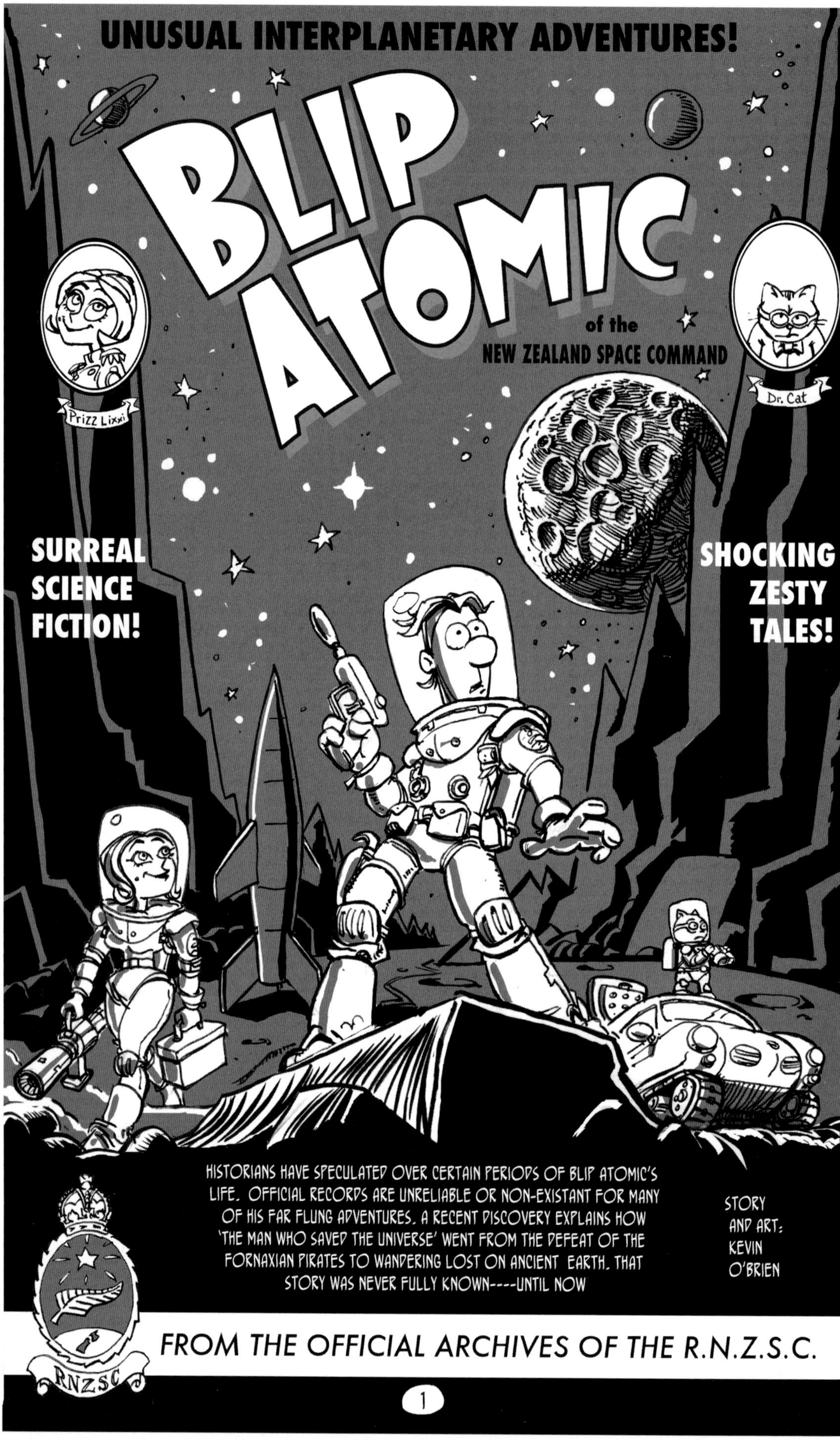
UNUSUAL INTERPLANETARY ADVENTURES!
BLIP ATOMIC
of the
NEW ZEALAND SPACE COMMAND
Prizz Lixxi
Dr. Cat
SURREAL SCIENCE FICTION!
SHOCKING ZESTY TALES!
HISTORIANS HAVE SPECULATED OVER CERTAIN PERIODS OF BLIP ATOMIC'S LIFE. OFFICIAL RECORDS ARE UNRELIABLE OR NON-EXISTANT FOR MANY OF HIS FAR FLUNG ADVENTURES. A RECENT DISCOVERY EXPLAINS HOW 'THE MAN WHO SAVED THE UNIVERSE' WENT FROM THE DEFEAT OF THE FORNAXIAN PIRATES TO WANDERING LOST ON ANCIENT EARTH. THAT STORY WAS NEVER FULLY KNOWN----UNTIL NOW
STORY AND ART: KEVIN O'BRIEN
RNZSC
FROM THE OFFICIAL ARCHIVES OF THE R.N.Z.S.C.

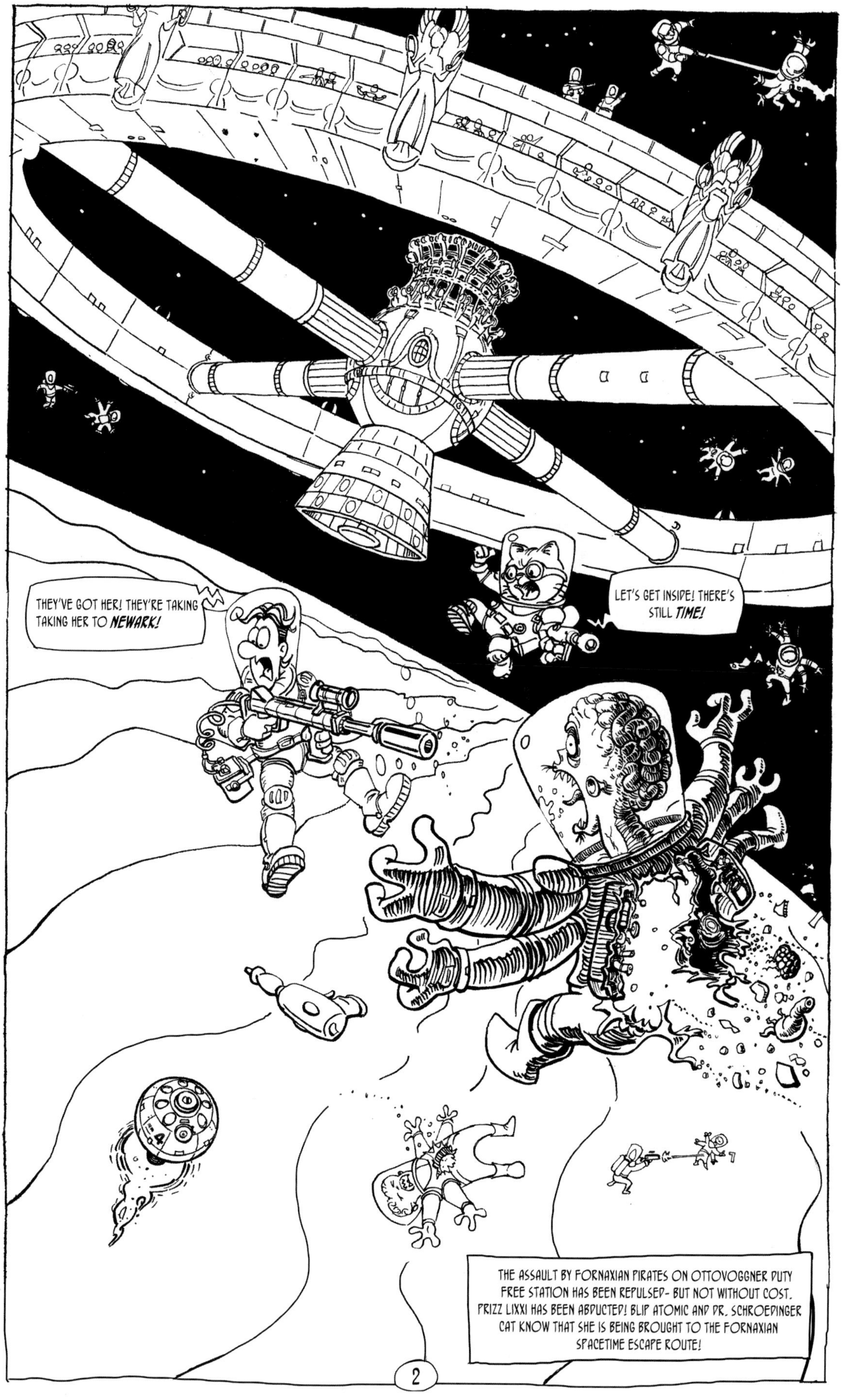
THEY'VE GOT HER! THEY'RE TAKING TAKING HER TO NEWARK!
LET'S GET INSIDE! THERE'S STILL TIME!
THE ASSAULT BY FORNAXIAN PIRATES ON OTTOVOGGNER DUTY FREE STATION HAS BEEN REPULSED- BUT NOT WITHOUT COST. PRIZZ LIXXI HAS BEEN ABDUCTED! BLIP ATOMIC AND DR. SCHROEDINGER CAT KNOW THAT SHE IS BEING BROUGHT TO THE FORNAXIAN SPACETIME ESCAPE ROUTE!

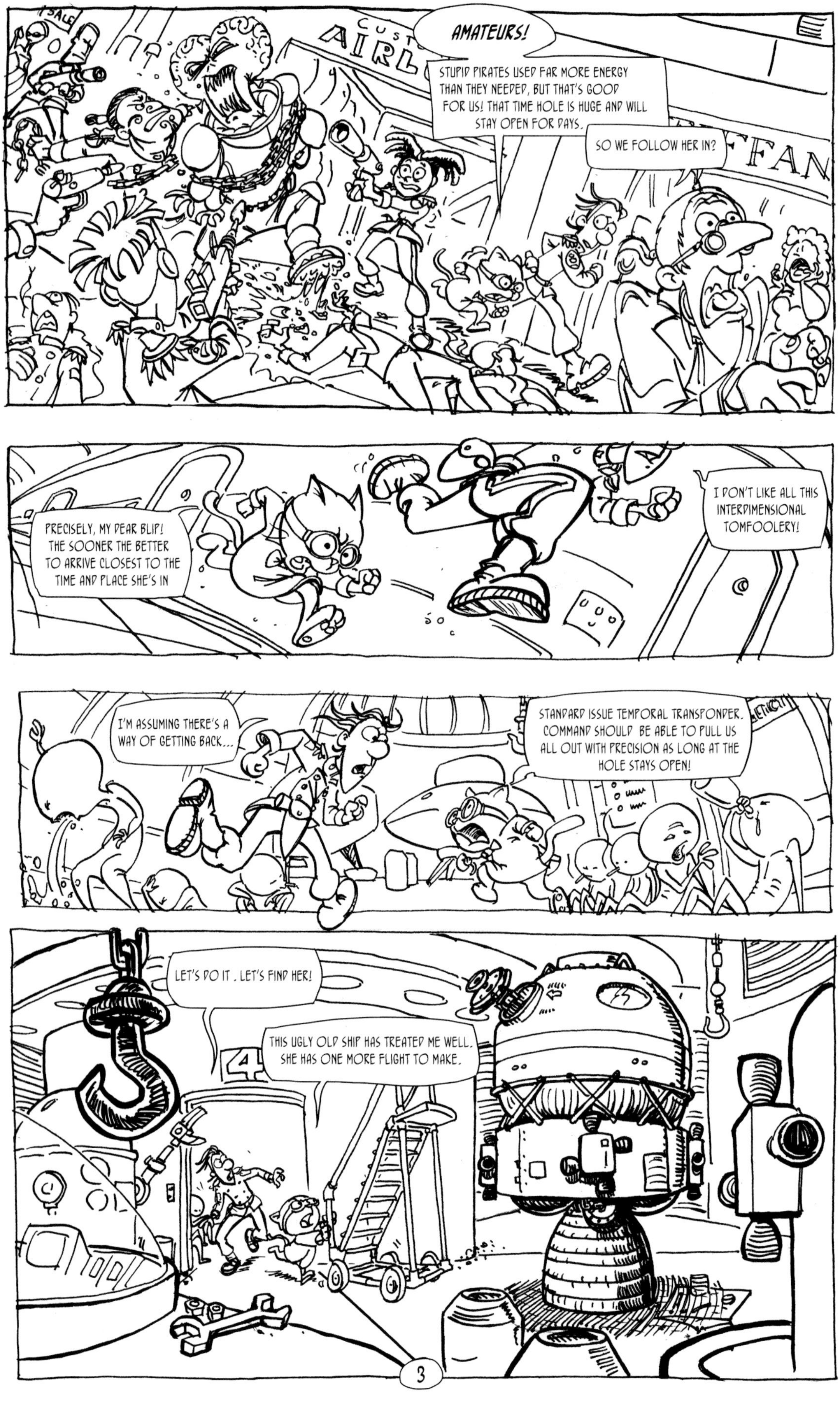

CUST
AIRL
AMATEURS!
STUPID PIRATES USED FAR MORE ENERGY THAN THEY NEEDED, BUT THAT'S GOOD FOR US! THAT TIME HOLE IS HUGE AND WILL STAY OPEN FOR DAYS.
SO WE FOLLOW HER IN?
FAN
PRECISELY, MY DEAR BLIP! THE SOONER THE BETTER TO ARRIVE CLOSEST TO THE TIME AND PLACE SHE'S IN
I DON'T LIKE ALL THIS INTERDIMENSIONAL TOMFOOLERY!
I'M ASSUMING THERE'S A WAY OF GETTING BACK...
STANDARD ISSUE TEMPORAL TRANSPONDER. COMMAND SHOULD BE ABLE TO PULL US ALL OUT WITH PRECISION AS LONG AT THE HOLE STAYS OPEN!
LET'S DO IT. LET'S FIND HER!
THIS UGLY OLD SHIP HAS TREATED ME WELL. SHE HAS ONE MORE FLIGHT TO MAKE.
4

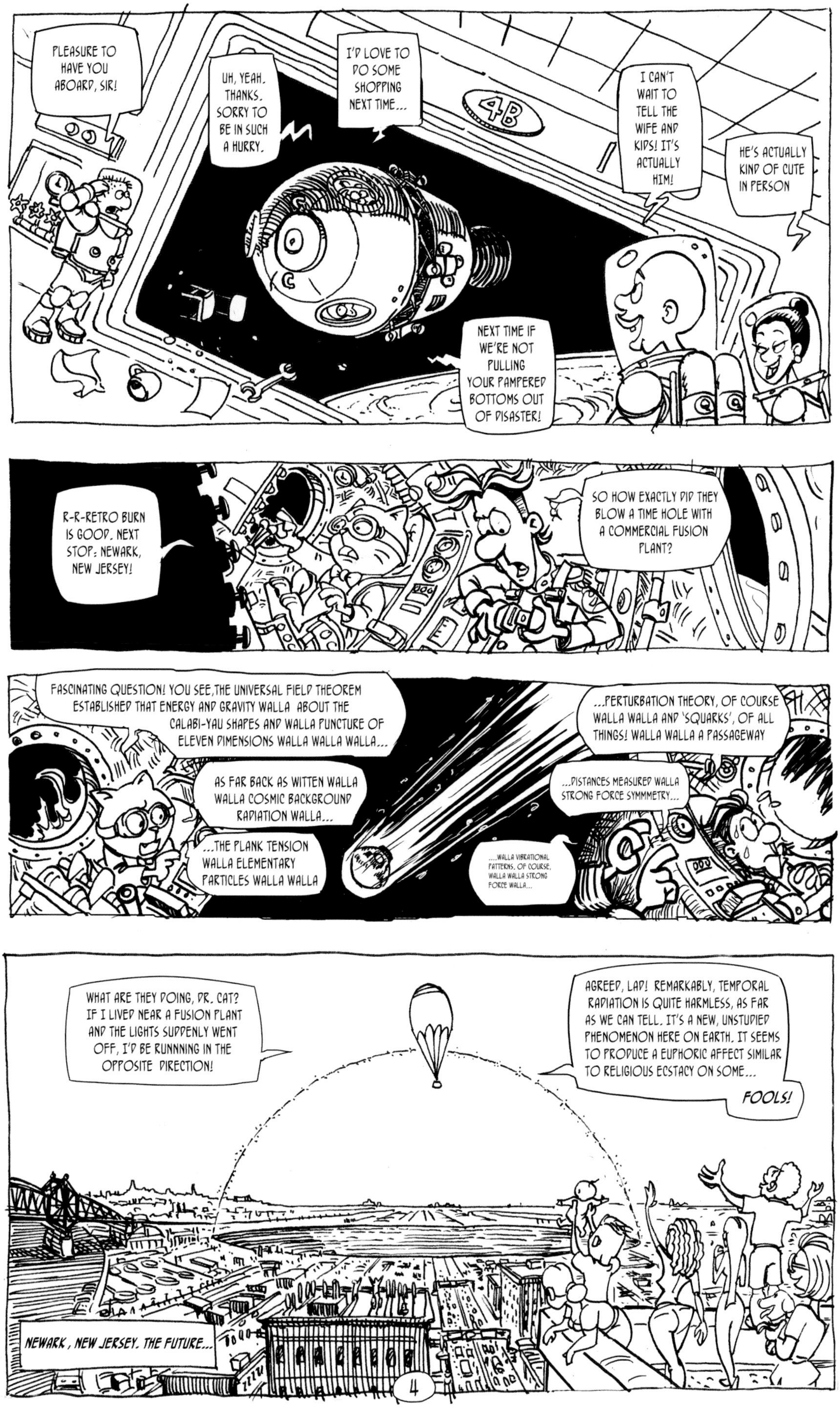
PLEASURE TO HAVE YOU ABOARD, SIR!
UH, YEAH. THANKS. SORRY TO BE IN SUCH A HURRY.
I'D LOVE TO DO SOME SHOPPING NEXT TIME...
4B
I CAN'T WAIT TO TELL THE WIFE AND KIDS! IT'S ACTUALLY HIM!
HE'S ACTUALLY KIND OF CUTE IN PERSON
NEXT TIME IF WE'RE NOT PULLING YOUR PAMPERED BOTTOMS OUT OF DISASTER!
R-R-RETRO BURN IS GOOD. NEXT STOP: NEWARK, NEW JERSEY!
SO HOW EXACTLY DID THEY BLOW A TIME HOLE WITH A COMMERCIAL FUSION PLANT?
FASCINATING QUESTION! YOU SEE,THE UNIVERSAL FIELD THEOREM ESTABLISHED THAT ENERGY AND GRAVITY WALLA ABOUT THE CALABI-YAU SHAPES AND WALLA PUNCTURE OF ELEVEN DIMENSIONS WALLA WALLA WALLA...
AS FAR BACK AS WITTEN WALLA WALLA COSMIC BACKGROUND RADIATION WALLA...
...THE PLANK TENSION WALLA ELEMENTARY PARTICLES WALLA WALLA
...PERTURBATION THEORY, OF COURSE WALLA WALLA AND 'SQUARKS', OF ALL THINGS! WALLA WALLA A PASSAGEWAY
...DISTANCES MEASURED WALLA STRONG FORCE SYMMMETRY...
....WALLA VIBRATIONAL PATTERNS. OF COURSE, WALLA WALLA STRONG FORCE WALLA...
WHAT ARE THEY DOING, DR. CAT? IF I LIVED NEAR A FUSION PLANT AND THE LIGHTS SUDDENLY WENT OFF, I'D BE RUNNNING IN THE OPPOSITE DIRECTION!
AGREED, LAD! REMARKABLY, TEMPORAL RADIATION IS QUITE HARMLESS, AS FAR AS WE CAN TELL. IT'S A NEW, UNSTUDIED PHENOMENON HERE ON EARTH. IT SEEMS TO PRODUCE A EUPHORIC AFFECT SIMILAR TO RELIGIOUS ECSTACY ON SOME...
FOOLS!
NEWARK, NEW JERSEY. THE FUTURE...

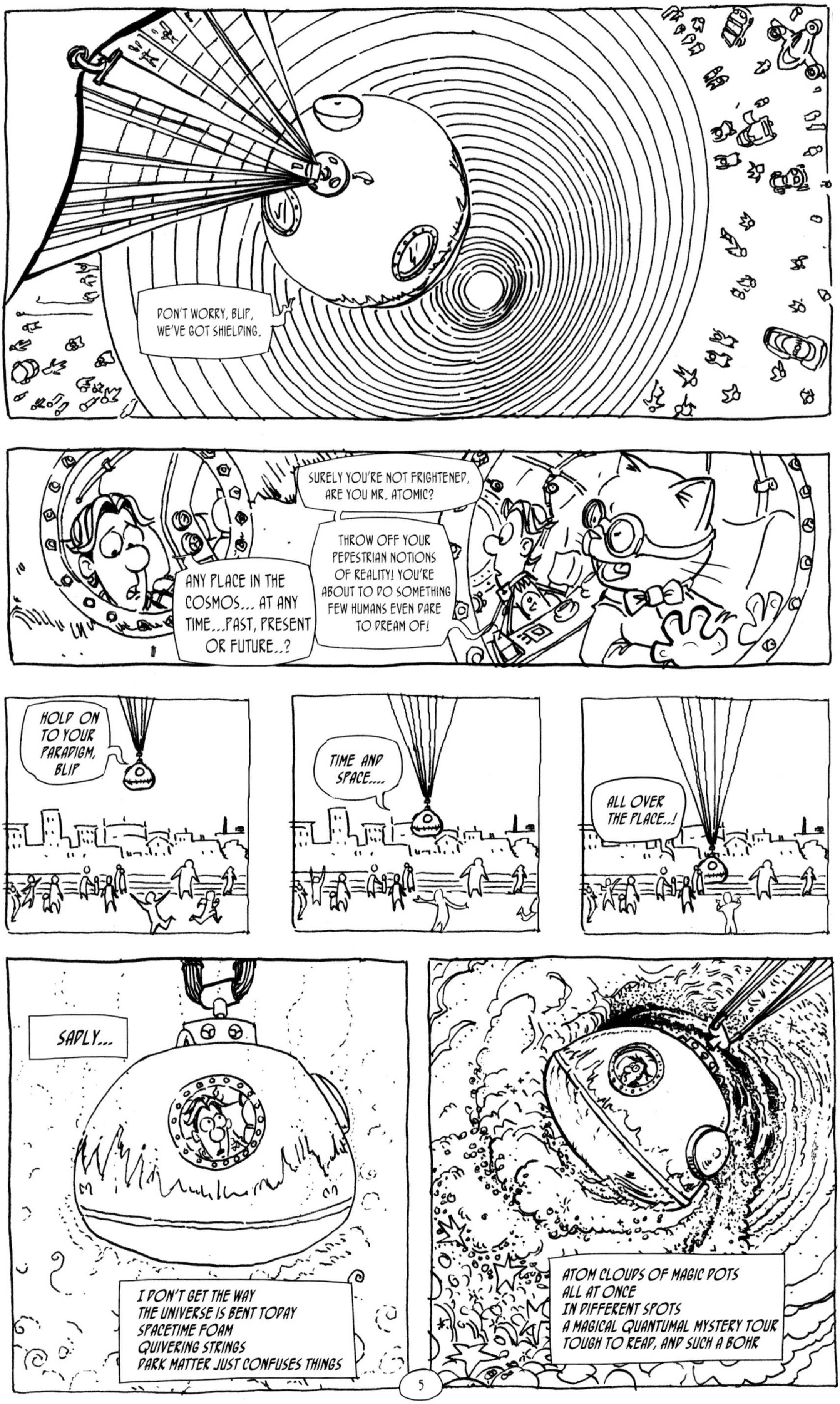
DON'T WORRY, BLIP, WE'VE GOT SHIELDING.
SURELY YOU'RE NOT FRIGHTENED, ARE YOU MR. ATOMIC?
ANY PLACE IN THE COSMOS... AT ANY TIME...PAST, PRESENT OR FUTURE..?
THROW OFF YOUR PEDESTRIAN NOTIONS OF REALITY! YOU'RE ABOUT TO DO SOMETHING FEW HUMANS EVEN DARE TO DREAM OF!
HOLD ON TO YOUR PARADIGM, BLIP
TIME AND SPACE....
ALL OVER THE PLACE..!
SADLY...
I DON'T GET THE WAY
THE UNIVERSE IS BENT TODAY
SPACETIME FOAM
QUIVERING STRINGS
DARK MATTER JUST CONFUSES THINGS
ATOM CLOUDS OF MAGIC DOTS
ALL AT ONCE
IN DIFFERENT SPOTS
A MAGICAL QUANTUMAL MYSTERY TOUR
TOUGH TO READ, AND SUCH A BOHR

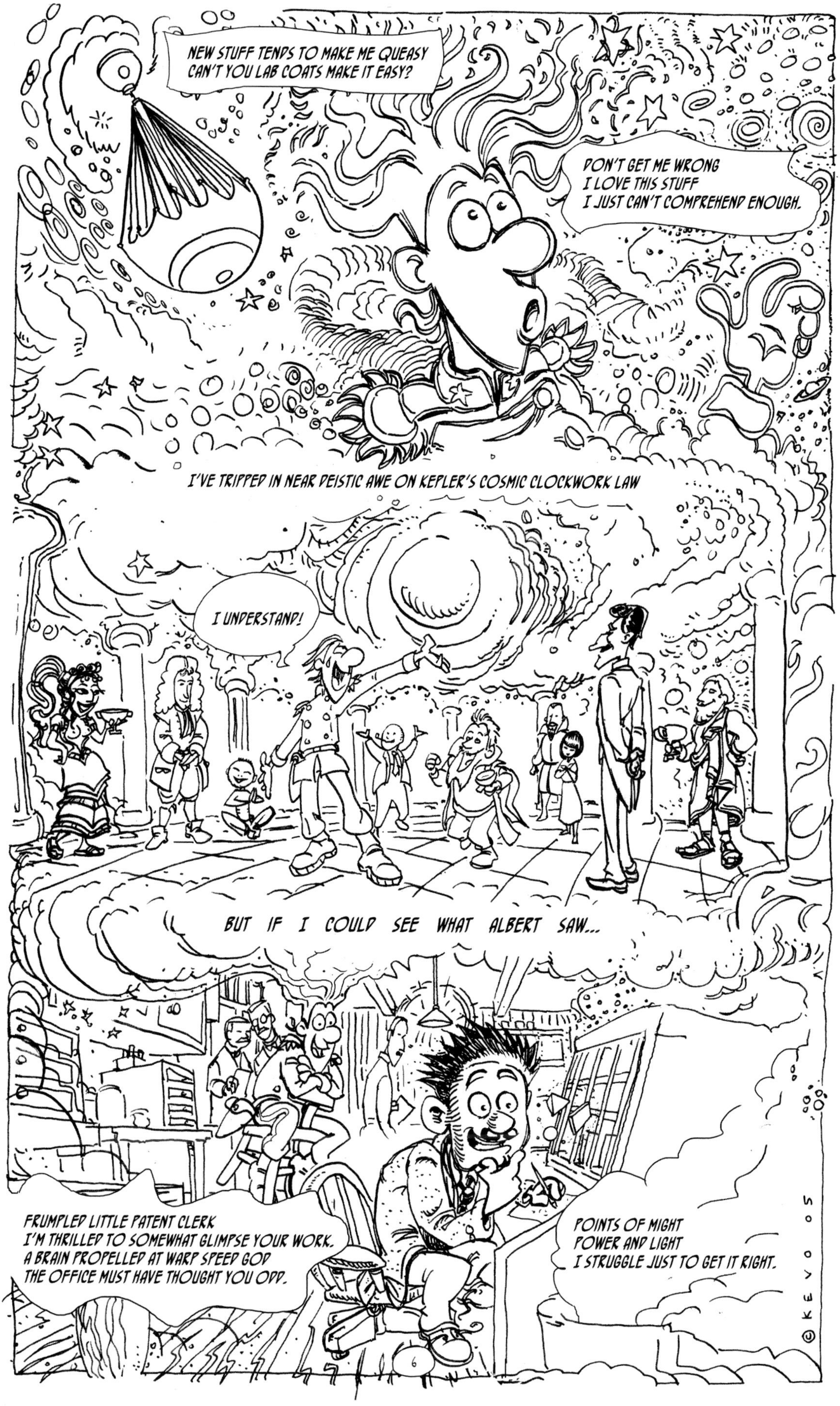

NEW STUFF TENDS TO MAKE ME QUEASY
CAN'T YOU LAB COATS MAKE IT EASY?
DON'T GET ME WRONG
I LOVE THIS STUFF
I JUST CAN'T COMPREHEND ENOUGH.
I'VE TRIPPED IN NEAR DEISTIC AWE ON KEPLER'S COSMIC CLOCKWORK LAW
I UNDERSTAND!
BUT IF I COULD SEE WHAT ALBERT SAW...
FRUMPLED LITTLE PATENT CLERK
I'M THRILLED TO SOMEWHAT GLIMPSE YOUR WORK.
A BRAIN PROPELLED AT WARP SPEED GOD
THE OFFICE MUST HAVE THOUGHT YOU ODD.
POINTS OF MIGHT
POWER AND LIGHT
I STRUGGLE JUST TO GET IT RIGHT.
© KEVO 05

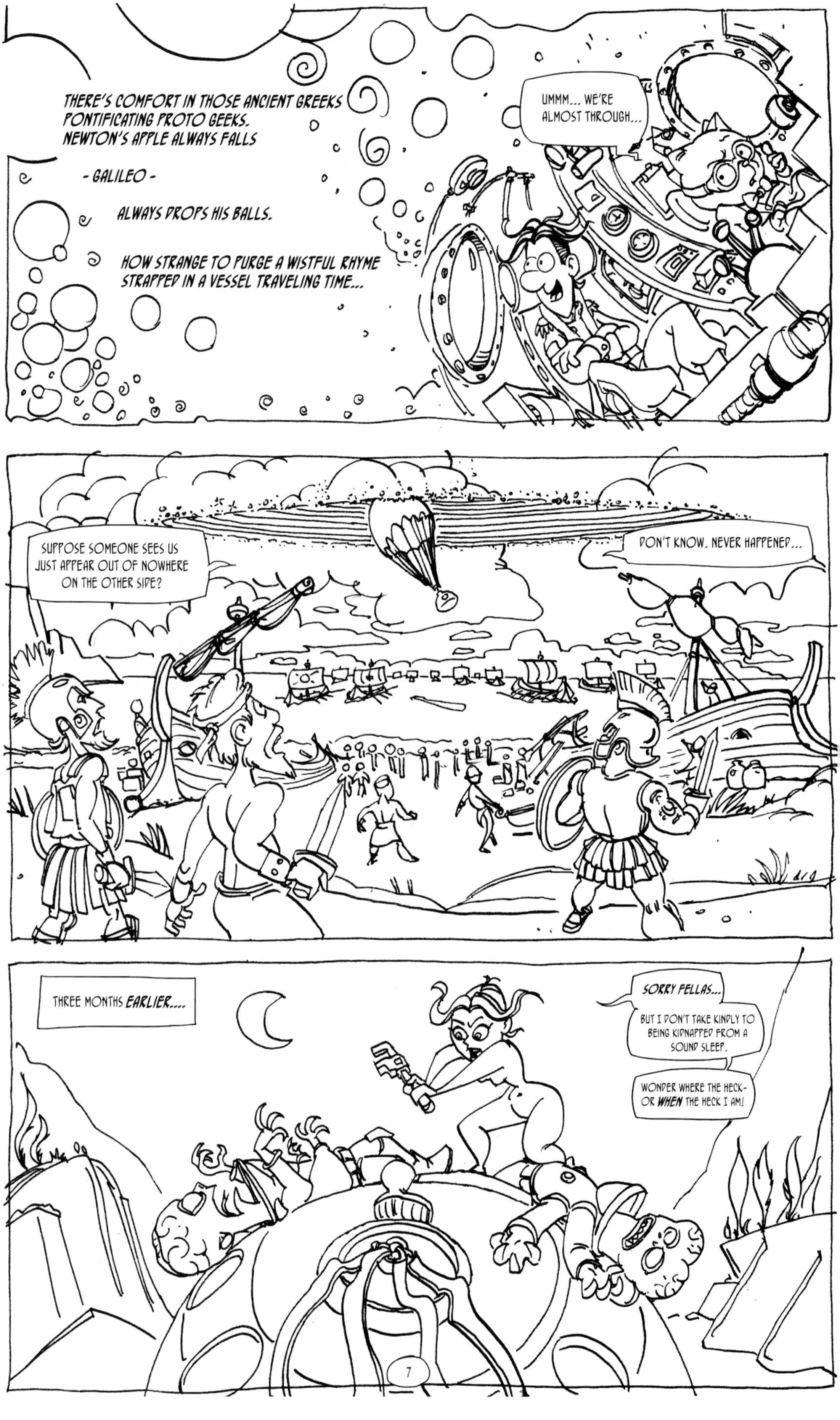
THERE'S COMFORT IN THOSE ANCIENT GREEKS
PONTIFICATING PROTO GEEKS.
NEWTON'S APPLE ALWAYS FALLS
- GALILEO -
ALWAYS DROPS HIS BALLS.
HOW STRANGE TO PURGE A WISTFUL RHYME
STRAPPED IN A VESSEL TRAVELING TIME...
UMMM... WE'RE ALMOST THROUGH...
SUPPOSE SOMEONE SEES US JUST APPEAR OUT OF NOWHERE ON THE OTHER SIDE?
DON'T KNOW. NEVER HAPPENED...
THREE MONTHS EARLIER....
SORRY FELLAS...
BUT I DON'T TAKE KINDLY TO BEING KIDNAPPED FROM A SOUND SLEEP.
WONDER WHERE THE HECK- OR WHEN THE HECK I AM!

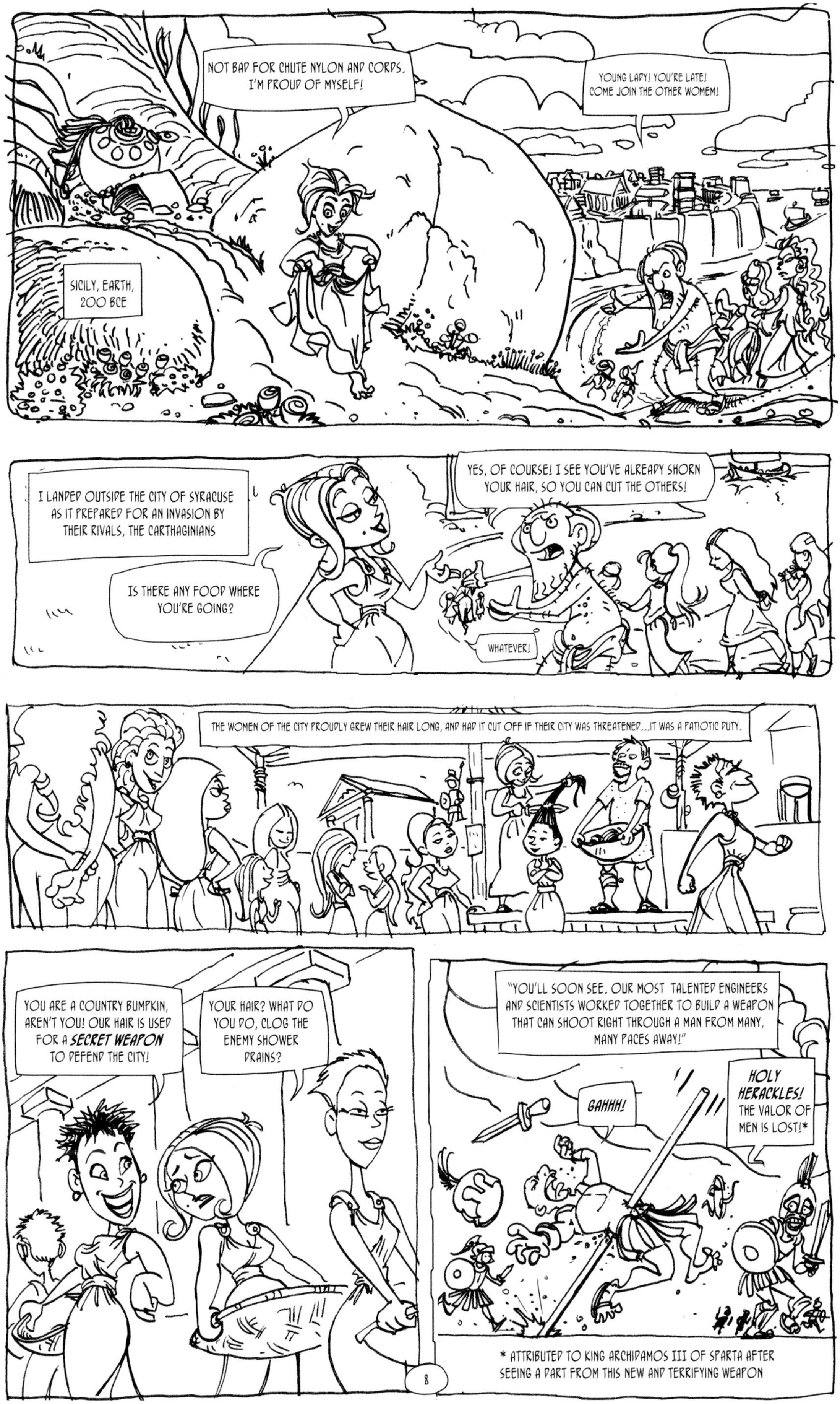
NOT BAD FOR CHUTE NYLON AND CORDS. I'M PROUD OF MYSELF!
YOUNG LADY! YOU'RE LATE! COME JOIN THE OTHER WOMEM!
SICILY, EARTH, 200 BCE
I LANDED OUTSIDE THE CITY OF SYRACUSE AS IT PREPARED FOR AN INVASION BY THEIR RIVALS, THE CARTHAGINIANS
IS THERE ANY FOOD WHERE YOU'RE GOING?
YES, OF COURSE! I SEE YOU'VE ALREADY SHORN YOUR HAIR, SO YOU CAN CUT THE OTHERS!
WHATEVER!
THE WOMEN OF THE CITY PROUDLY GREW THEIR HAIR LONG, AND HAD IT CUT OFF IF THEIR CITY WAS THREATENED...IT WAS A PATIOTIC DUTY.
YOU ARE A COUNTRY BUMPKIN, AREN'T YOU! OUR HAIR IS USED FOR A SECRET WEAPON TO DEFEND THE CITY!
YOUR HAIR? WHAT DO YOU DO, CLOG THE ENEMY SHOWER DRAINS?
"YOU'LL SOON SEE. OUR MOST TALENTED ENGINEERS AND SCIENTISTS WORKED TOGETHER TO BUILD A WEAPON THAT CAN SHOOT RIGHT THROUGH A MAN FROM MANY, MANY PACES AWAY!"
GAHHH!
HOLY HERACKLES! THE VALOR OF MEN IS LOST!*
* ATTRIBUTED TO KING ARCHIDAMOS III OF SPARTA AFTER SEEING A DART FROM THIS NEW AND TERRIFYING WEAPON

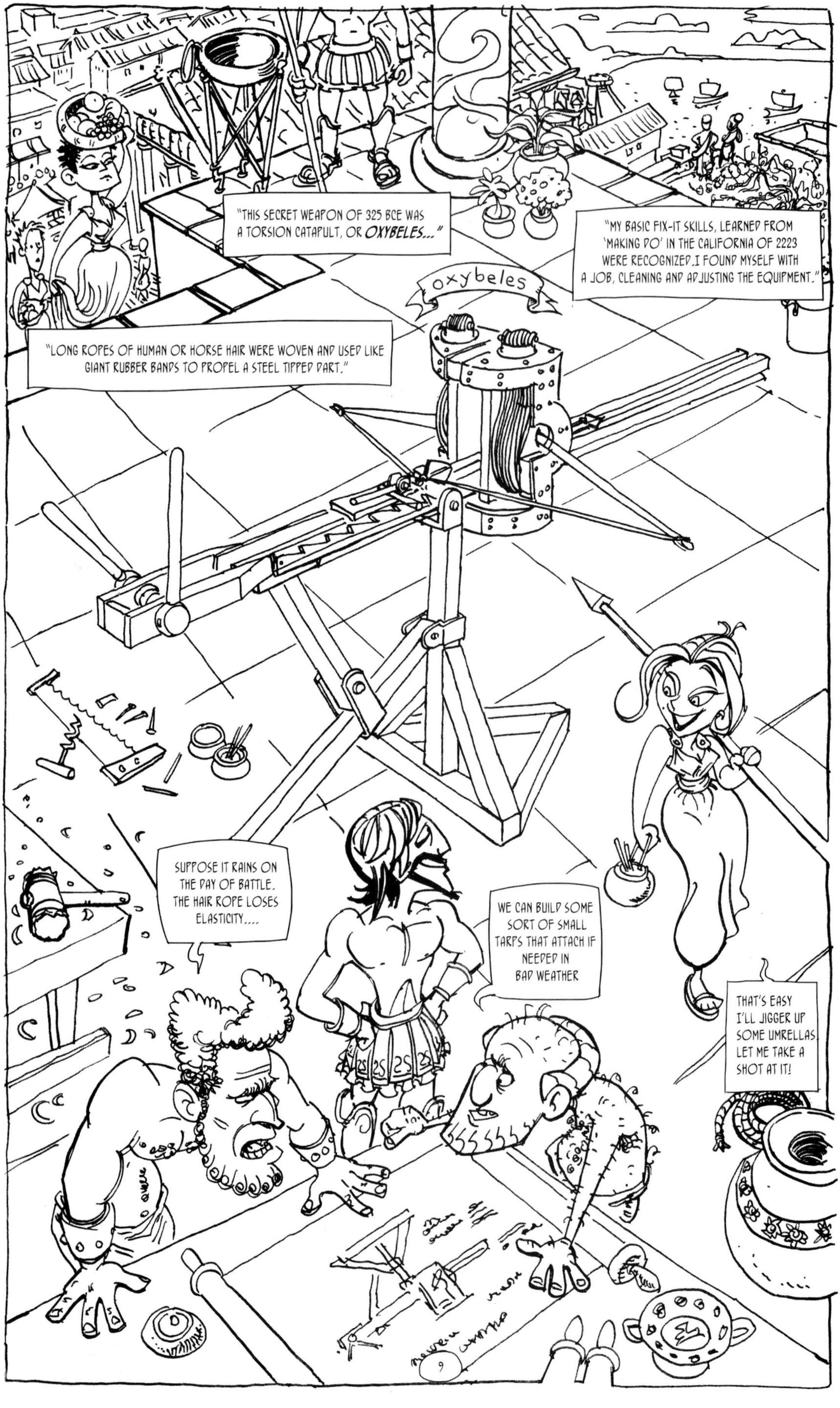
"THIS SECRET WEAPON OF 325 BCE WAS A TORSION CATAPULT, OR OXYBELES..."
"MY BASIC FIX-IT SKILLS, LEARNED FROM 'MAKING DO' IN THE CALIFORNIA OF 2223 WERE RECOGNIZED. I FOUND MYSELF WITH A JOB, CLEANING AND ADJUSTING THE EQUIPMENT."
oxybeles
"LONG ROPES OF HUMAN OR HORSE HAIR WERE WOVEN AND USED LIKE GIANT RUBBER BANDS TO PROPEL A STEEL TIPPED DART."
SUPPOSE IT RAINS ON THE DAY OF BATTLE. THE HAIR ROPE LOSES ELASTICITY....
WE CAN BUILD SOME SORT OF SMALL TARPS THAT ATTACH IF NEEDED IN BAD WEATHER
THAT'S EASY I'LL JIGGER UP SOME UMRELLAS. LET ME TAKE A SHOT AT IT!

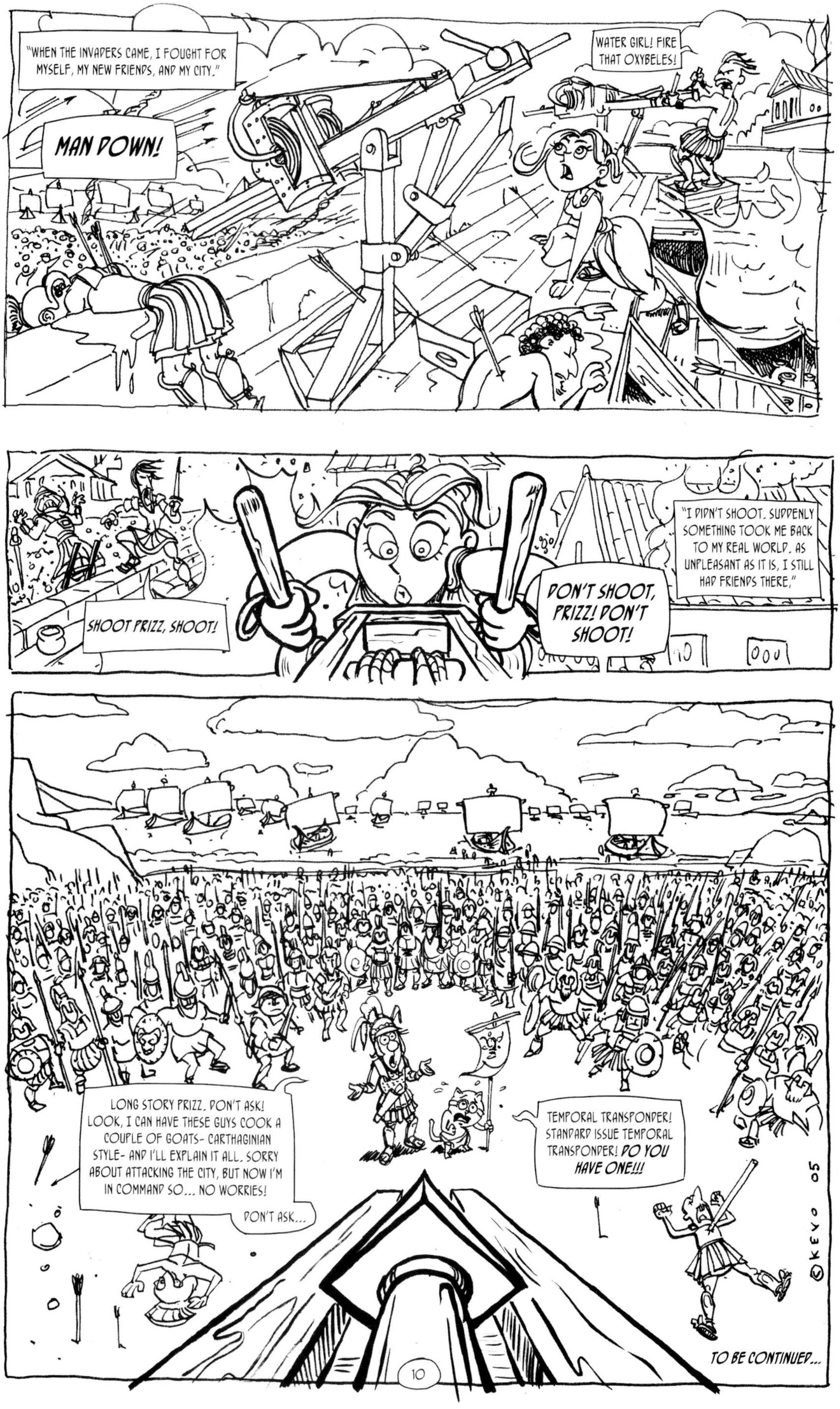
"WHEN THE INVADERS CAME, I FOUGHT FOR MYSELF, MY NEW FRIENDS, AND MY CITY."
MAN DOWN!
WATER GIRL! FIRE THAT OXYBELES!
SHOOT PRIZZ, SHOOT!
DON'T SHOOT, PRIZZ! DON'T SHOOT!
"I DIDN'T SHOOT. SUDDENLY SOMETHING TOOK ME BACK TO MY REAL WORLD. AS UNPLEASANT AS IT IS, I STILL HAD FRIENDS THERE."
LONG STORY PRIZZ. DON'T ASK! LOOK, I CAN HAVE THESE GUYS COOK A COUPLE OF GOATS- CARTHAGINIAN STYLE- AND I'LL EXPLAIN IT ALL. SORRY ABOUT ATTACKING THE CITY, BUT NOW I'M IN COMMAND SO... NO WORRIES!
DON'T ASK...
TEMPORAL TRANSPONDER! STANDARD ISSUE TEMPORAL TRANSPONDER! DO YOU HAVE ONE!!!
©KEYO 05
TO BE CONTINUED...

louis gonzales

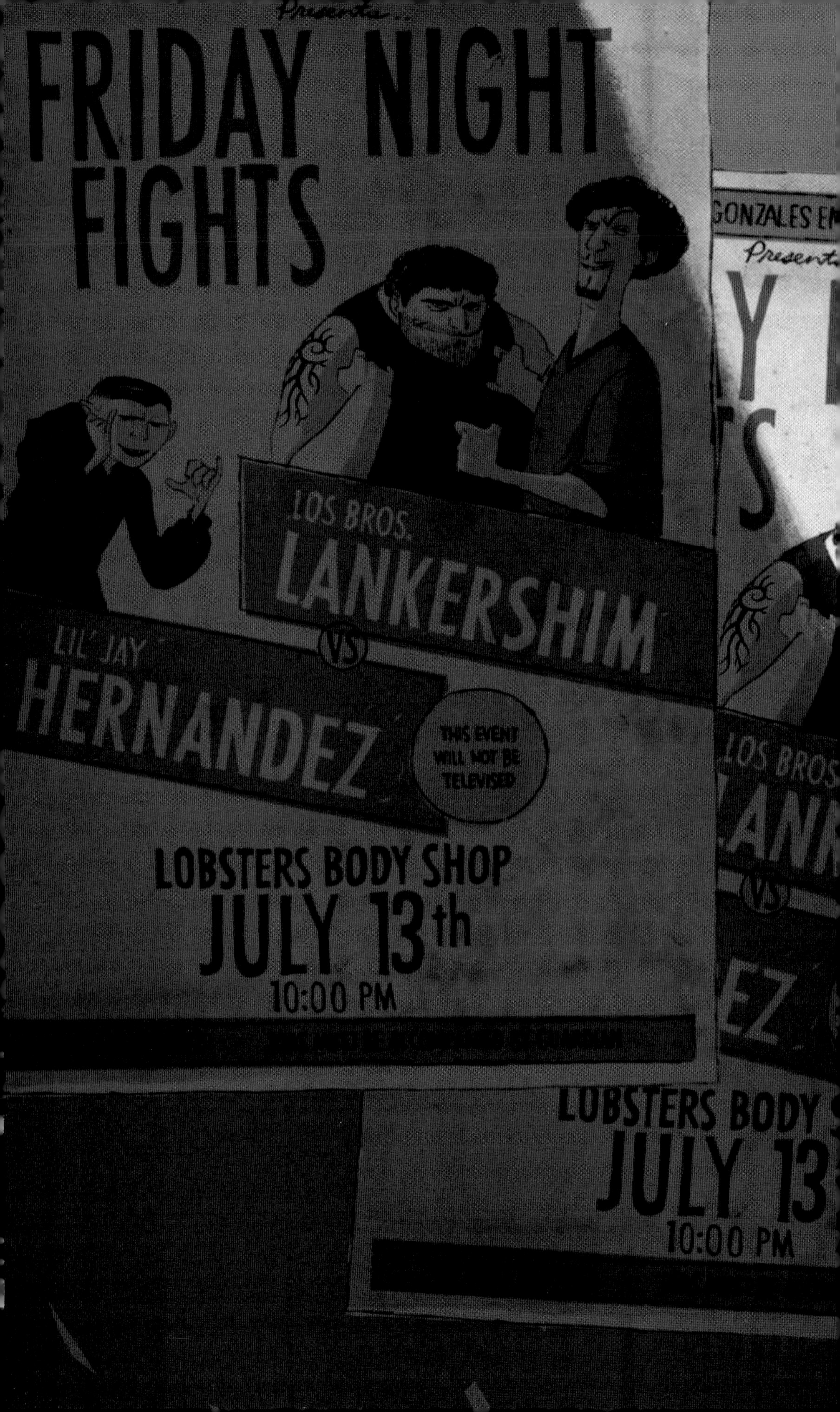

FRIDAY NIGHT FIGHTS
LOS BROS. LANKERSHIM
VS
LIL' JAY HERNANDEZ
THIS EVENT WILL NOT BE TELEVISED
LOBSTERS BODY SHOP
JULY 13th
10:00 PM
LOBSTERS BODY
JULY 13
10:00 PM

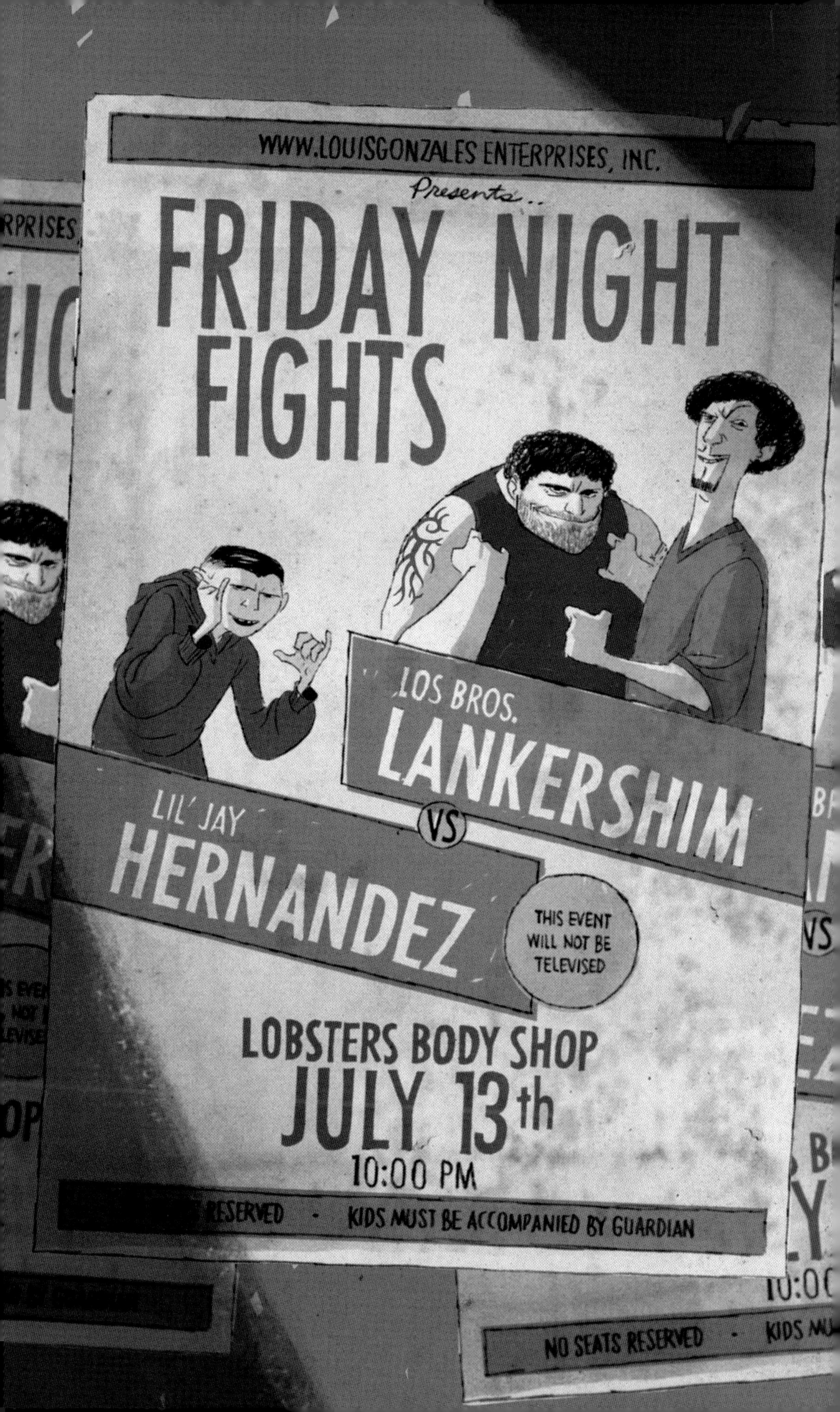
WWW.LOUISGONZALES ENTERPRISES, INC.
Presents..
FRIDAY NIGHT FIGHTS
LOS BROS.
LANKERSHIM
VS
LIL' JAY
HERNANDEZ
THIS EVENT WILL NOT BE TELEVISED
LOBSTERS BODY SHOP
JULY 13th
10:00 PM
RESERVED · KIDS MUST BE ACCOMPANIED BY GUARDIAN
NO SEATS RESERVED

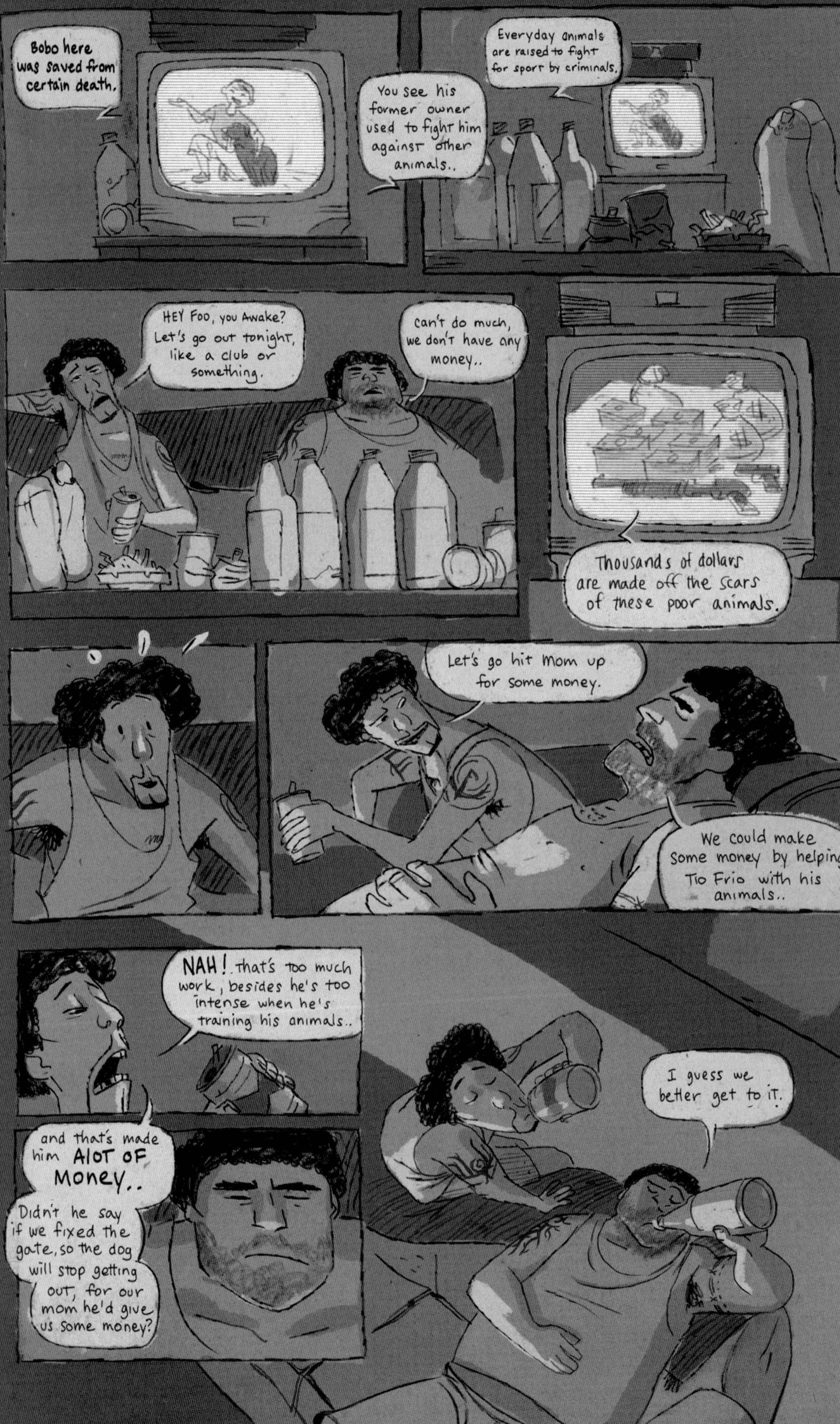
Bobo here was saved from certain death.
You see his former owner used to fight him against other animals..
Everyday animals are raised to fight for sport by criminals.
HEY FOO, you Awake? Let's go out tonight, like a club or something.
can't do much, we don't have any money..
Thousands of dollars are made off the scars of these poor animals.
Let's go hit Mom up for some money.
We could make some money by helping Tio Frio with his animals..
NAH! that's too much work, besides he's too intense when he's training his animals..
and that's made him AlOT OF Money..
Didn't he say if we fixed the gate, so the dog will stop getting out, for our mom he'd give us some money?
I guess we better get to it.

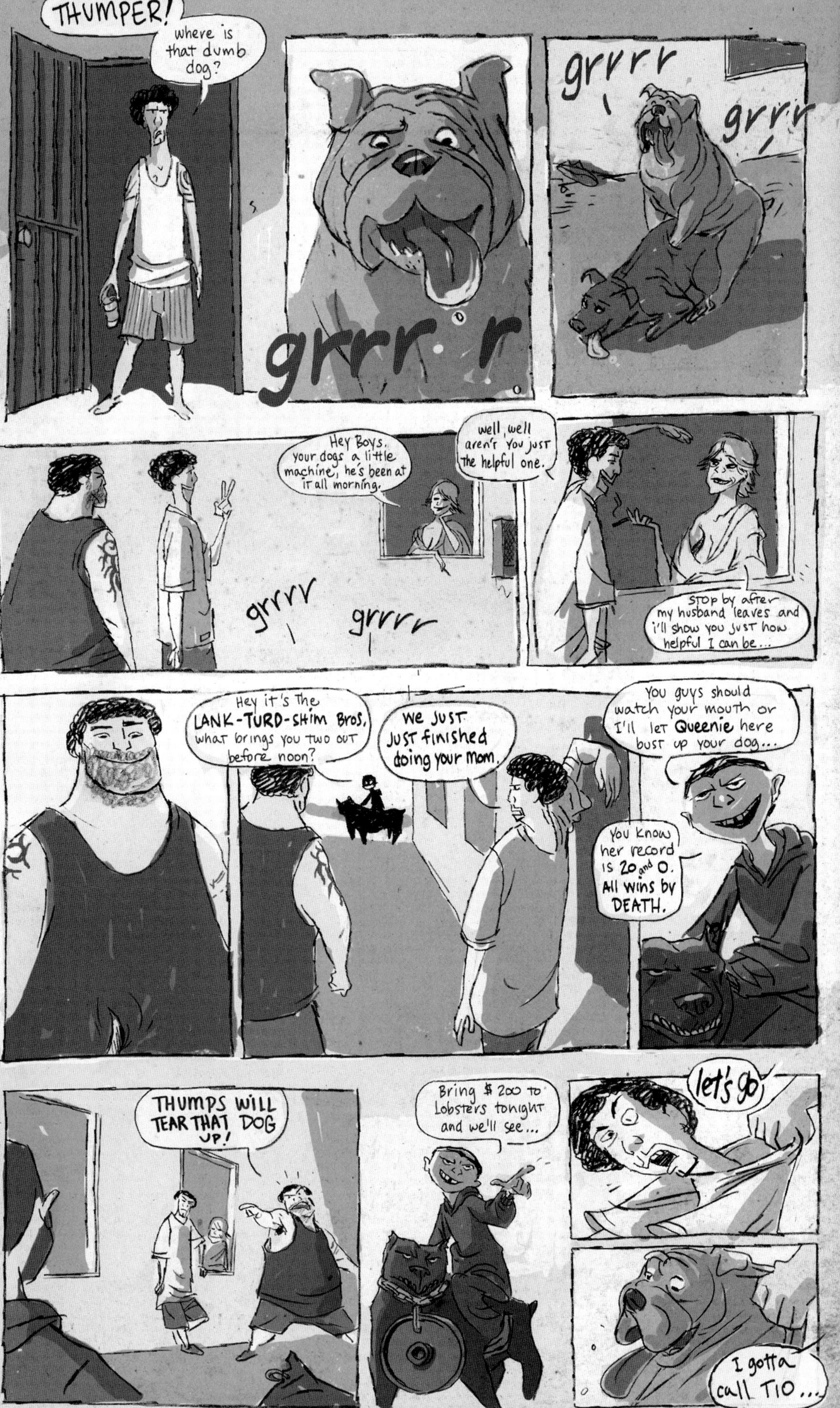

THUMPER!
where is that dumb dog?
grrr r
grrr
grrr
Hey Boys. your dogs a little machine, he's been at it all morning.
well, well aren't you just the helpful one.
grrrr
grrrr
STOP by after my husband leaves and i'll show you just how helpful I can be...
Hey it's The LANK-TURD-SHIM Bros, what brings you two out before noon?
We JUST JUST finished doing your mom.
You guys should watch your mouth or I'll let Queenie here bust up your dog...
You know her record is 20 and 0. All wins by DEATH.
THUMPS WILL TEAR THAT DOG UP!
Bring $200 to Lobsters tonight and we'll see...
let's go
I gotta call TIO...

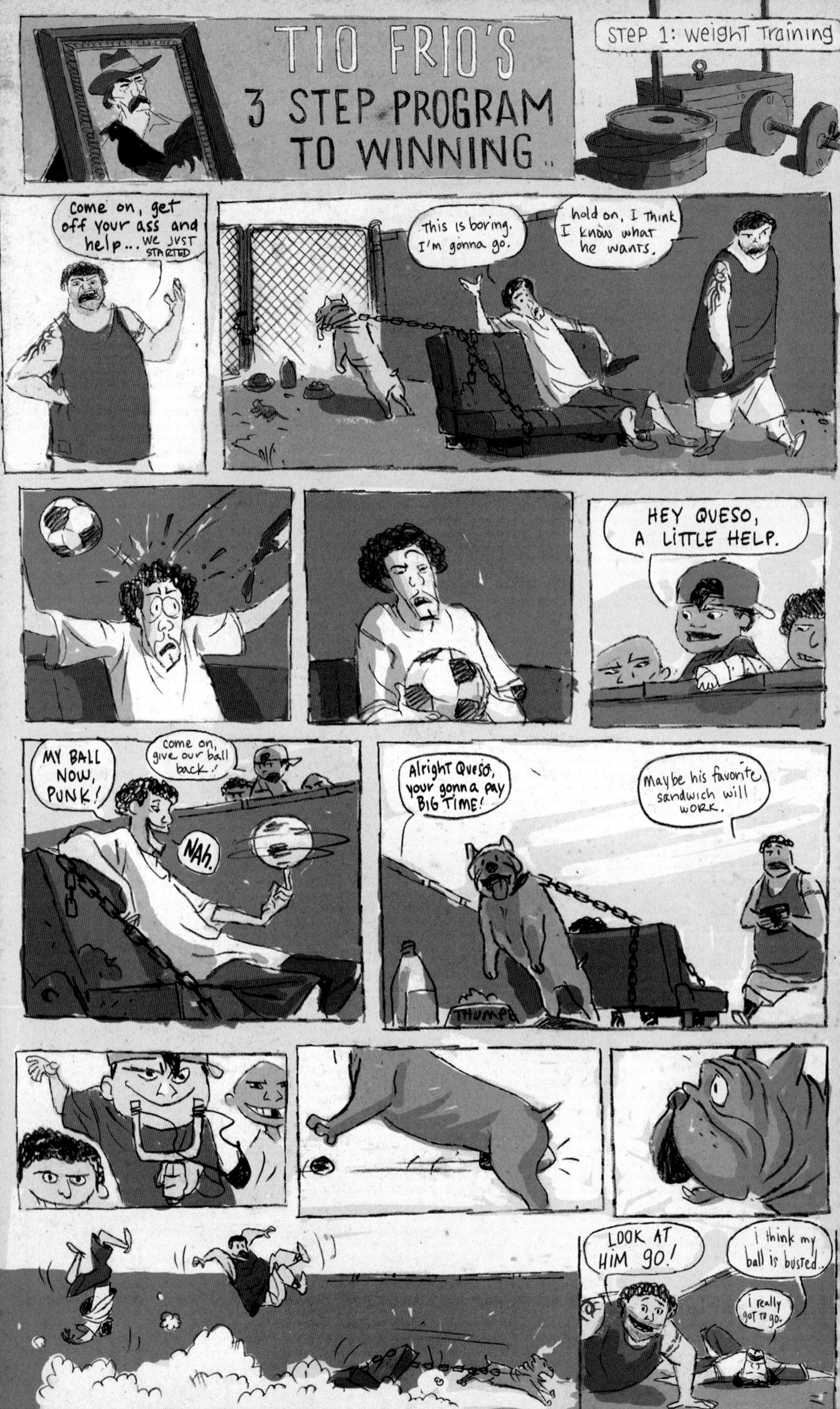
TIO FRIO'S
3 STEP PROGRAM
TO WINNING..
STEP 1: WEIGHT TRAINING
Come on, get off your ass and help... WE JUST STARTED
This is boring. I'm gonna go.
hold on, I think I know what he wants.
HEY QUESO, A LITTLE HELP.
MY BALL NOW, PUNK!
come on, give our ball back!
NAh.
Alright Queso, your gonna pay BIG TIME!
Maybe his favorite sandwich will WORK.
THUMP
LOOK AT HIM GO!
i think my ball is busted..
i really got to go.

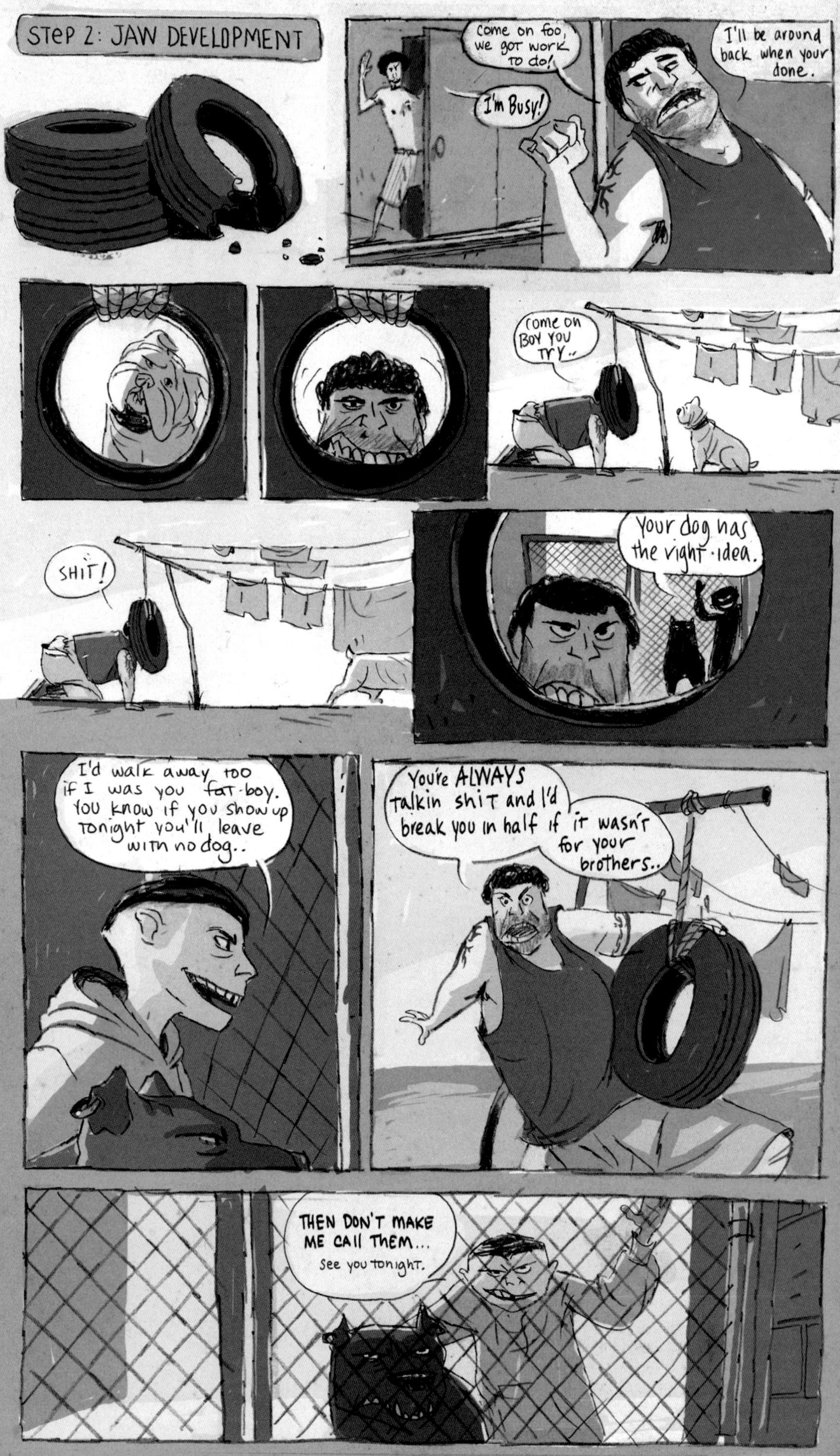
Step 2: JAW DEVELOPMENT
Come on foo, we got work to do!
I'm Busy!
I'll be around back when your done.
Come on Boy you try..
SHIT!
Your dog has the right idea.
I'd walk away too if I was you fat-boy. You know if you show up tonight you'll leave with no dog..
You're ALWAYS talkin shit and I'd break you in half if it wasn't for your brothers..
THEN DON'T MAKE ME CAll THEM...
See you tonight.

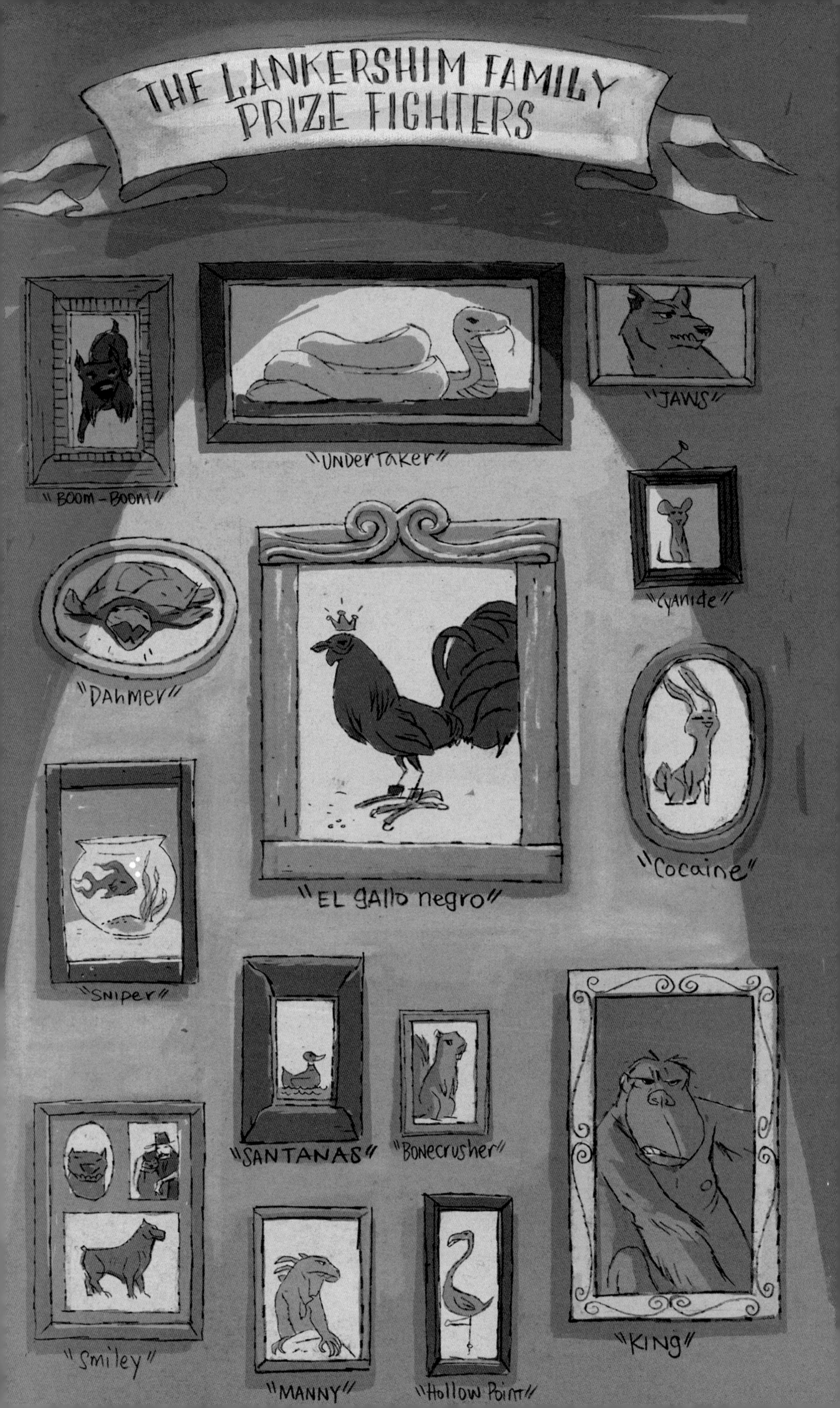
THE LANKERSHIM FAMILY PRIZE FIGHTERS
"BOOM-BOOM"
"UNDERTAKER"
"JAWS"
"CYANIDE"
"DAHMER"
"EL GALLO NEGRO"
"COCAINE"
"SNIPER"
"SANTANAS"
"BONECRUSHER"
"KING"
"SMILEY"
"MANNY"
"HOLLOW POINT"

"THUMPER"

simon dunsdon

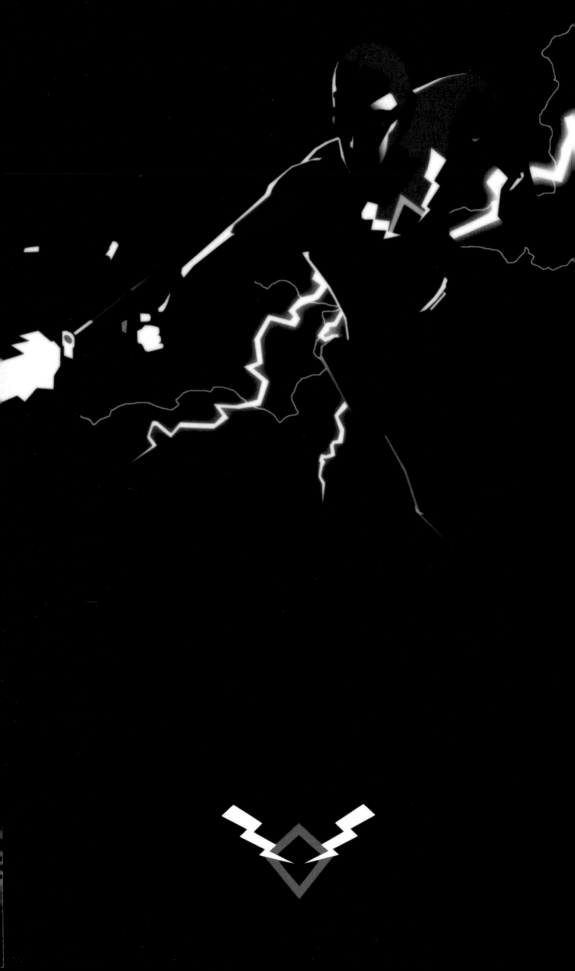

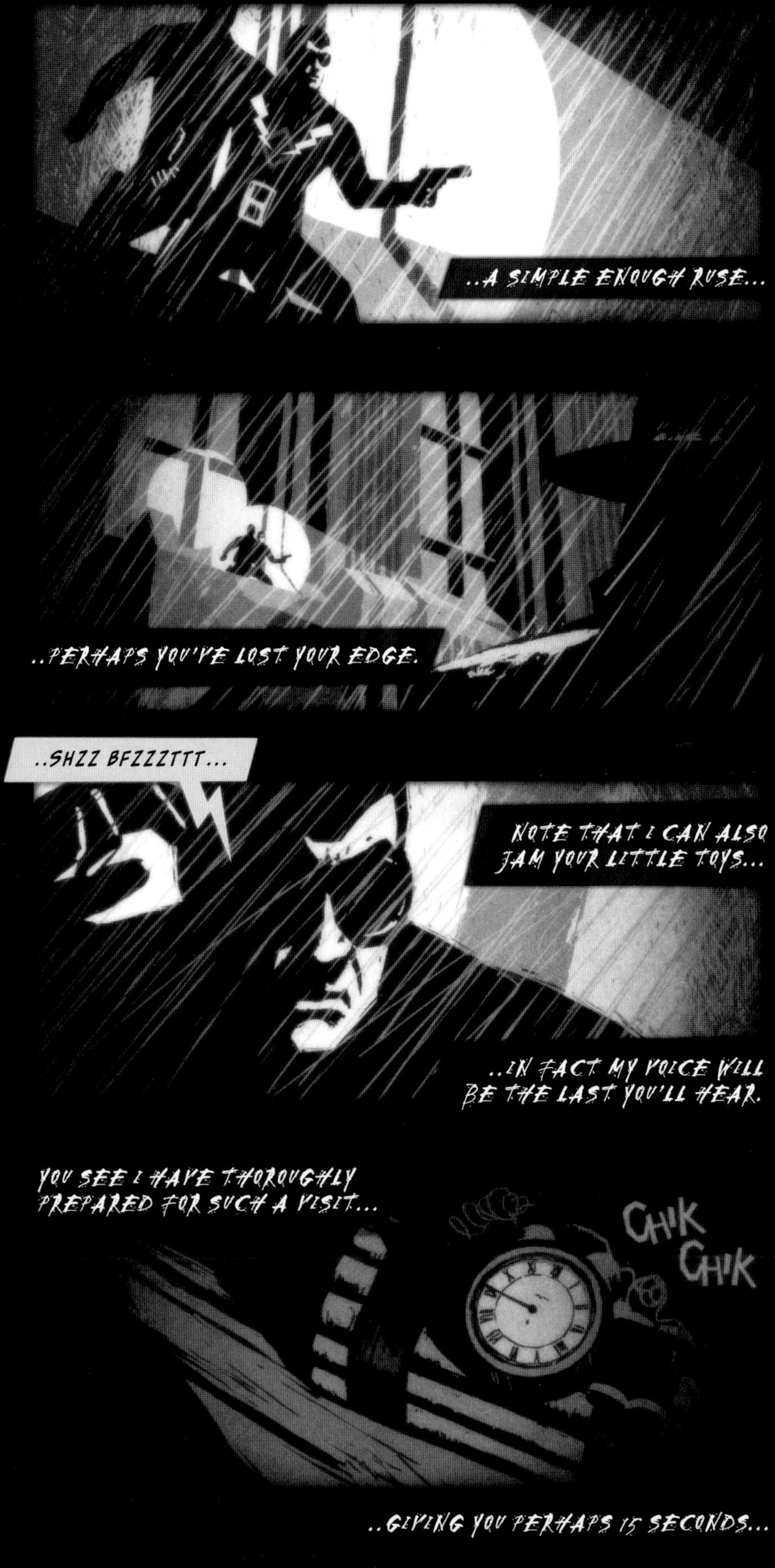
..A SIMPLE ENOUGH RUSE...
..PERHAPS YOU'VE LOST YOUR EDGE.
..SHZZ BFZZZTTT...
NOTE THAT I CAN ALSO JAM YOUR LITTLE TOYS...
..IN FACT MY VOICE WILL BE THE LAST YOU'LL HEAR.
YOU SEE I HAVE THOROUGHLY PREPARED FOR SUCH A VISIT...
CHIK CHIK
..GIVING YOU PERHAPS 15 SECONDS...

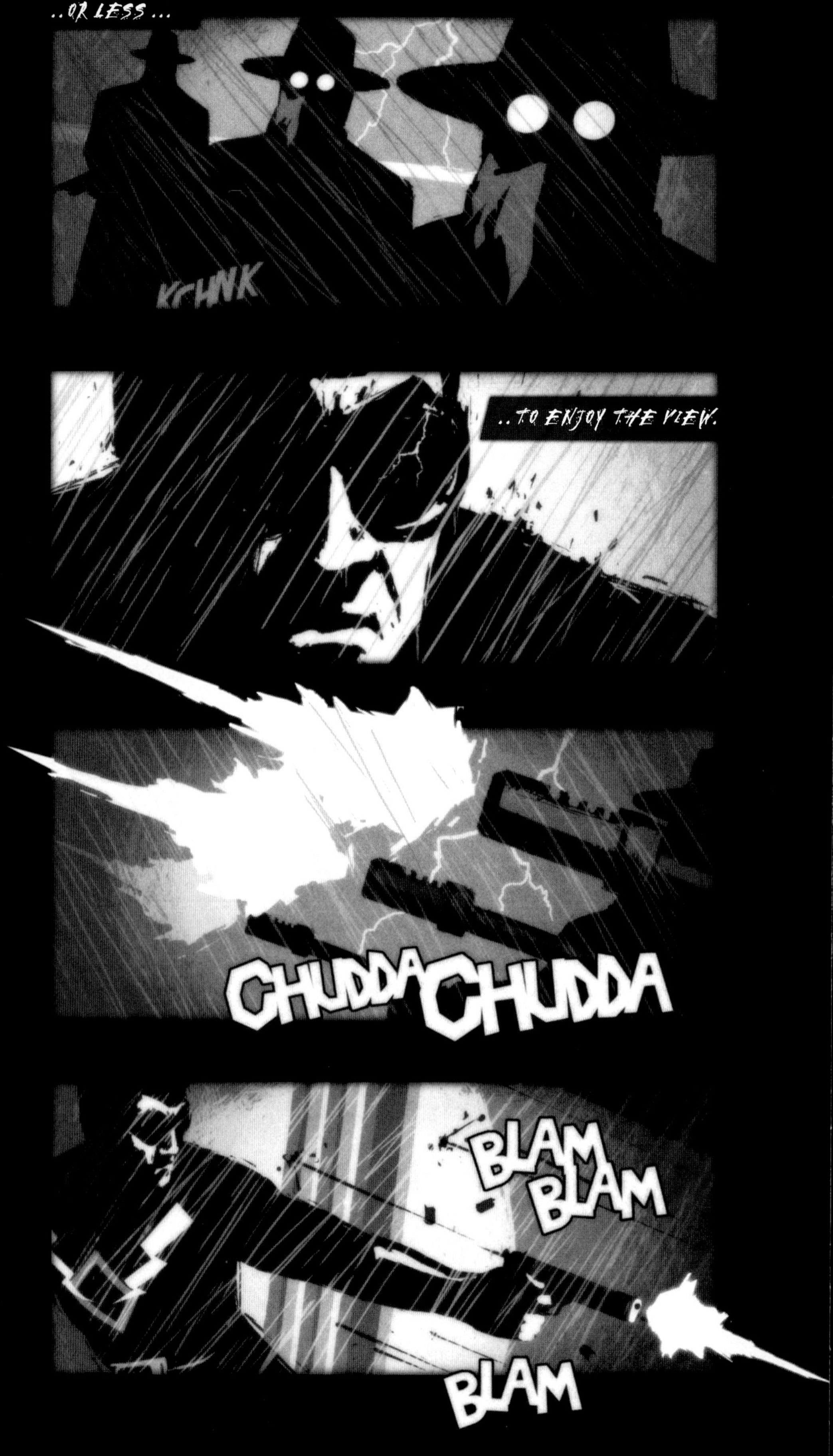
..OR LESS...
KCHNK
..TO ENJOY THE VIEW.
CHUDDA CHUDDA
BLAM
BLAM
BLAM

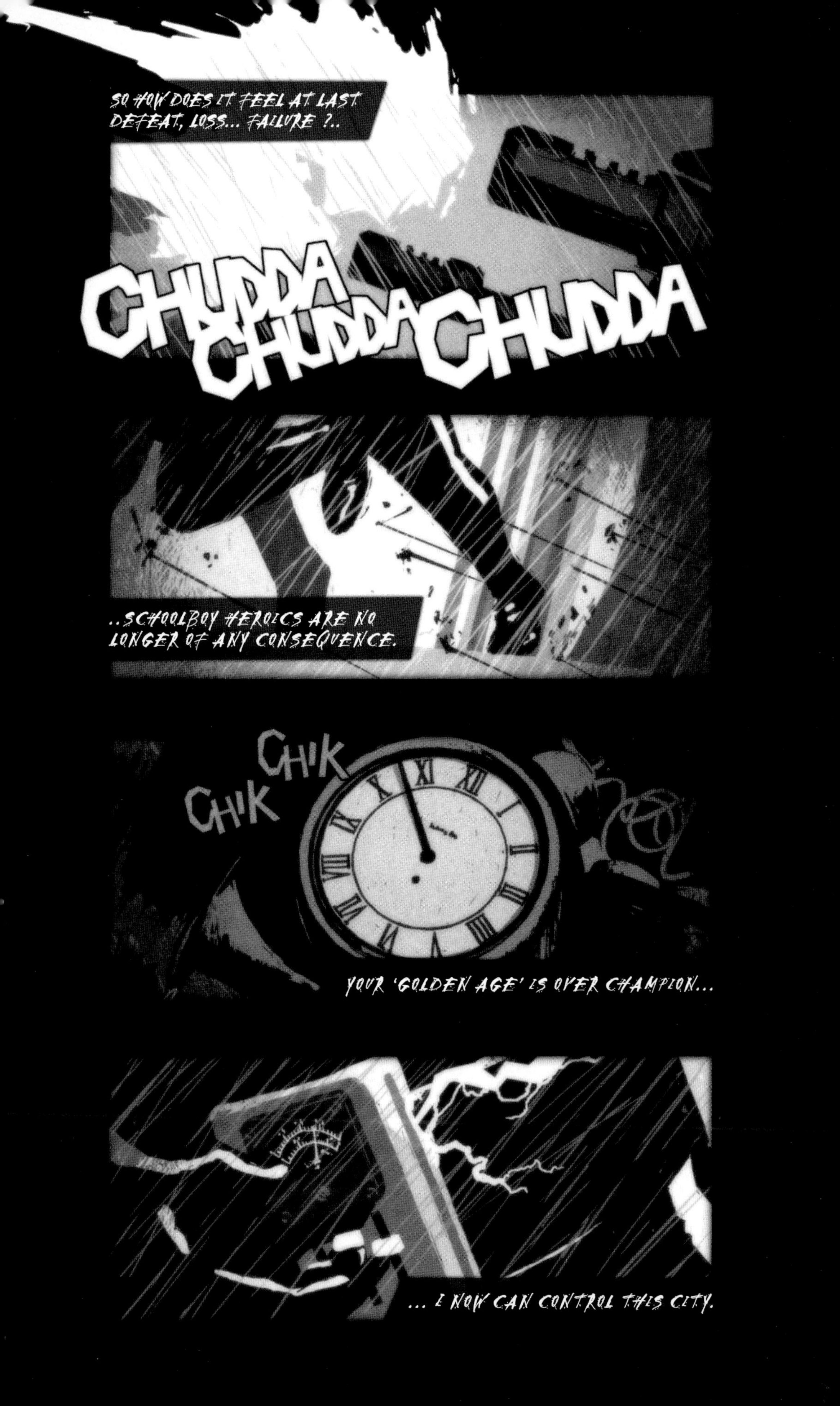
SO HOW DOES IT FEEL AT LAST DEFEAT, LOSS... FAILURE ?..
CHUDDA CHUDDA CHUDDA
..SCHOOLBOY HEROICS ARE NO LONGER OF ANY CONSEQUENCE.
CHIK CHIK
YOUR 'GOLDEN AGE' IS OVER CHAMPION...
... I NOW CAN CONTROL THIS CITY.

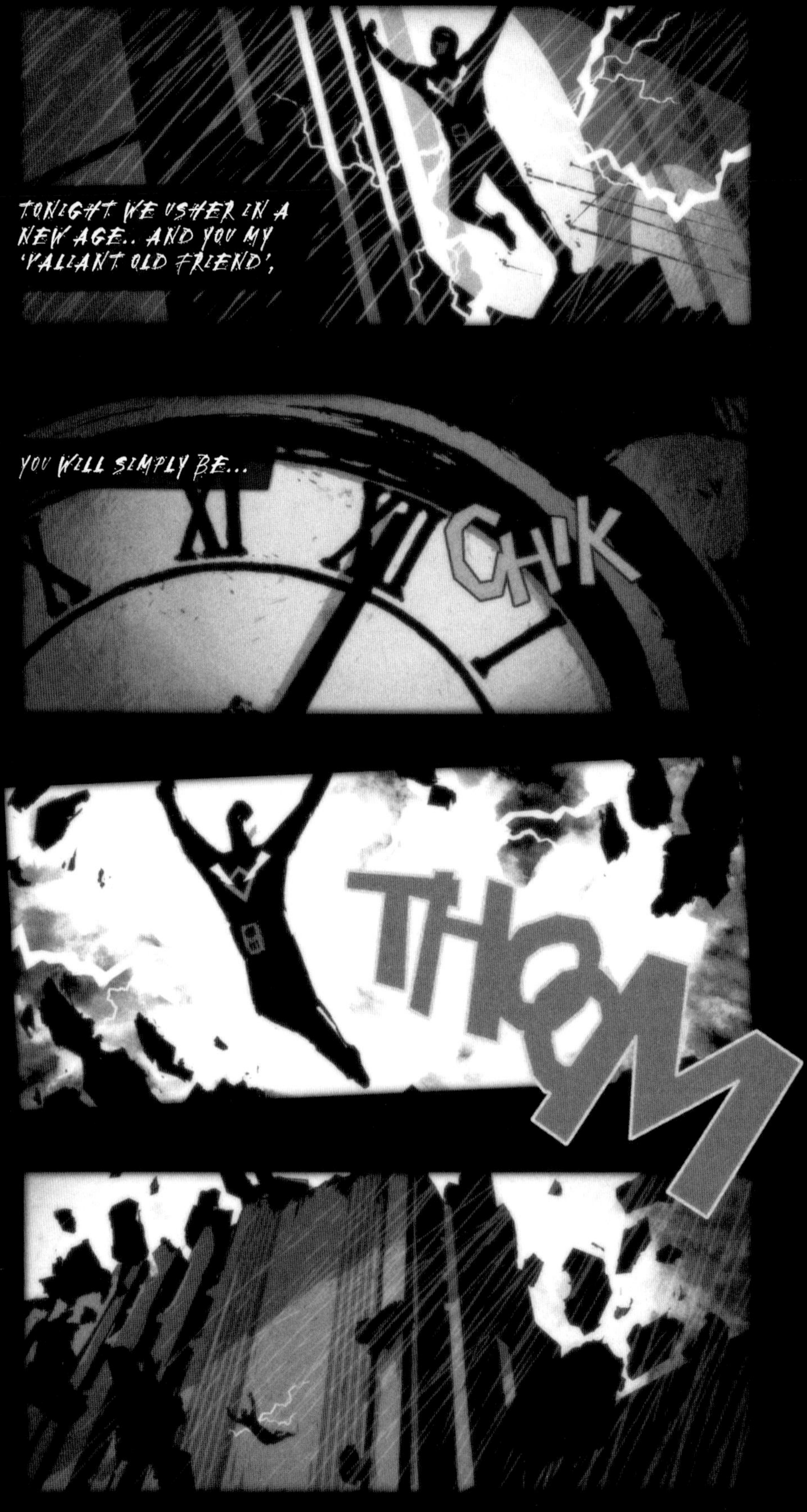

TONIGHT WE USHER IN A NEW AGE.. AND YOU MY 'VALIANT OLD FRIEND',
YOU WILL SIMPLY BE...
CHIK
THOOM
... FORGOTTEN.

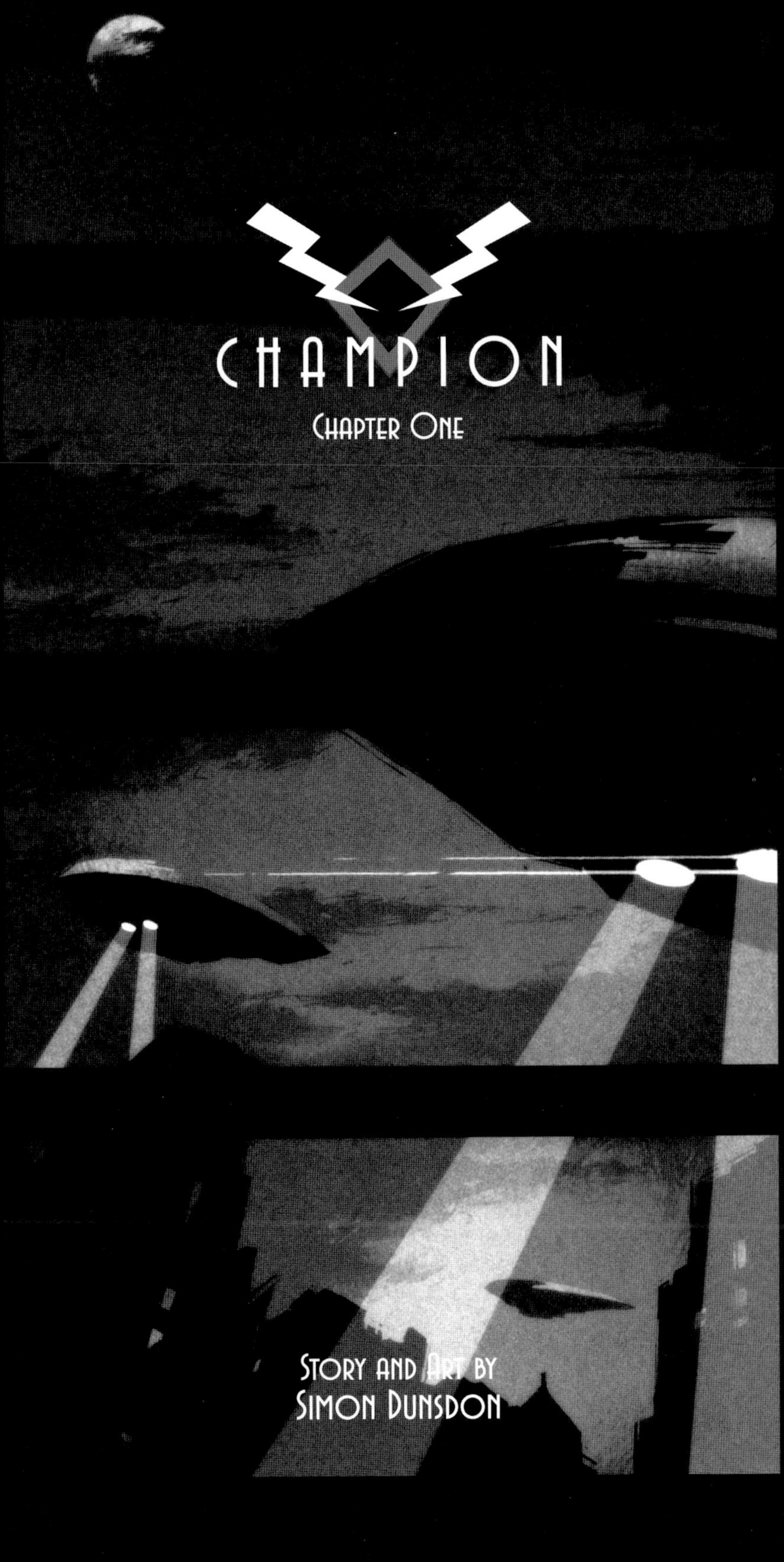
CHAMPION
Chapter One
Story and Art by
Simon Dunsdon

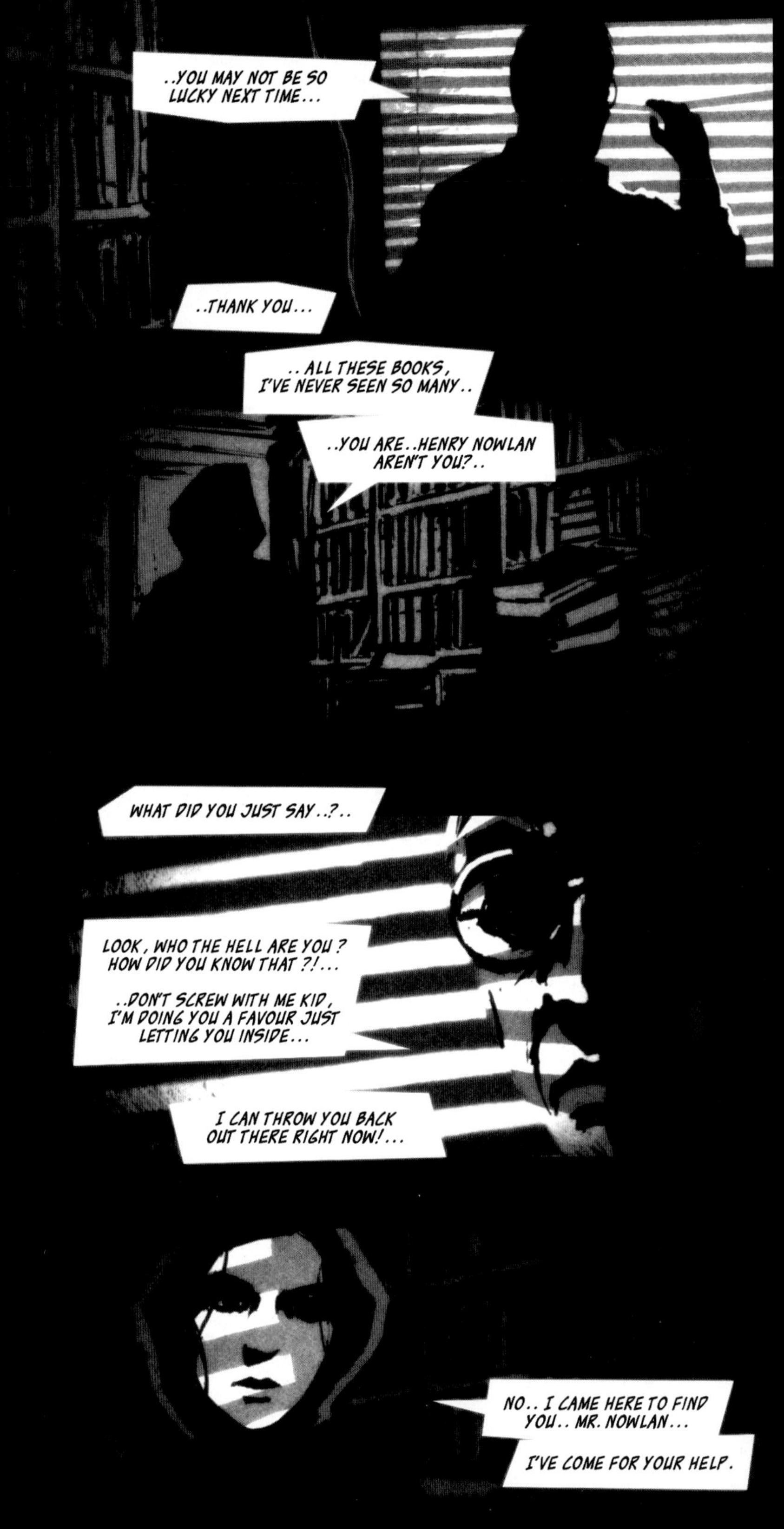
..YOU MAY NOT BE SO LUCKY NEXT TIME...
..THANK YOU...
.. ALL THESE BOOKS, I'VE NEVER SEEN SO MANY..
..YOU ARE..HENRY NOWLAN AREN'T YOU?..
WHAT DID YOU JUST SAY..?..
LOOK, WHO THE HELL ARE YOU? HOW DID YOU KNOW THAT?!...
..DON'T SCREW WITH ME KID, I'M DOING YOU A FAVOUR JUST LETTING YOU INSIDE...
I CAN THROW YOU BACK OUT THERE RIGHT NOW!...
NO.. I CAME HERE TO FIND YOU.. MR. NOWLAN...
I'VE COME FOR YOUR HELP.

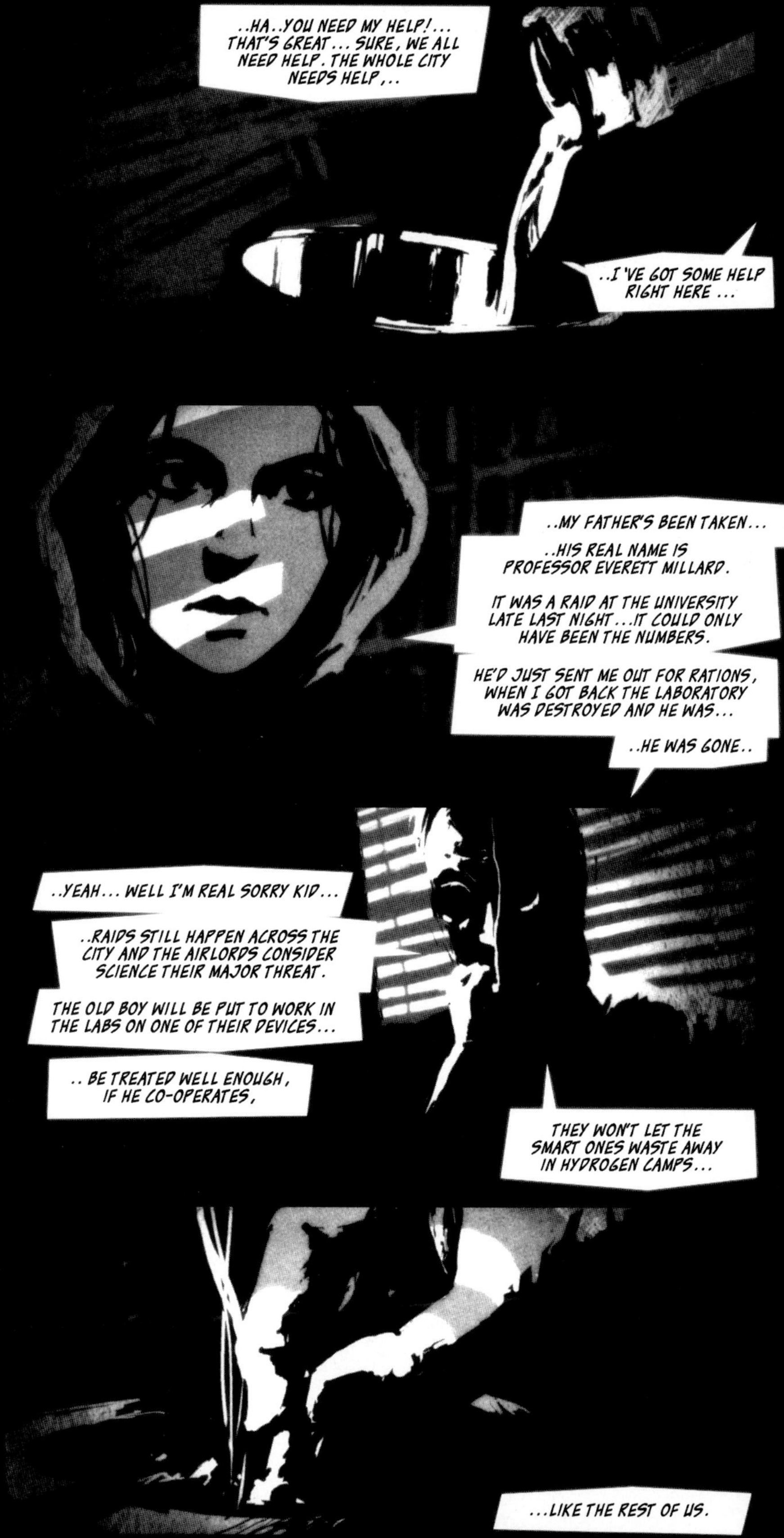

..HA..YOU NEED MY HELP!... THAT'S GREAT... SURE, WE ALL NEED HELP. THE WHOLE CITY NEEDS HELP,..
..I'VE GOT SOME HELP RIGHT HERE ...
..MY FATHER'S BEEN TAKEN...
..HIS REAL NAME IS PROFESSOR EVERETT MILLARD.
IT WAS A RAID AT THE UNIVERSITY LATE LAST NIGHT...IT COULD ONLY HAVE BEEN THE NUMBERS.
HE'D JUST SENT ME OUT FOR RATIONS, WHEN I GOT BACK THE LABORATORY WAS DESTROYED AND HE WAS...
..HE WAS GONE..
..YEAH... WELL I'M REAL SORRY KID...
..RAIDS STILL HAPPEN ACROSS THE CITY AND THE AIRLORDS CONSIDER SCIENCE THEIR MAJOR THREAT.
THE OLD BOY WILL BE PUT TO WORK IN THE LABS ON ONE OF THEIR DEVICES...
.. BE TREATED WELL ENOUGH, IF HE CO-OPERATES,
THEY WON'T LET THE SMART ONES WASTE AWAY IN HYDROGEN CAMPS...
...LIKE THE REST OF US.

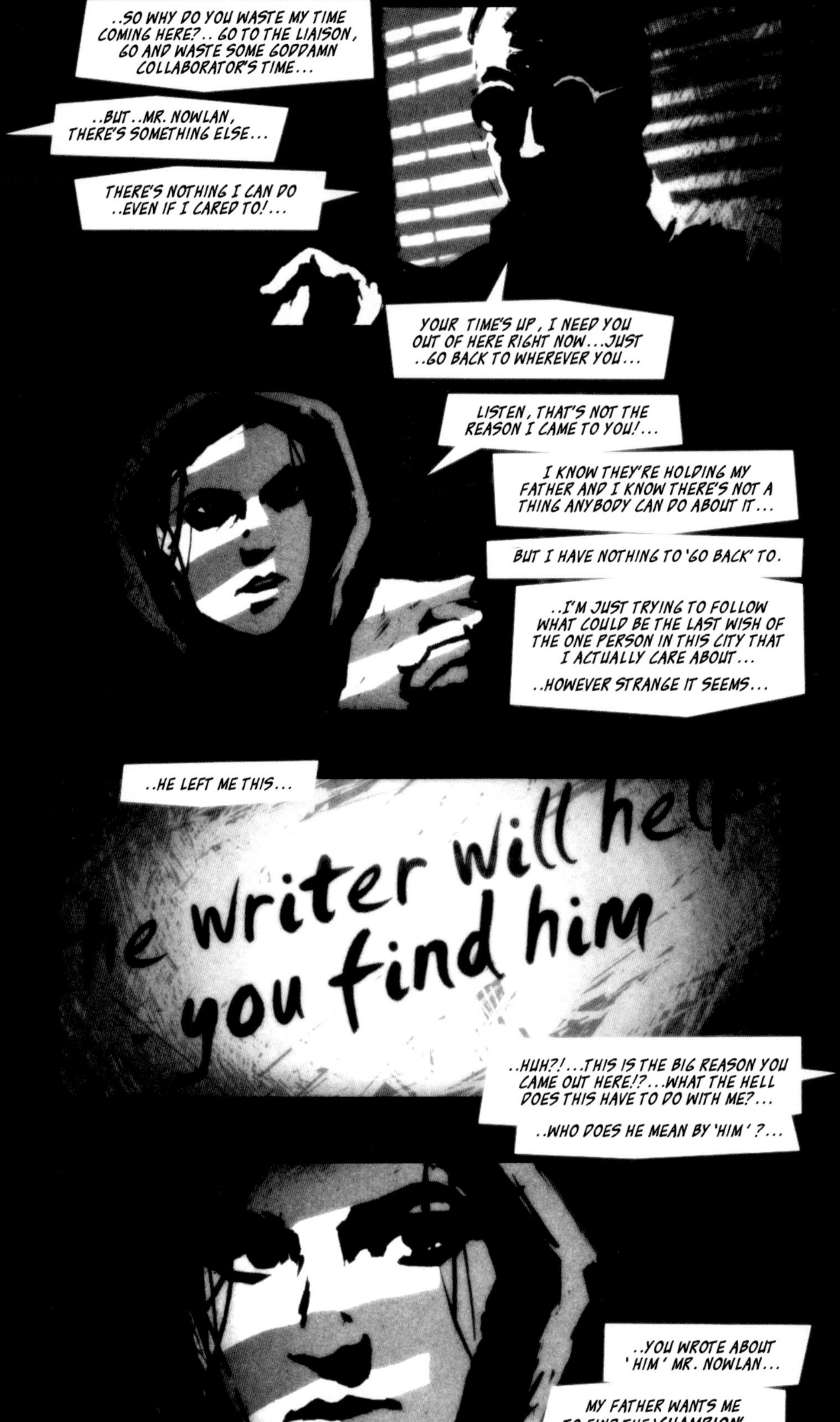
..SO WHY DO YOU WASTE MY TIME COMING HERE?.. GO TO THE LIAISON, GO AND WASTE SOME GODDAMN COLLABORATOR'S TIME...
..BUT..MR. NOWLAN, THERE'S SOMETHING ELSE...
THERE'S NOTHING I CAN DO ..EVEN IF I CARED TO!...
YOUR TIME'S UP, I NEED YOU OUT OF HERE RIGHT NOW...JUST ..GO BACK TO WHEREVER YOU...
LISTEN, THAT'S NOT THE REASON I CAME TO YOU!...
I KNOW THEY'RE HOLDING MY FATHER AND I KNOW THERE'S NOT A THING ANYBODY CAN DO ABOUT IT...
BUT I HAVE NOTHING TO 'GO BACK' TO.
..I'M JUST TRYING TO FOLLOW WHAT COULD BE THE LAST WISH OF THE ONE PERSON IN THIS CITY THAT I ACTUALLY CARE ABOUT...
..HOWEVER STRANGE IT SEEMS...
..HE LEFT ME THIS...
writer will hel
you find him
..HUH?!...THIS IS THE BIG REASON YOU CAME OUT HERE!?...WHAT THE HELL DOES THIS HAVE TO DO WITH ME?...
..WHO DOES HE MEAN BY 'HIM'?...
..YOU WROTE ABOUT 'HIM' MR. NOWLAN...
MY FATHER WANTS ME TO FIND THE 'CHAMPION'...

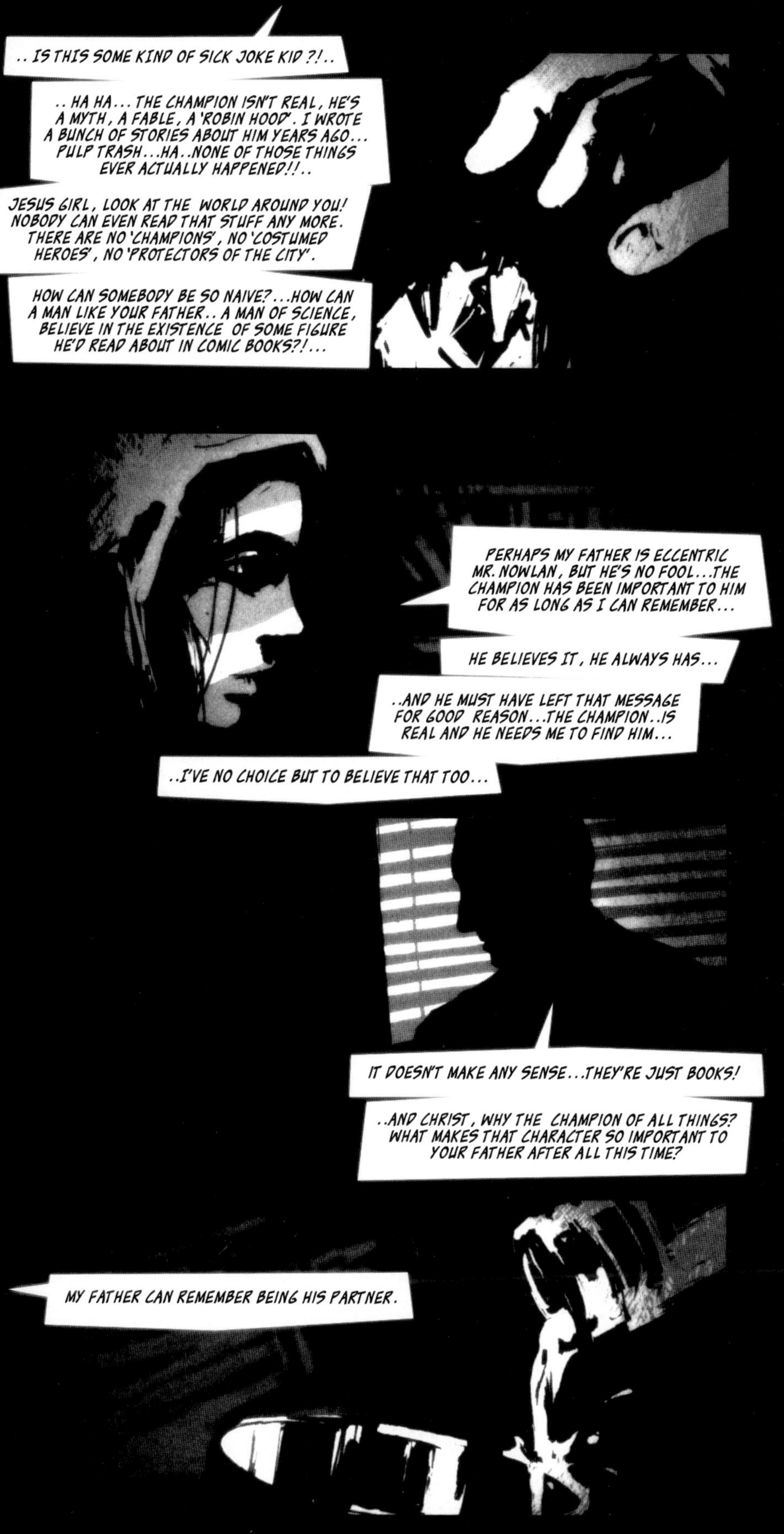
.. IS THIS SOME KIND OF SICK JOKE KID ?!..
.. HA HA... THE CHAMPION ISN'T REAL, HE'S A MYTH, A FABLE, A 'ROBIN HOOD'. I WROTE A BUNCH OF STORIES ABOUT HIM YEARS AGO... PULP TRASH...HA..NONE OF THOSE THINGS EVER ACTUALLY HAPPENED!!..
JESUS GIRL, LOOK AT THE WORLD AROUND YOU! NOBODY CAN EVEN READ THAT STUFF ANY MORE. THERE ARE NO 'CHAMPIONS', NO 'COSTUMED HEROES', NO 'PROTECTORS OF THE CITY'.
HOW CAN SOMEBODY BE SO NAIVE?...HOW CAN A MAN LIKE YOUR FATHER.. A MAN OF SCIENCE, BELIEVE IN THE EXISTENCE OF SOME FIGURE HE'D READ ABOUT IN COMIC BOOKS?!...
PERHAPS MY FATHER IS ECCENTRIC MR. NOWLAN, BUT HE'S NO FOOL...THE CHAMPION HAS BEEN IMPORTANT TO HIM FOR AS LONG AS I CAN REMEMBER...
HE BELIEVES IT, HE ALWAYS HAS...
..AND HE MUST HAVE LEFT THAT MESSAGE FOR GOOD REASON...THE CHAMPION..IS REAL AND HE NEEDS ME TO FIND HIM...
..I'VE NO CHOICE BUT TO BELIEVE THAT TOO...
IT DOESN'T MAKE ANY SENSE...THEY'RE JUST BOOKS!
..AND CHRIST, WHY THE CHAMPION OF ALL THINGS? WHAT MAKES THAT CHARACTER SO IMPORTANT TO YOUR FATHER AFTER ALL THIS TIME?
MY FATHER CAN REMEMBER BEING HIS PARTNER.

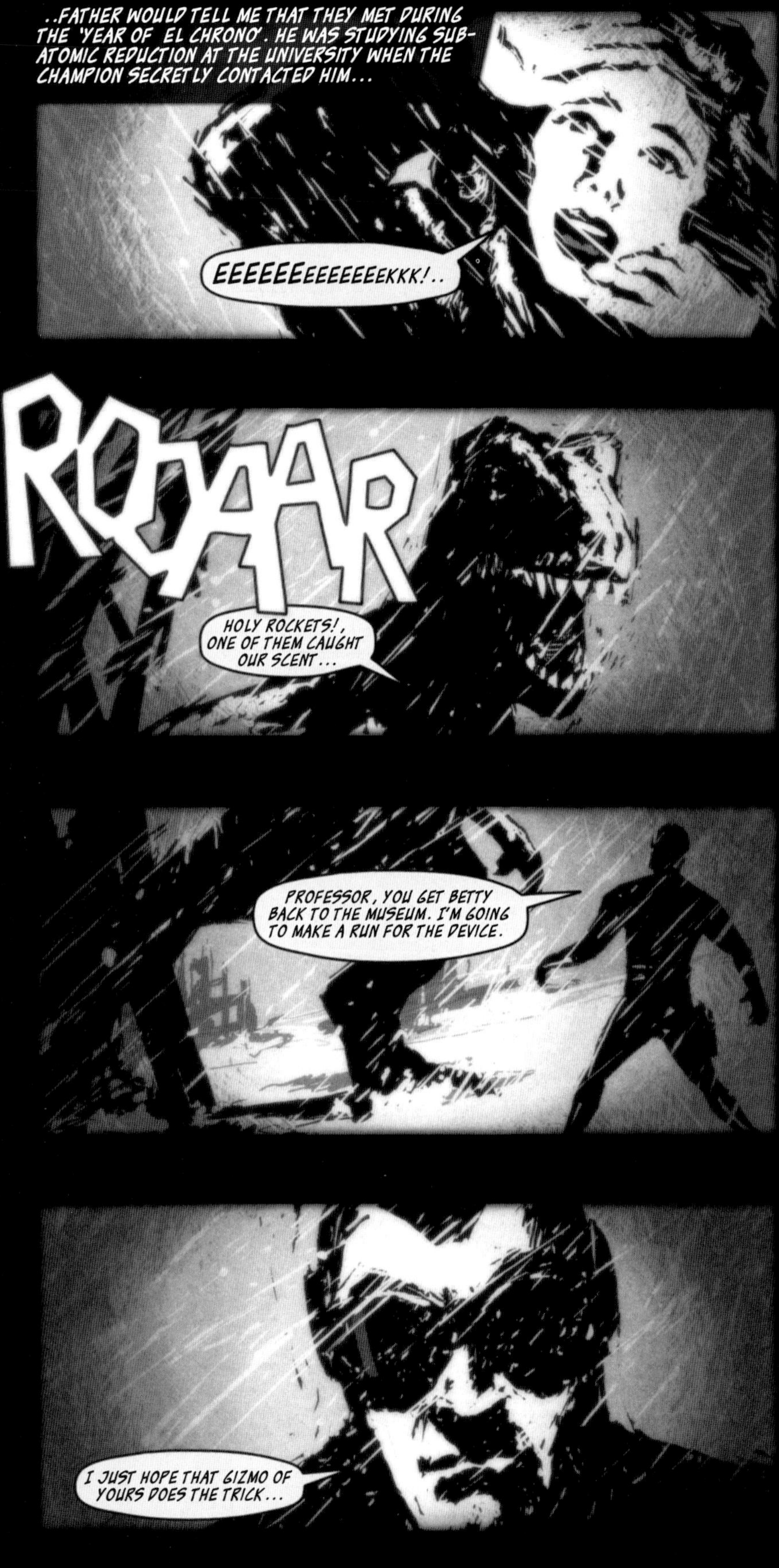
..FATHER WOULD TELL ME THAT THEY MET DURING THE 'YEAR OF EL CHRONO'. HE WAS STUDYING SUB-ATOMIC REDUCTION AT THE UNIVERSITY WHEN THE CHAMPION SECRETLY CONTACTED HIM...
EEEEEEEEEEEEEKKK!..
ROOAAR
HOLY ROCKETS!, ONE OF THEM CAUGHT OUR SCENT...
PROFESSOR, YOU GET BETTY BACK TO THE MUSEUM. I'M GOING TO MAKE A RUN FOR THE DEVICE.
I JUST HOPE THAT GIZMO OF YOURS DOES THE TRICK...

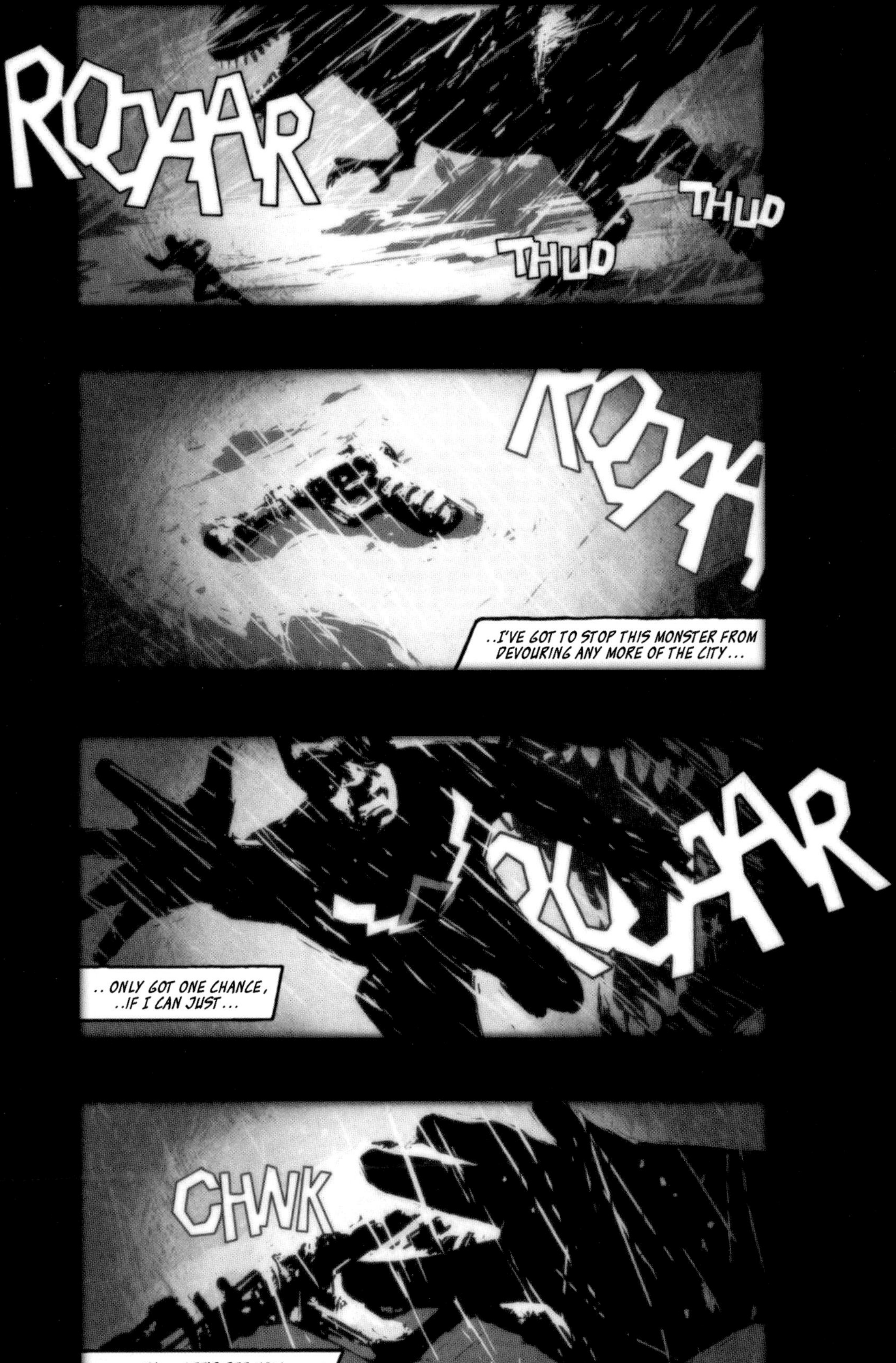
ROOAAR
THUD
THUD
..I'VE GOT TO STOP THIS MONSTER FROM DEVOURING ANY MORE OF THE CITY...
.. ONLY GOT ONE CHANCE, ..IF I CAN JUST...
CHNK
..HA... LET'S SEE HOW YOU LIKE THE TASTE OF THIS...

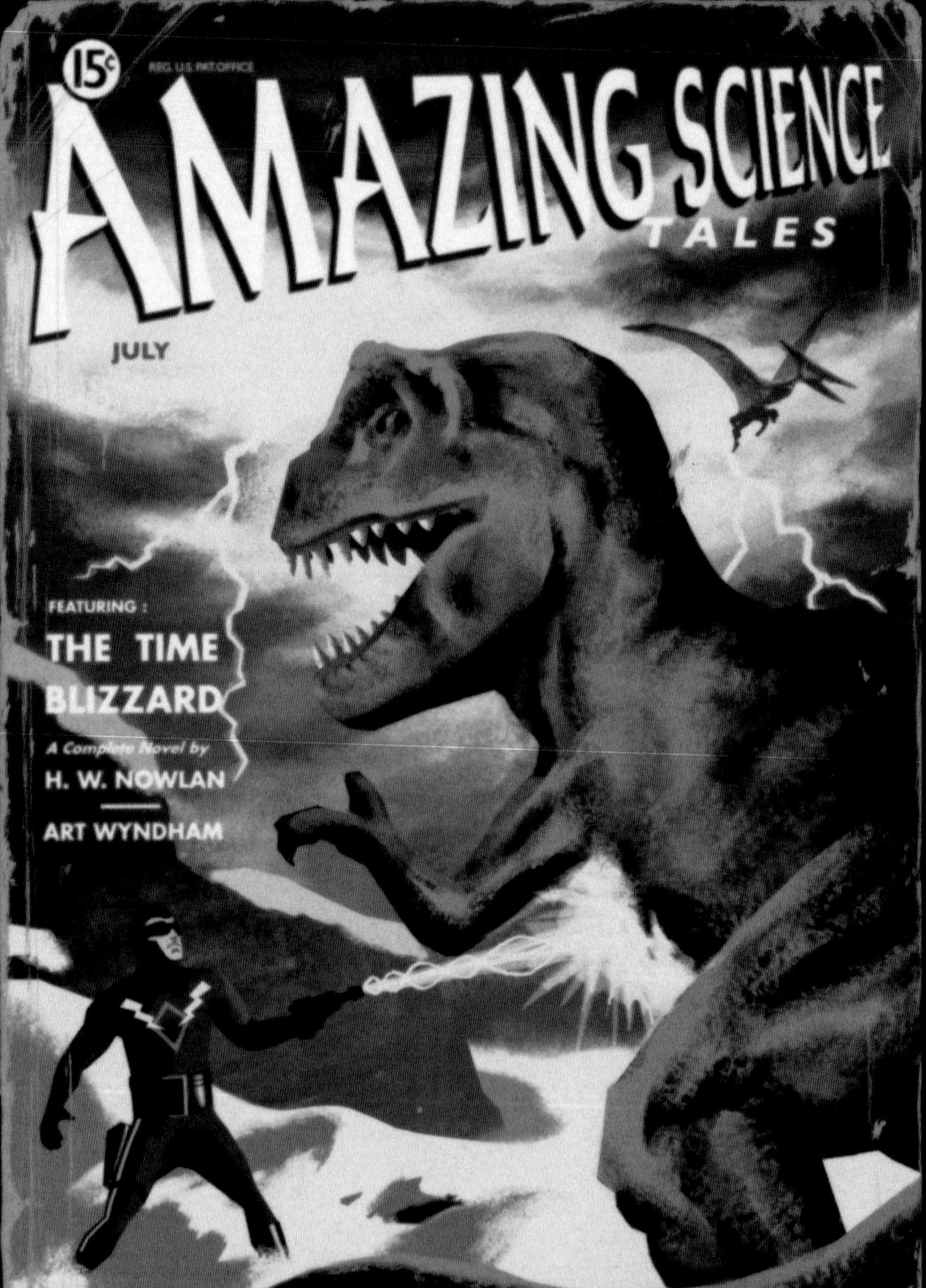
15¢
REG. U.S. PAT. OFFICE
AMAZING SCIENCE
TALES
JULY
FEATURING :
THE TIME
BLIZZARD
A Complete Novel by
H. W. NOWLAN
ART WYNDHAM
FANTASTIC STORIES of ADVENTURE
A THRILLING
PUBLICATION

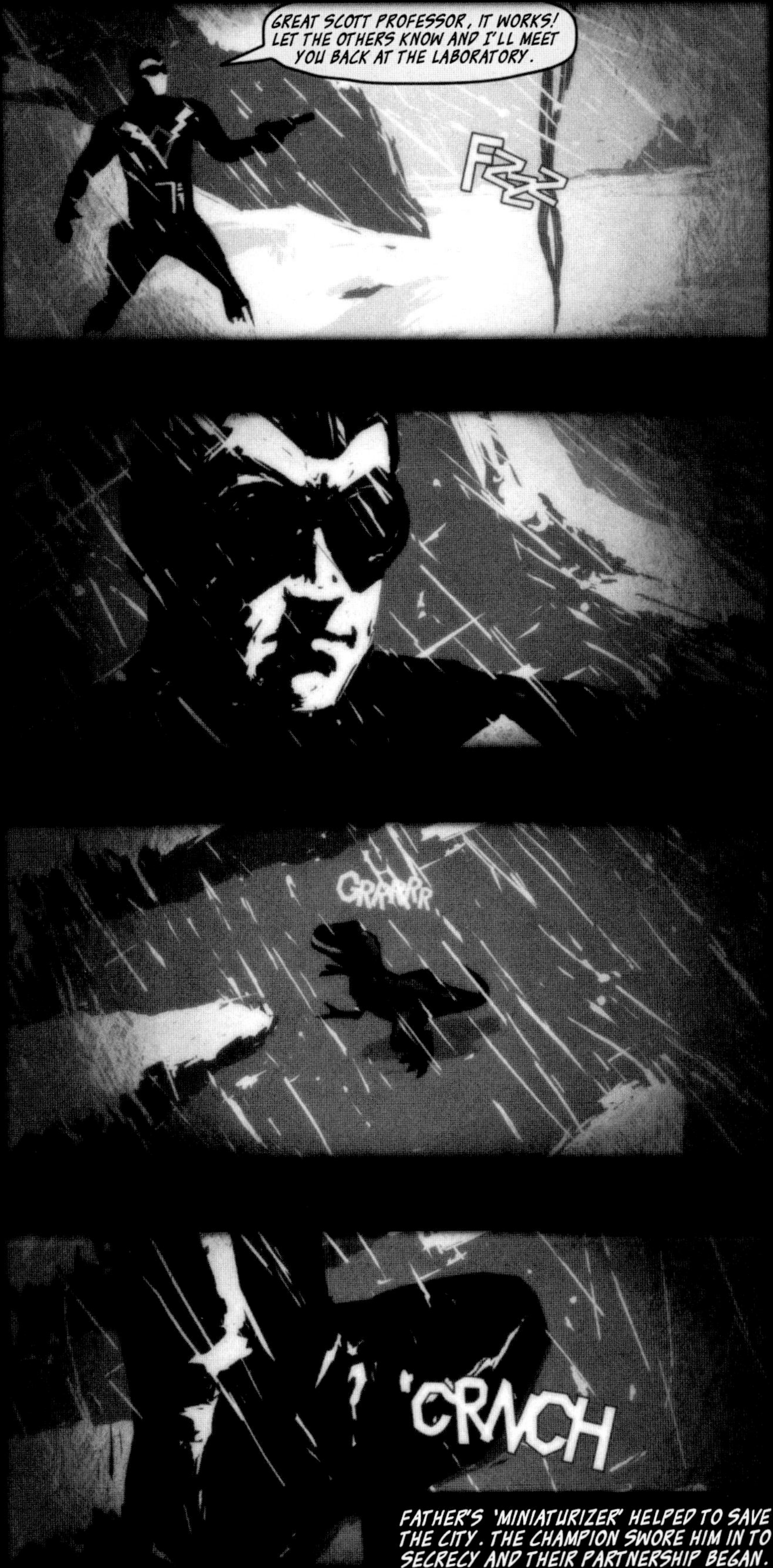
GREAT SCOTT PROFESSOR, IT WORKS! LET THE OTHERS KNOW AND I'LL MEET YOU BACK AT THE LABORATORY.
FZZZ
GRRRRR
CRNCH
FATHER'S 'MINIATURIZER' HELPED TO SAVE THE CITY. THE CHAMPION SWORE HIM IN TO SECRECY AND THEIR PARTNERSHIP BEGAN.

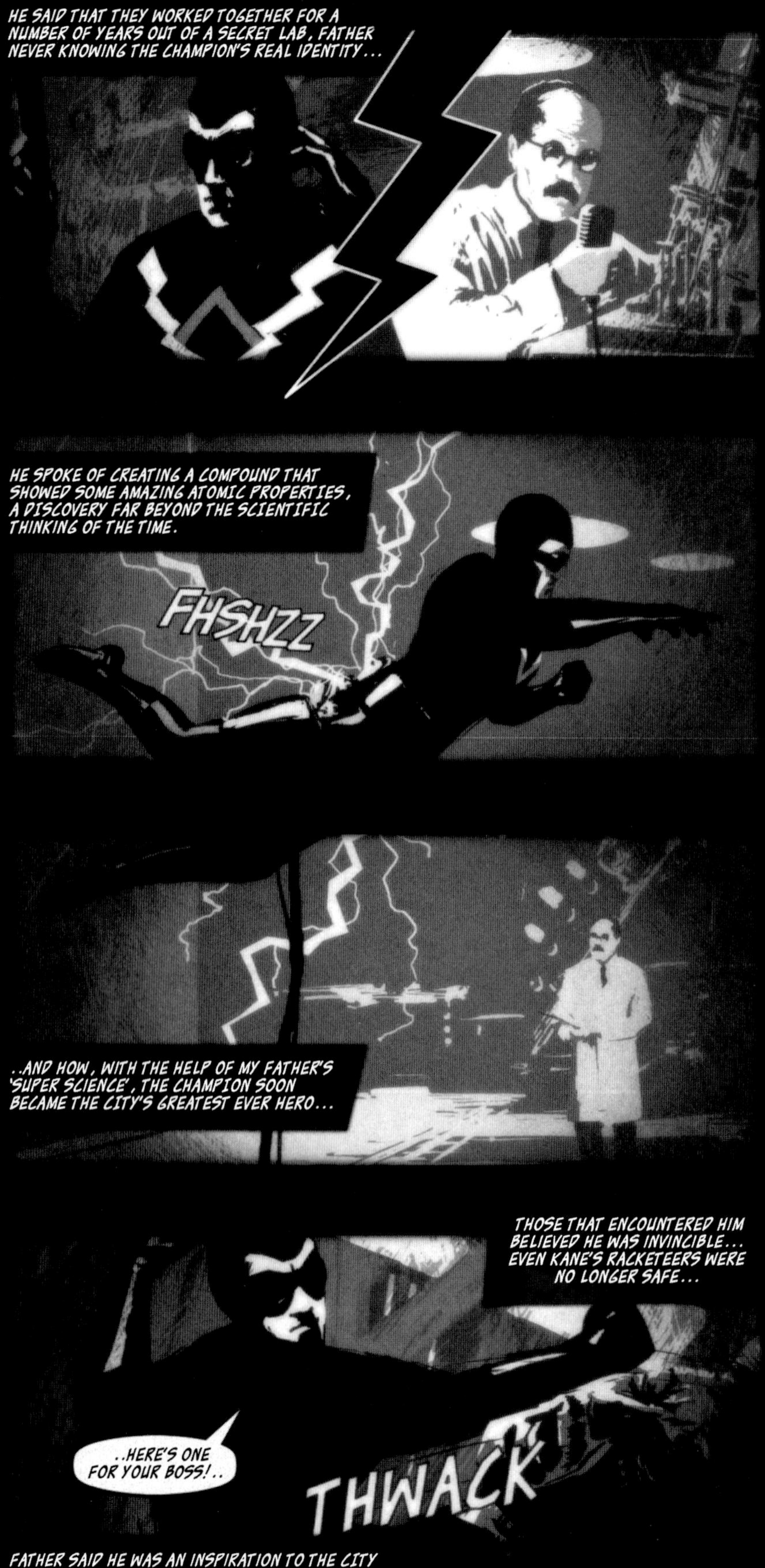
HE SAID THAT THEY WORKED TOGETHER FOR A NUMBER OF YEARS OUT OF A SECRET LAB, FATHER NEVER KNOWING THE CHAMPION'S REAL IDENTITY...
HE SPOKE OF CREATING A COMPOUND THAT SHOWED SOME AMAZING ATOMIC PROPERTIES, A DISCOVERY FAR BEYOND THE SCIENTIFIC THINKING OF THE TIME.
FHSHZZ
..AND HOW, WITH THE HELP OF MY FATHER'S 'SUPER SCIENCE', THE CHAMPION SOON BECAME THE CITY'S GREATEST EVER HERO...
THOSE THAT ENCOUNTERED HIM BELIEVED HE WAS INVINCIBLE... EVEN KANE'S RACKETEERS WERE NO LONGER SAFE...
..HERE'S ONE FOR YOUR BOSS!..
THWACK
FATHER SAID HE WAS AN INSPIRATION TO THE CITY AND A THORN IN THE SIDE OF THE...

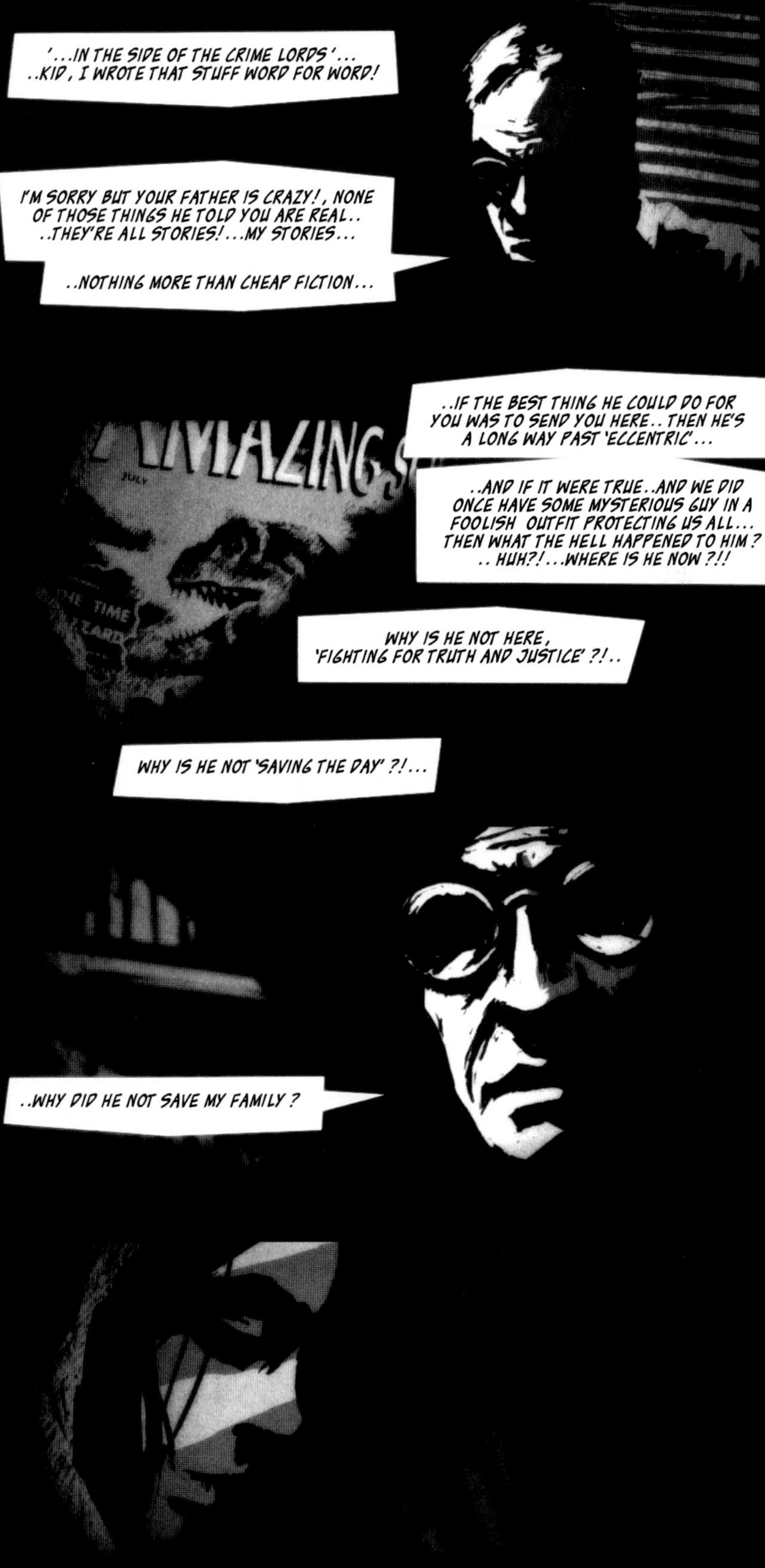
'...IN THE SIDE OF THE CRIME LORDS'... ..KID, I WROTE THAT STUFF WORD FOR WORD!
I'M SORRY BUT YOUR FATHER IS CRAZY!, NONE OF THOSE THINGS HE TOLD YOU ARE REAL.. ..THEY'RE ALL STORIES!...MY STORIES...
..NOTHING MORE THAN CHEAP FICTION...
AMAZING
..IF THE BEST THING HE COULD DO FOR YOU WAS TO SEND YOU HERE.. THEN HE'S A LONG WAY PAST 'ECCENTRIC'...
..AND IF IT WERE TRUE..AND WE DID ONCE HAVE SOME MYSTERIOUS GUY IN A FOOLISH OUTFIT PROTECTING US ALL... THEN WHAT THE HELL HAPPENED TO HIM? .. HUH?!...WHERE IS HE NOW?!!
WHY IS HE NOT HERE, 'FIGHTING FOR TRUTH AND JUSTICE'?!..
WHY IS HE NOT 'SAVING THE DAY'?!...
..WHY DID HE NOT SAVE MY FAMILY?

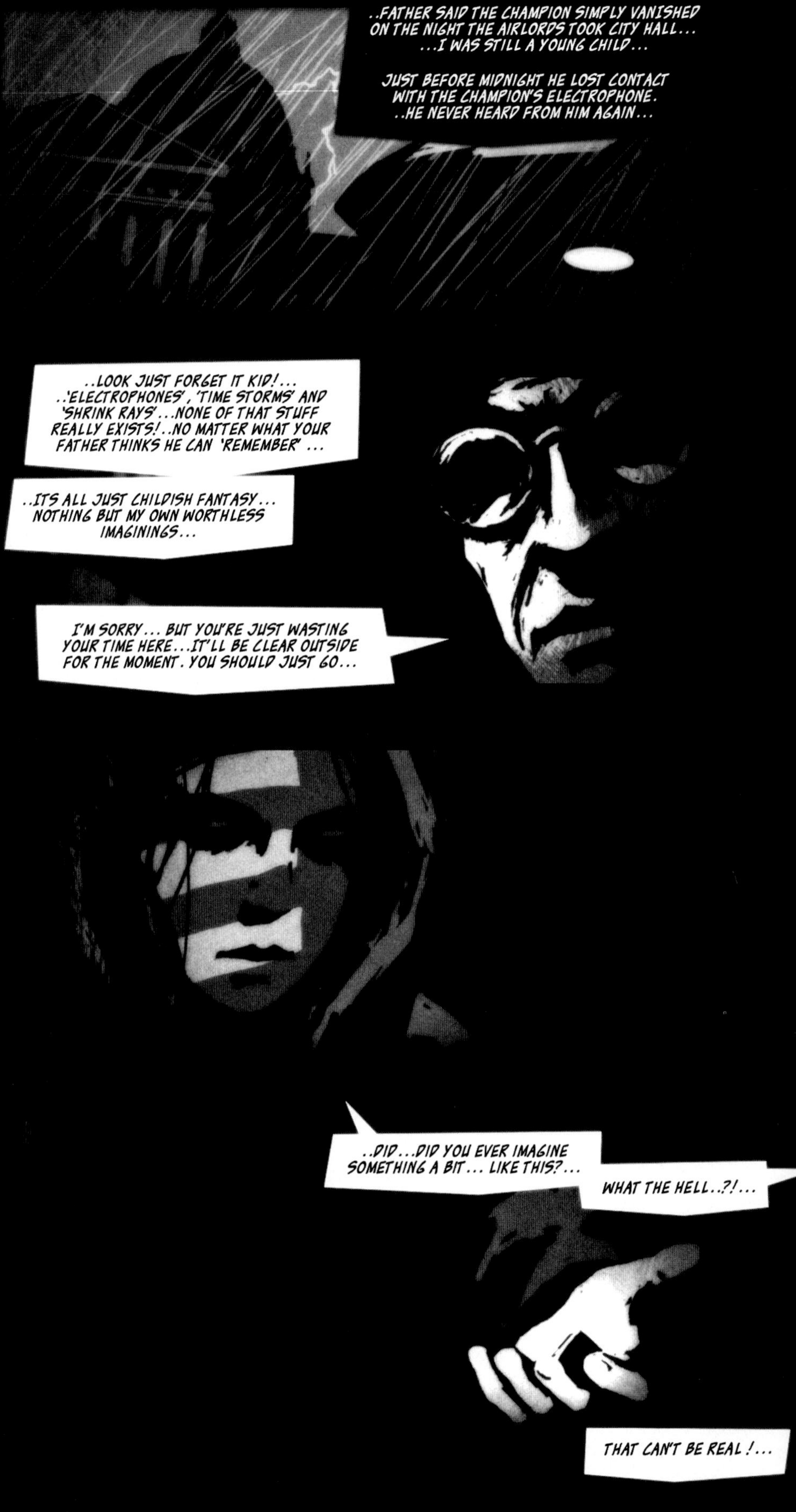
..FATHER SAID THE CHAMPION SIMPLY VANISHED ON THE NIGHT THE AIRLORDS TOOK CITY HALL... ...I WAS STILL A YOUNG CHILD...
JUST BEFORE MIDNIGHT HE LOST CONTACT WITH THE CHAMPION'S ELECTROPHONE. ..HE NEVER HEARD FROM HIM AGAIN...
..LOOK JUST FORGET IT KID!... ..'ELECTROPHONES', 'TIME STORMS' AND 'SHRINK RAYS'...NONE OF THAT STUFF REALLY EXISTS!..NO MATTER WHAT YOUR FATHER THINKS HE CAN 'REMEMBER'...
..ITS ALL JUST CHILDISH FANTASY... NOTHING BUT MY OWN WORTHLESS IMAGININGS...
I'M SORRY... BUT YOU'RE JUST WASTING YOUR TIME HERE...IT'LL BE CLEAR OUTSIDE FOR THE MOMENT. YOU SHOULD JUST GO...
..DID...DID YOU EVER IMAGINE SOMETHING A BIT... LIKE THIS?...
WHAT THE HELL..?!...
THAT CAN'T BE REAL!...

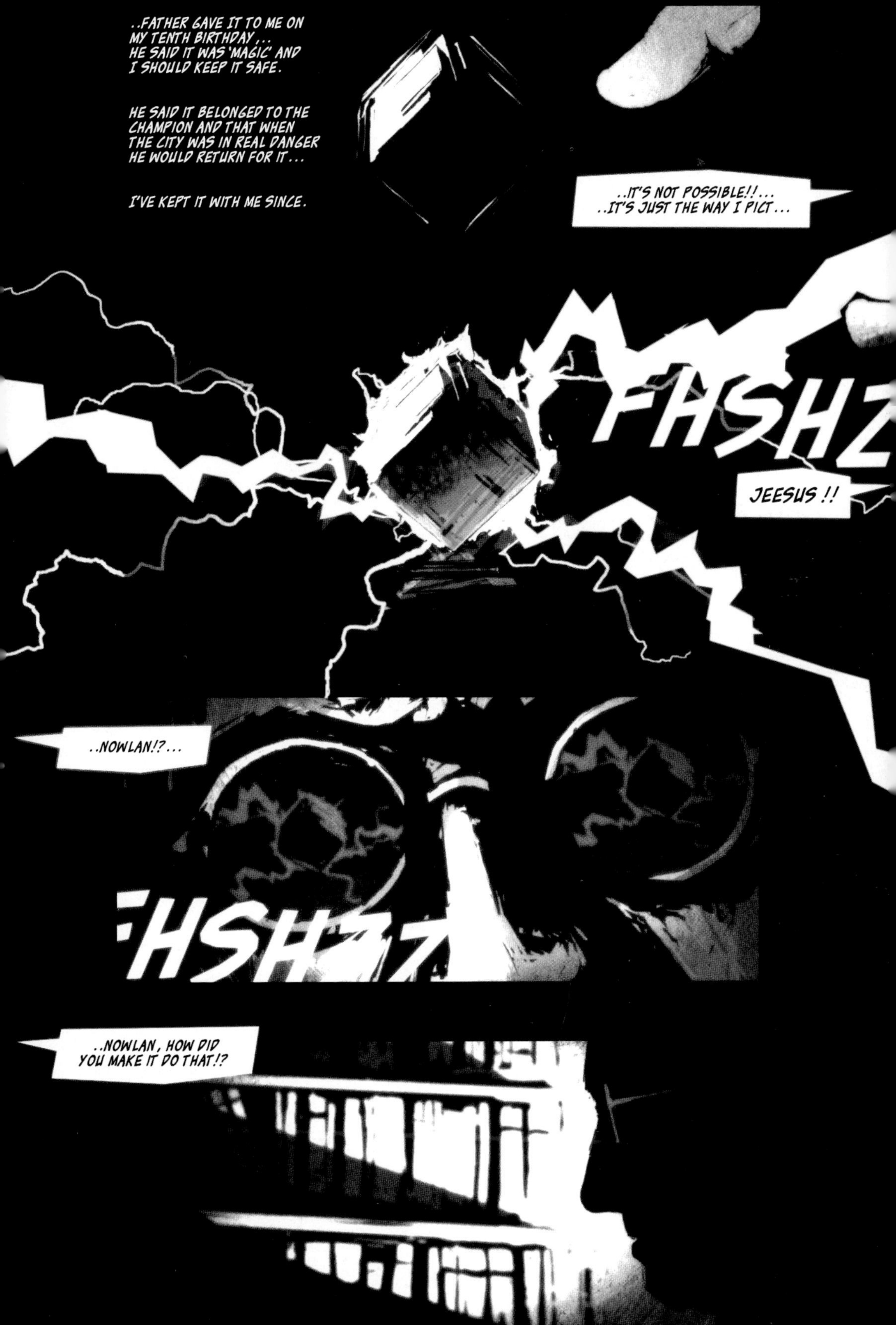
..FATHER GAVE IT TO ME ON MY TENTH BIRTHDAY,.. HE SAID IT WAS 'MAGIC' AND I SHOULD KEEP IT SAFE.
HE SAID IT BELONGED TO THE CHAMPION AND THAT WHEN THE CITY WAS IN REAL DANGER HE WOULD RETURN FOR IT...
I'VE KEPT IT WITH ME SINCE.
..IT'S NOT POSSIBLE!!... ..IT'S JUST THE WAY I PICT...
FHSHZ
JEESUS !!
..NOWLAN!?...
FHSHZZ
..NOWLAN, HOW DID YOU MAKE IT DO THAT!?

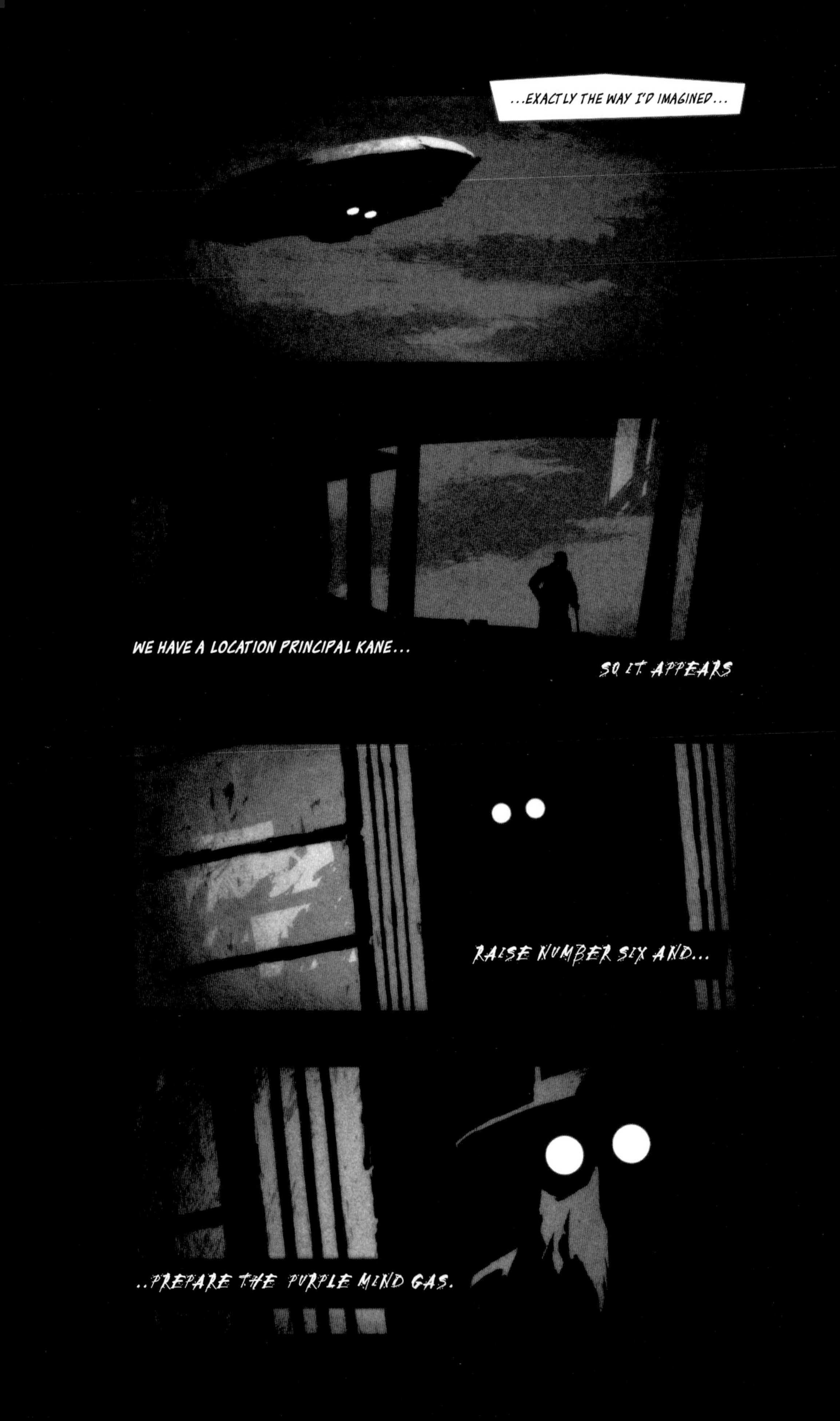
...EXACTLY THE WAY I'D IMAGINED...
WE HAVE A LOCATION PRINCIPAL KANE...
SO IT APPEARS
RAISE NUMBER SIX AND...
..PREPARE THE PURPLE MIND GAS.

PIN-UPS

One of the coolest things about doing a comic book,
is getting your friends who happen to be proper artists
to do their very own take on your character.

Steve Purcell

The twisted genius creator of 'Sam and Max', hands down the
funniest comic and computer game ever made, started at Pixar
on the same day as me.. but I'm sure he tells everybody that
too. Steve, we all still await those sociopathic rabbit toys.

Ryan Church

Truly as charming and geeky as he is talented, Ryan spearheaded
concept design on the last two 'Star Wars' prequels. So needs
to appear here for some real publicity...You can almost touch
him by downloading his brushes at: WWW.RYANCHURCH.COM

Bill Presing

Creator of 'Rex Steele Nazi Smasher'. Bill seems harmless enough
at first, but beneath that mild-mannered exterior beats the heart
of wisecracking, butt-kicking, all-American pulp slugger. Truly a
dangerous man with a pencil. WWW.REXSTEELE.COM

Ronnie Del Carmen

Pixar is choc full of extremely talented people. Ask any of
them and without exception they will say; "Yeah, that guy
Ronnie, he's really good...". But then what do extremely
talented people know? WWW.RONNIEDELCARMEN.COM

Thanks Again Gentlemen

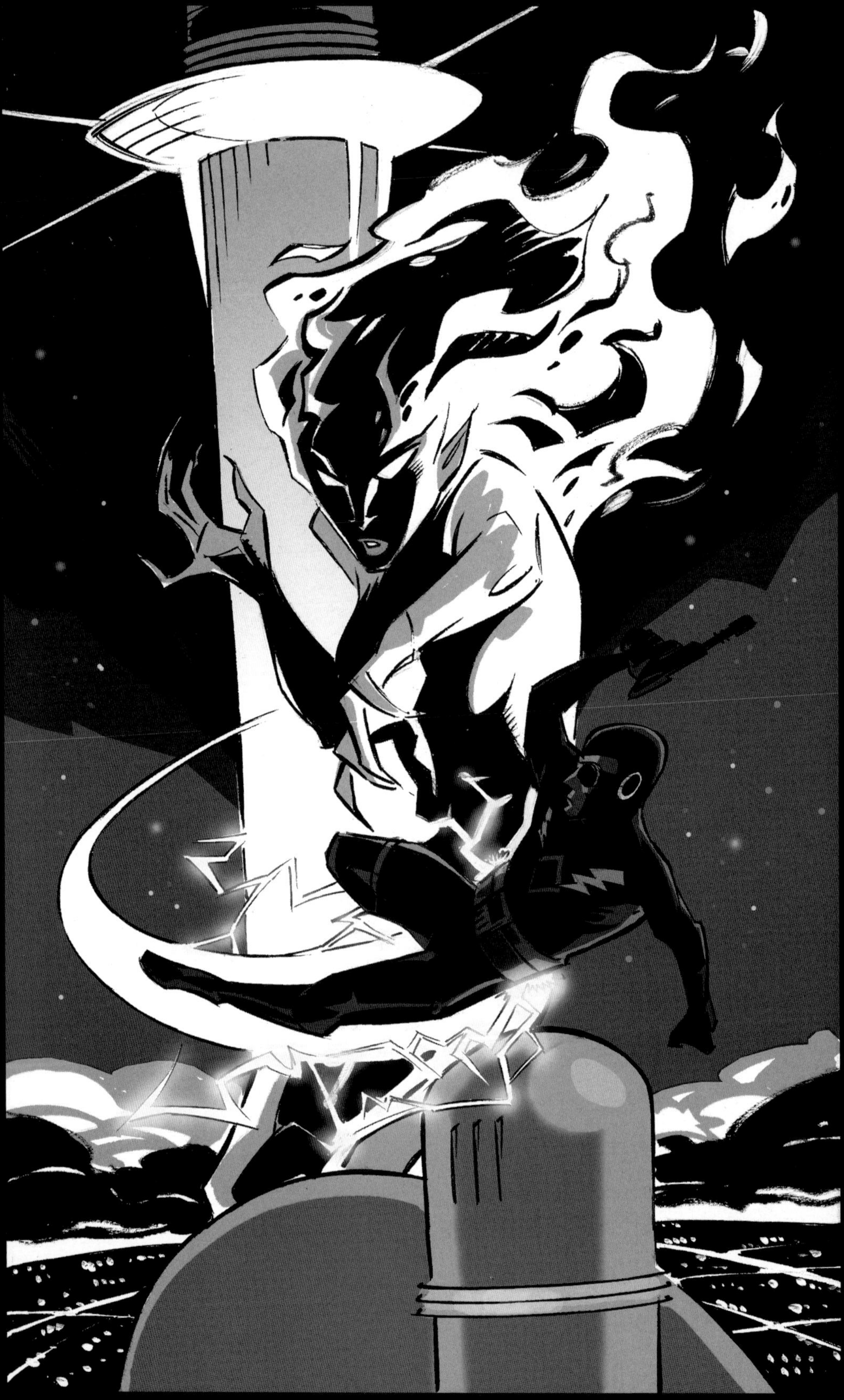

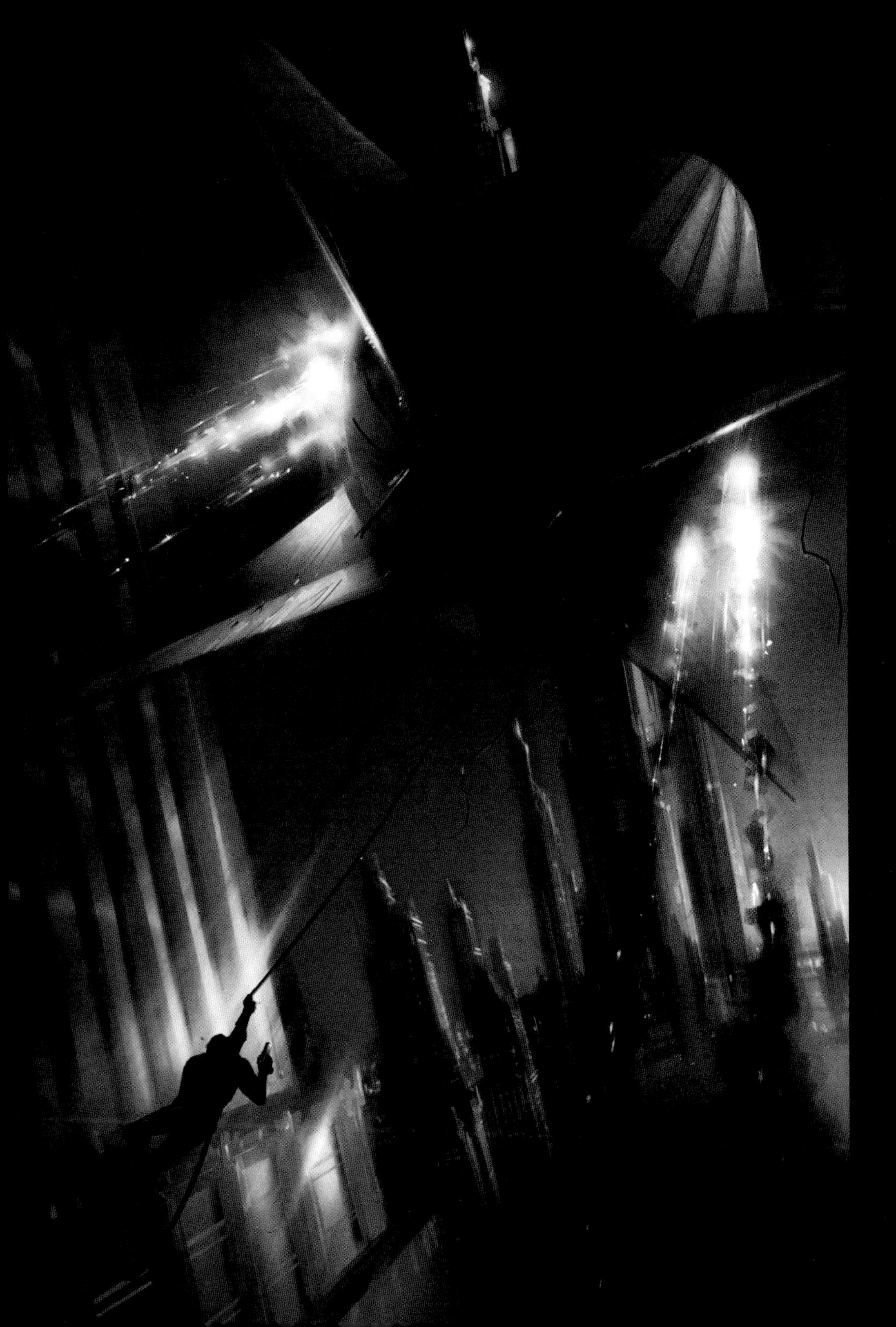

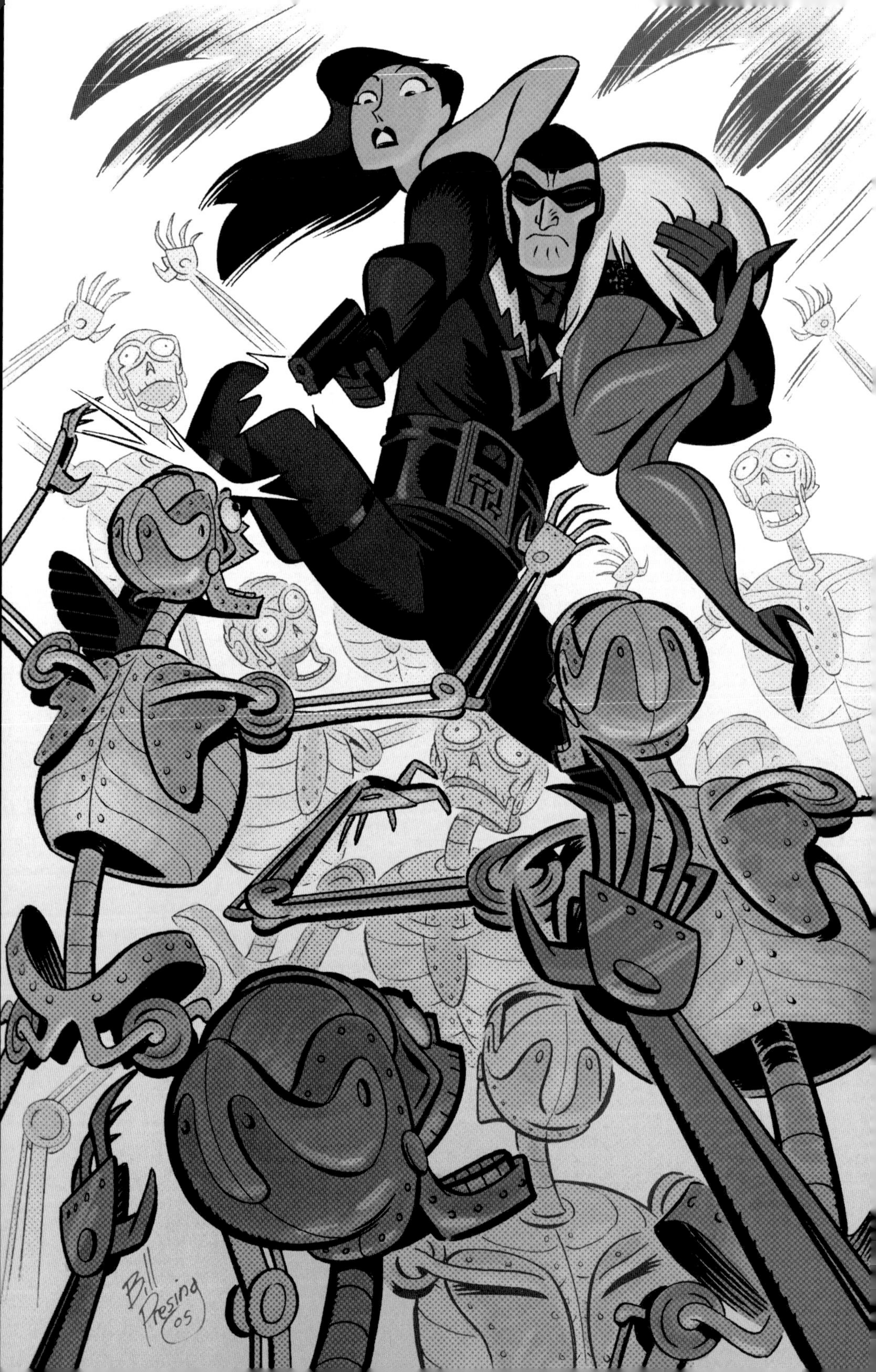
Bill Presing '05

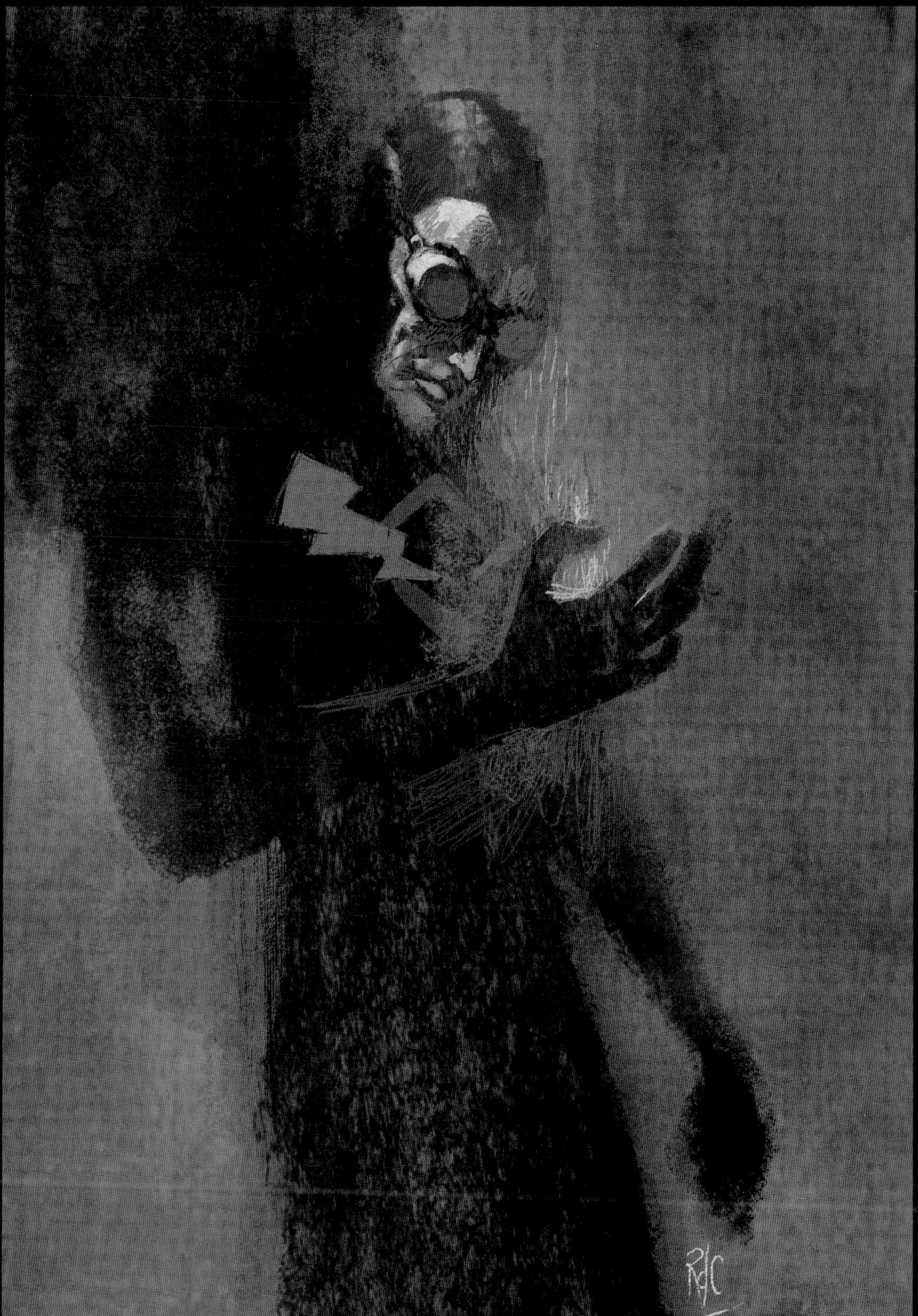

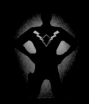

To Be Continued...

The Champion Commends

Brian Christian
&
Robert Kondo

Salutes the
Amazing Work of

Frank R Paul
Philip F Nowlan

Recognises the
Additional Heroism of

Jay Shuster
Kevin O'Brien
Ronnie Del Carmen
Louis Gonzales
Ted Mathot
Nate Stanton
Jim Capobianco
Enrico Casarosa
Max Brace
Sanjay Patel
Mark Andrews
Richard Meibers
E-Ville Press
Pixar

Gives an Enigmatic
Wink to

Lisa
Mum & Dad
Karen

simon.dunsdon@sbcglobal.net

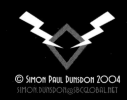

Fig(3).

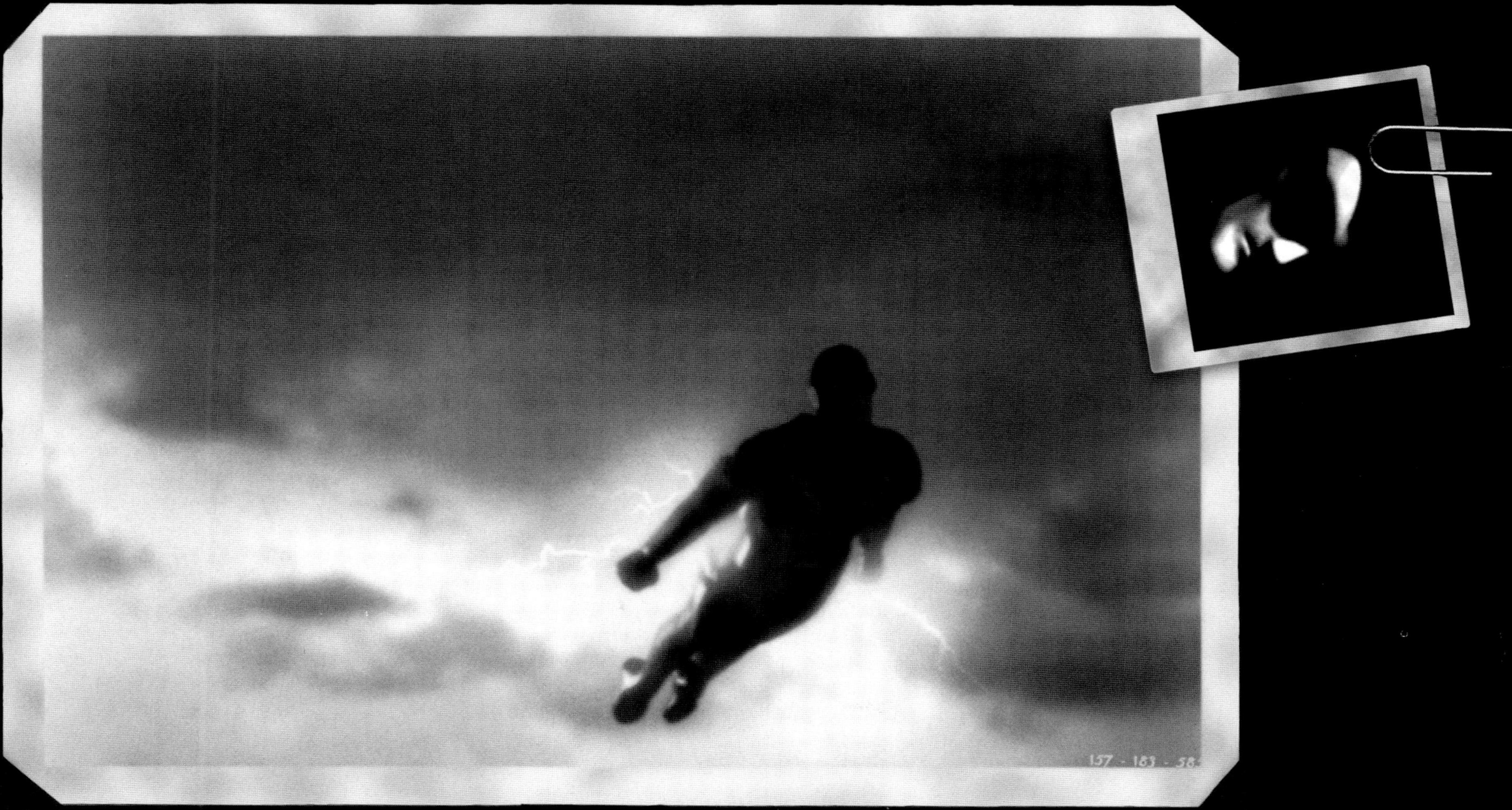
157 - 183 - 58

Fig(3). A uniquely substantiated exposure of the Champion during full'atomic flight'.
Taken by noted journalist P.G. Webley through the rear port window glass of a Domier Sea-Plane.

DEDICATED TO
MY LOVELY AND AMAZING WIFE ESTHER PEARL WITHOUT WHOM THIS COMIC WOULD NOT EXIST

THANKS TO

MAX BRACE

ROBERT KONDO

BRIAN CHRISTIAN

SANJAY PATEL

RONNIE DEL CARMEN

KEVIN O BRIEN

SIMON DUNSDON

BILL PRESING

TED MATHOT

MARK ANDREWS

ENRICO CASAROSA

LOUIS GONZALES

MATT STANTON

ANDREW STANTON

MIKE MERELL

DEREK THOMPSON

FOR ALL THE SUPPORT AND INSPIRATION

THE VISIT

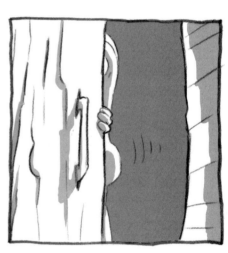

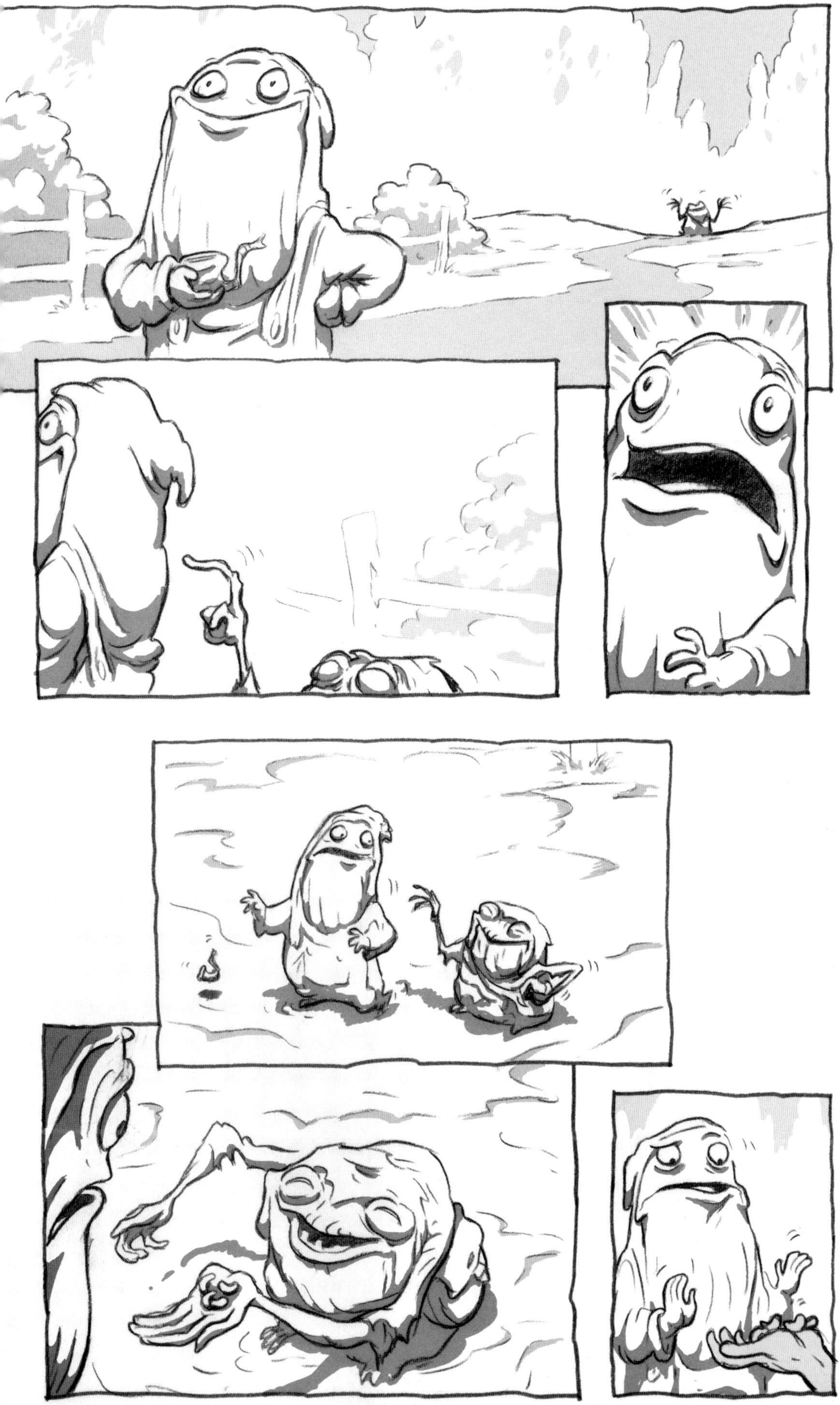

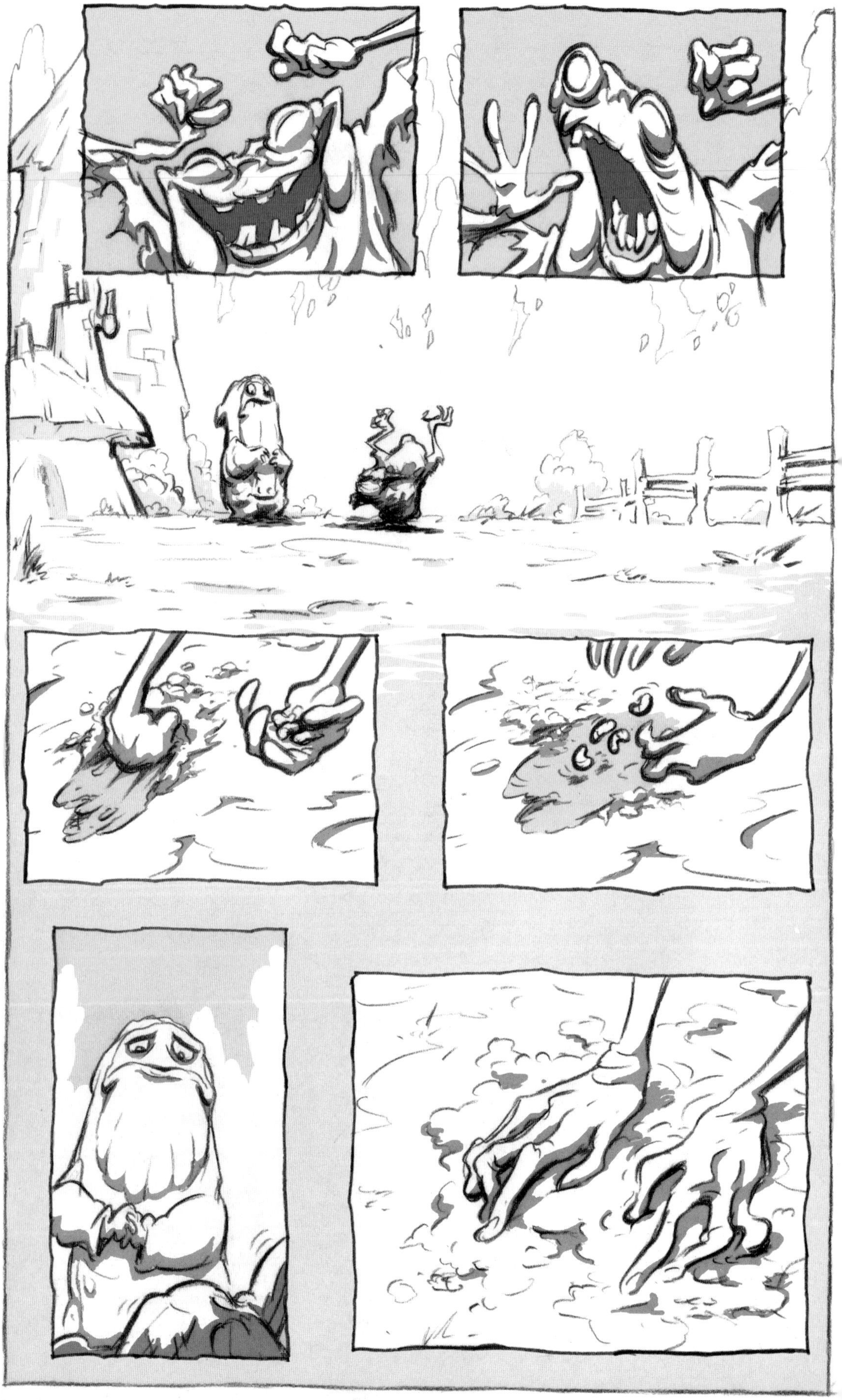

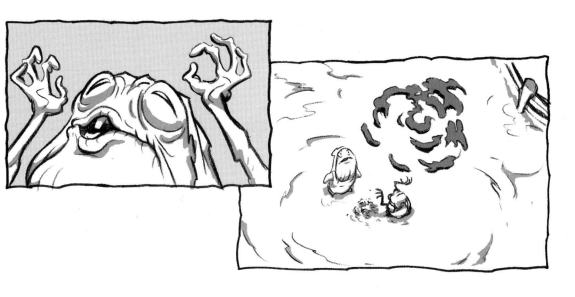

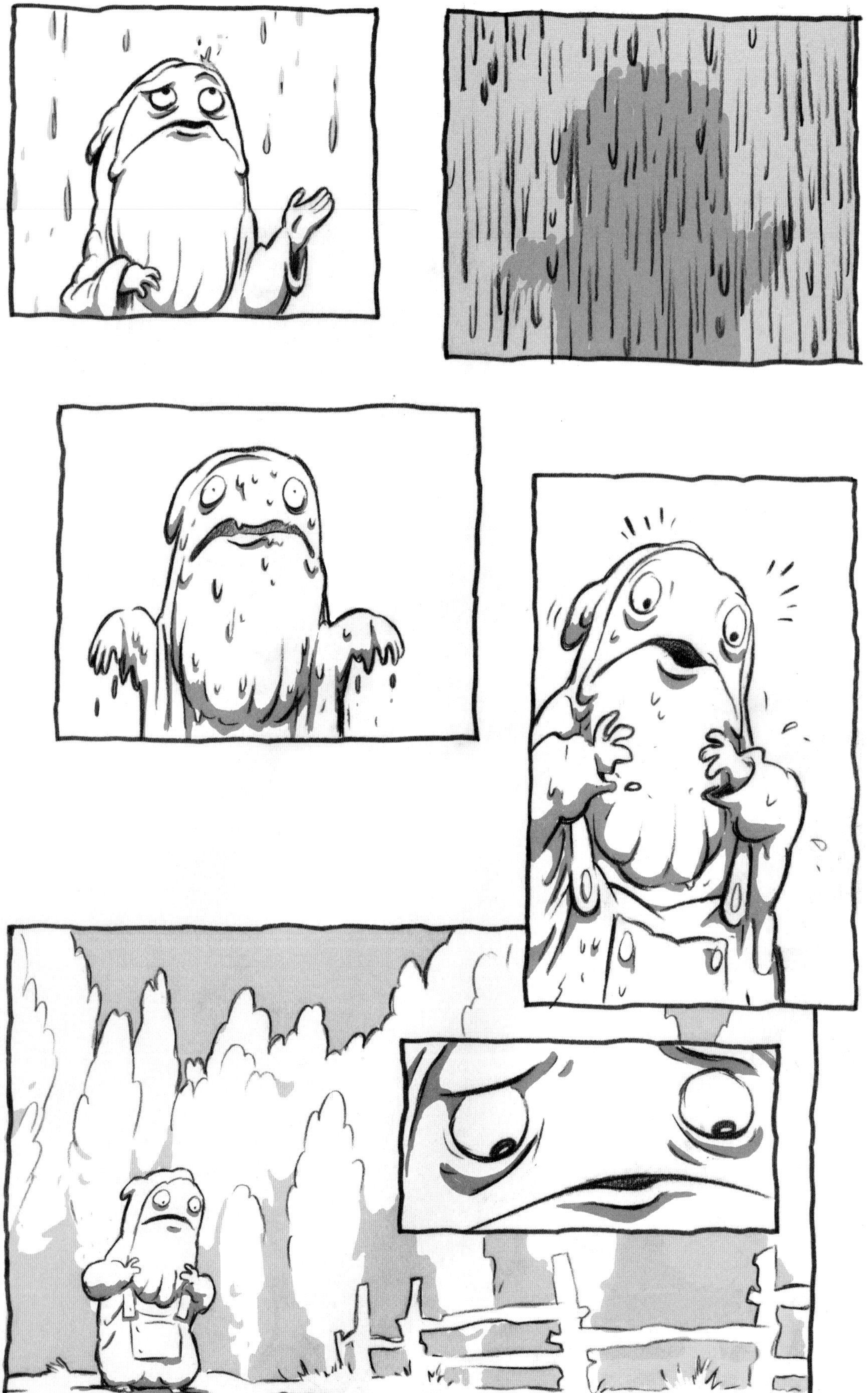

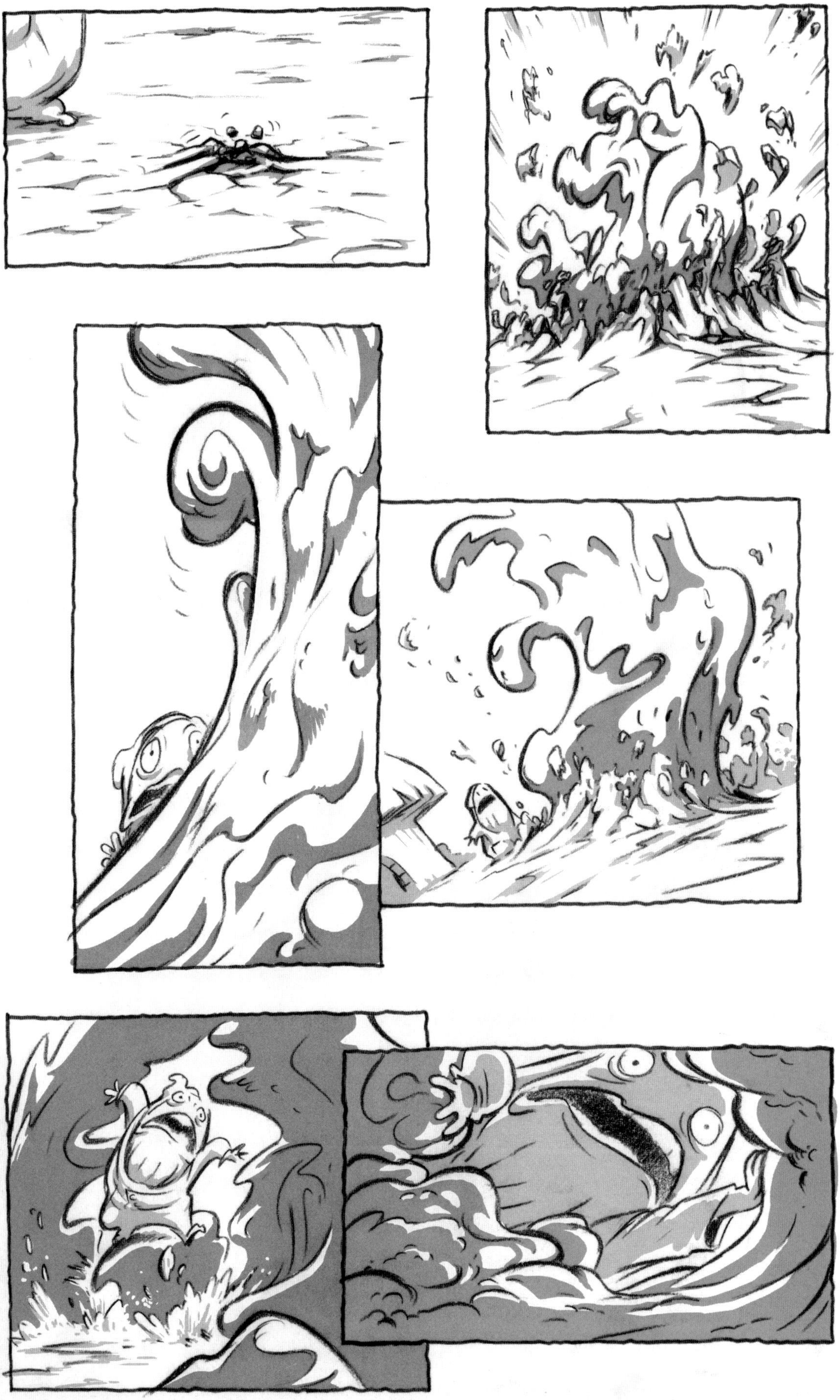

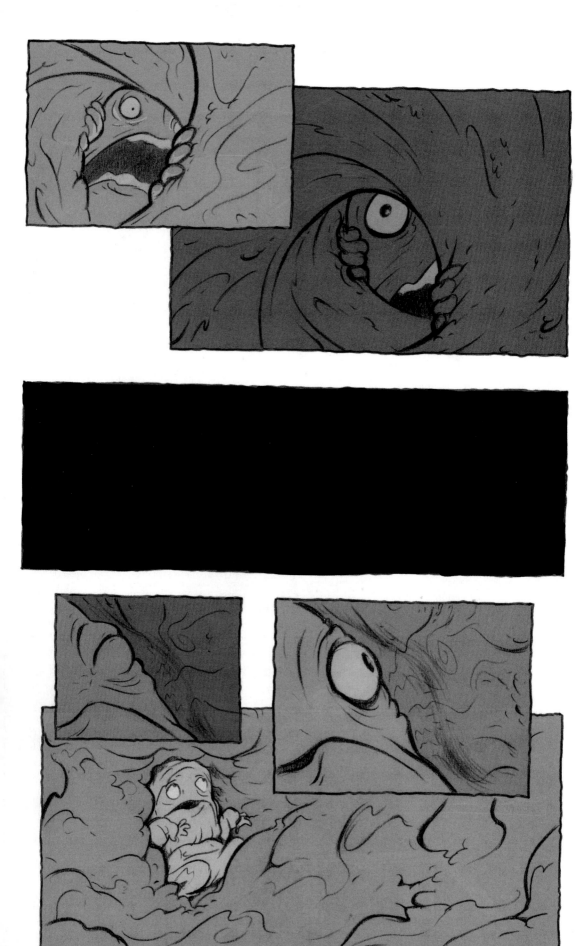

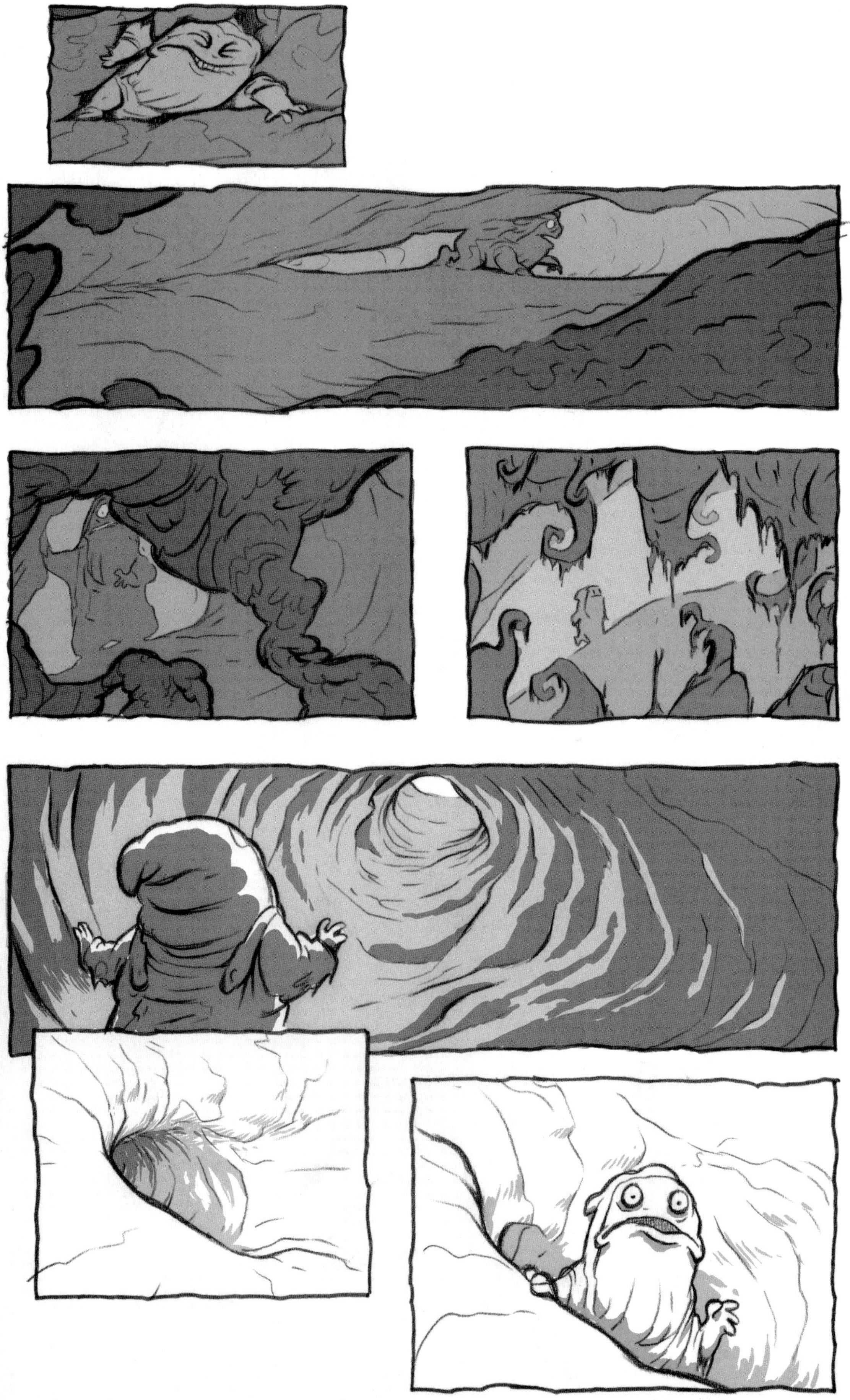

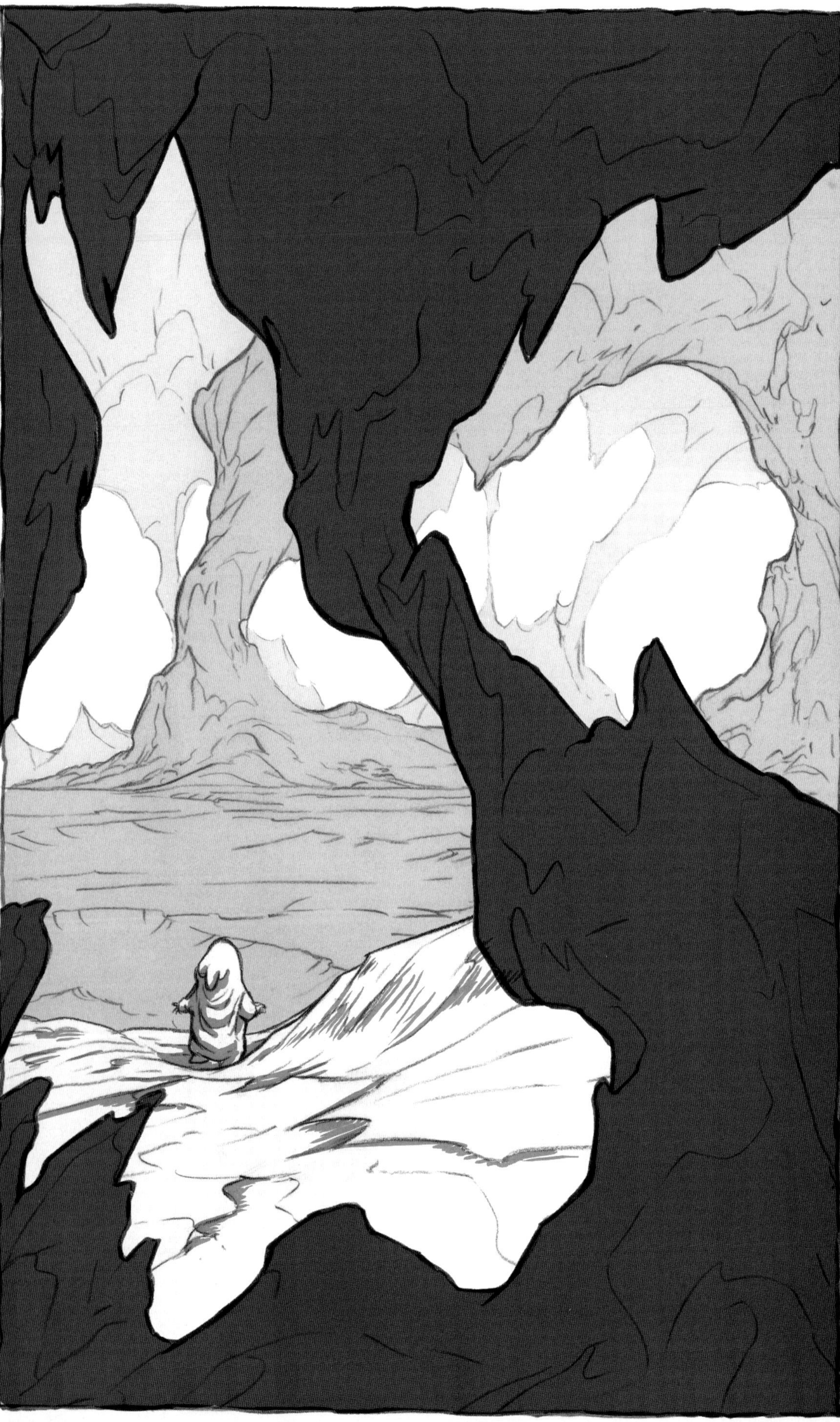

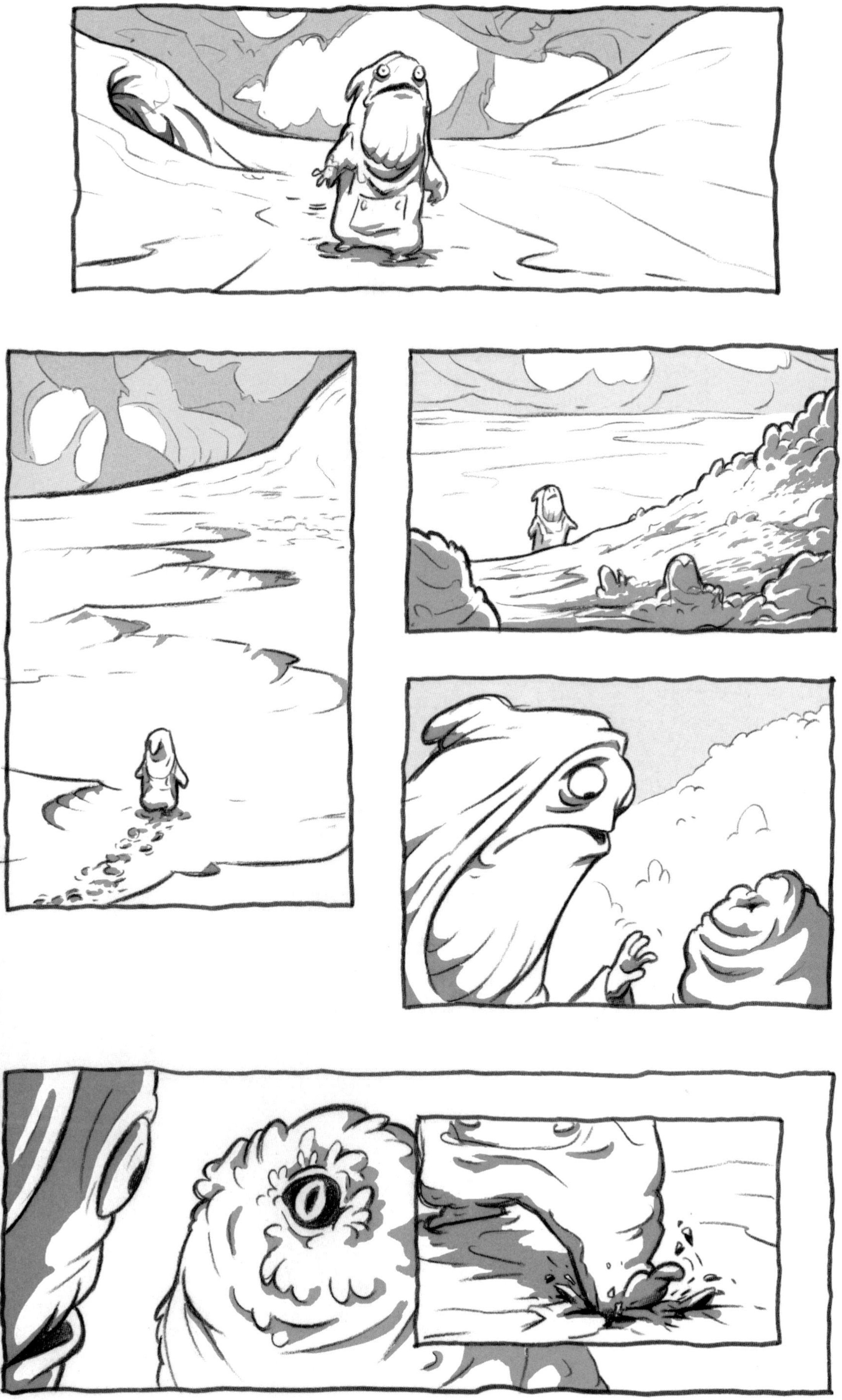

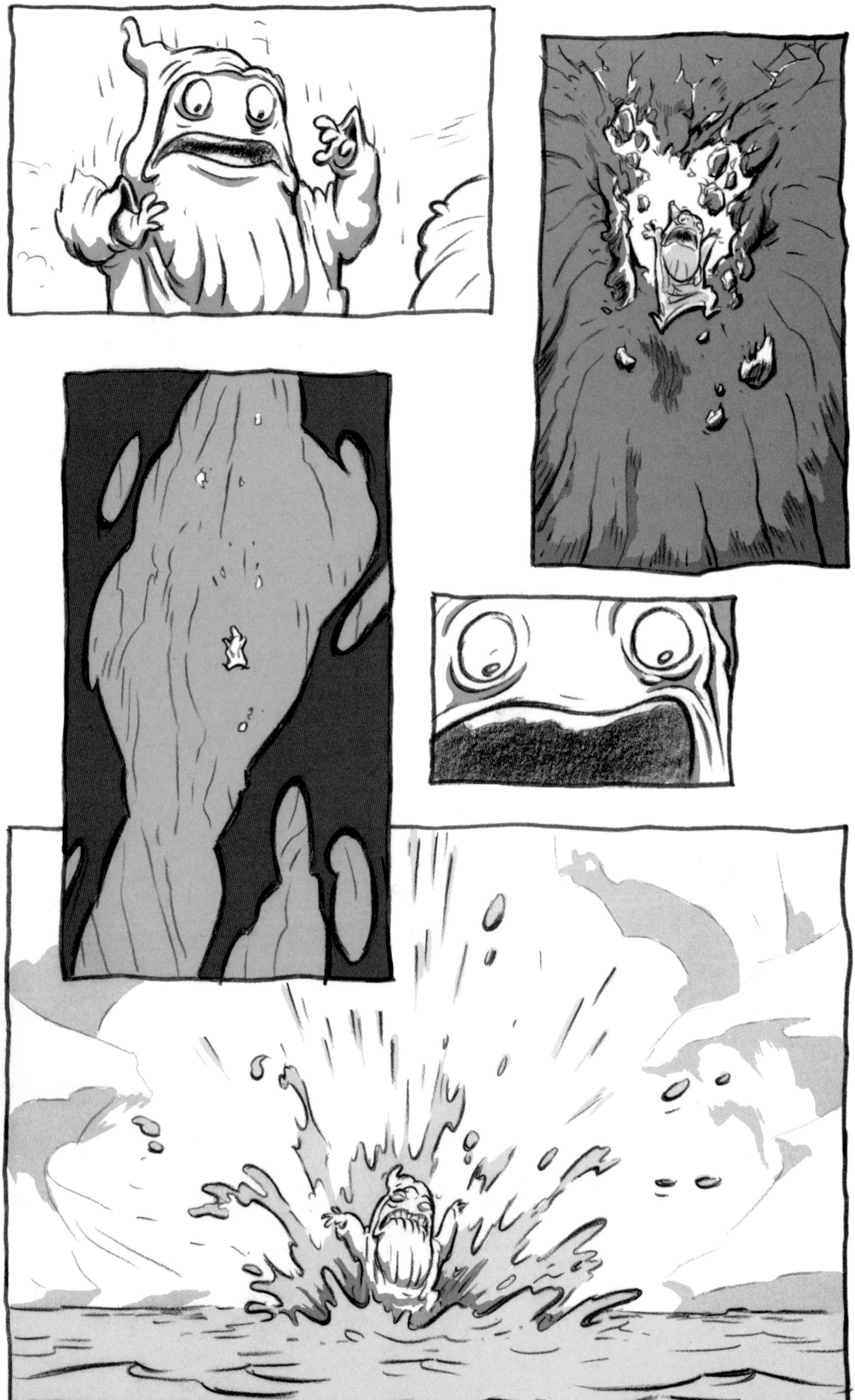

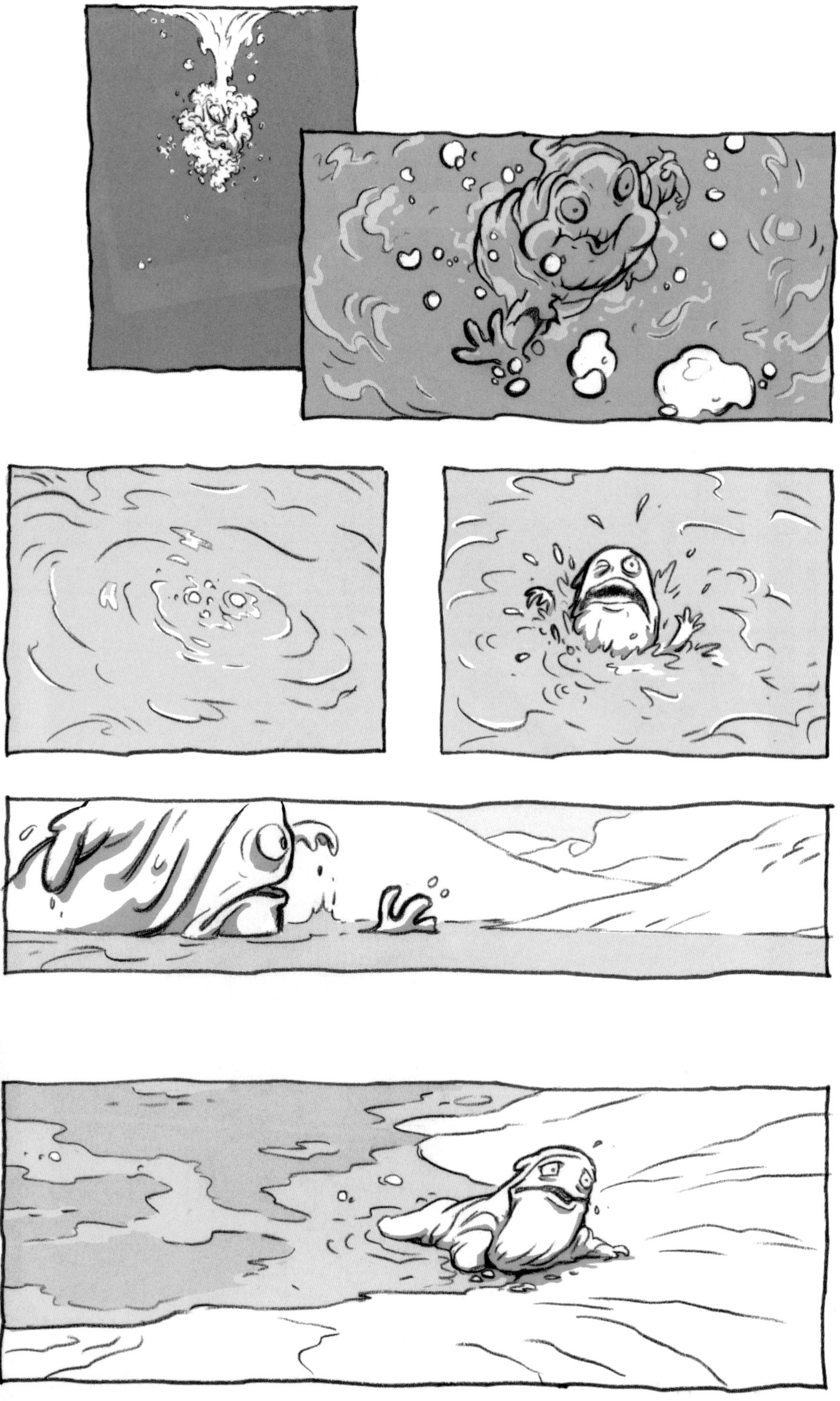

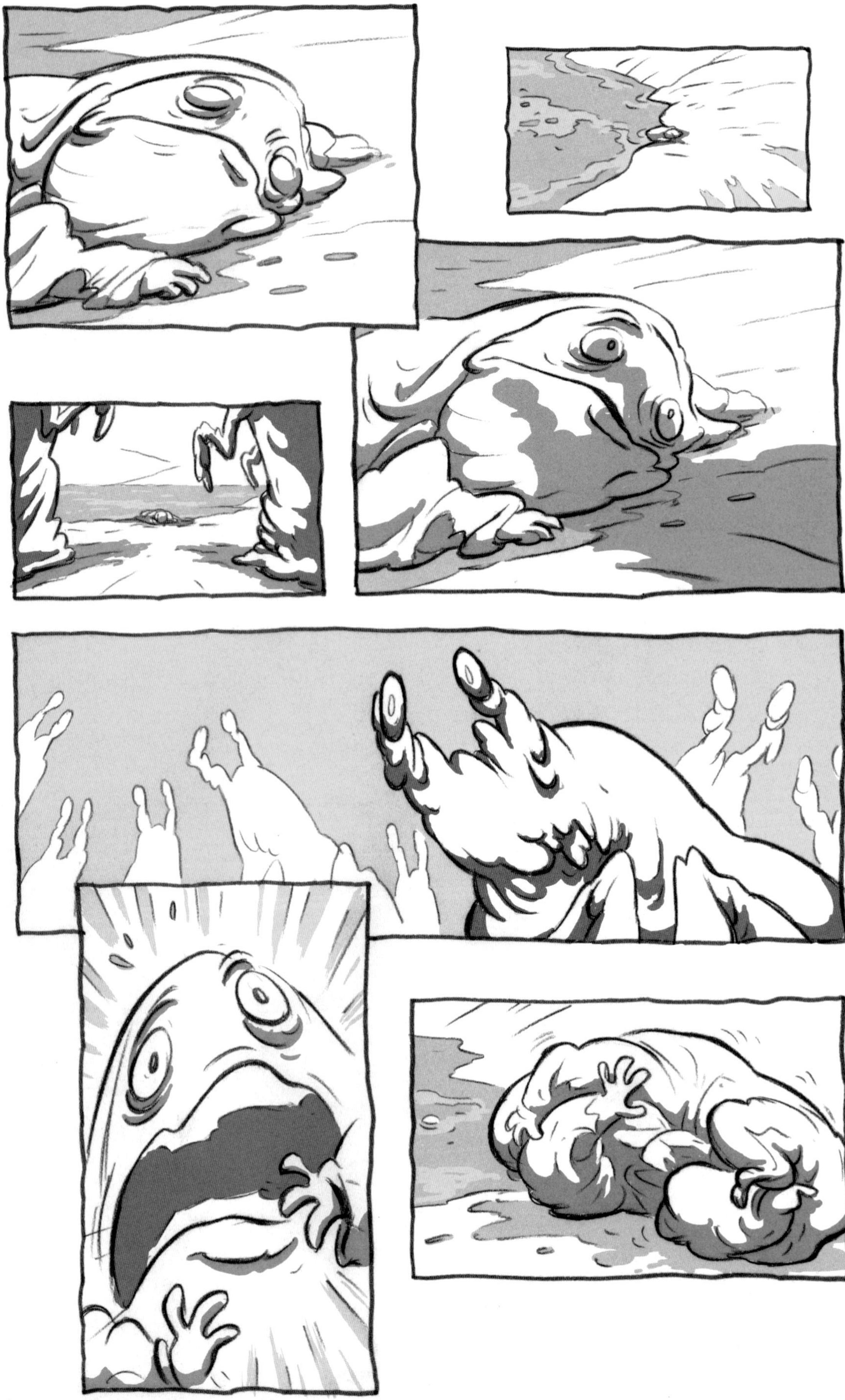

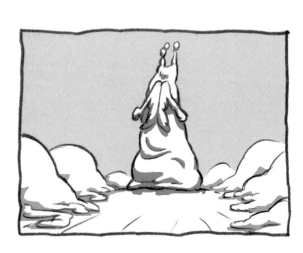

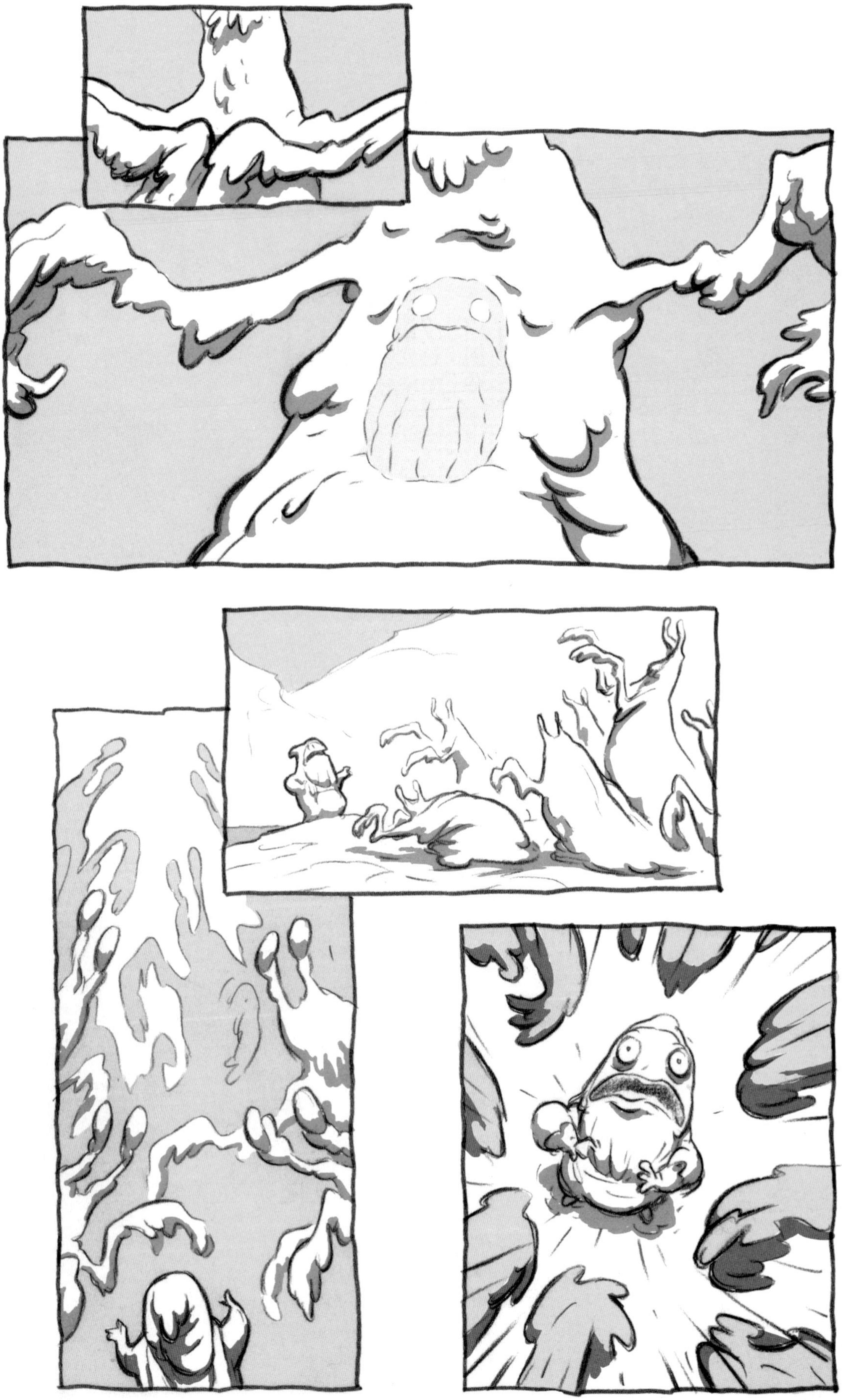

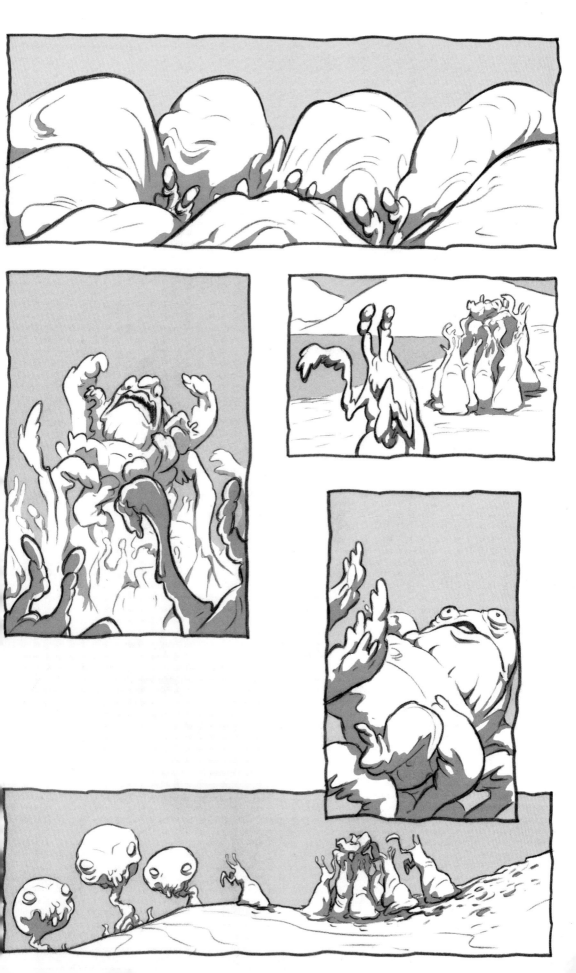

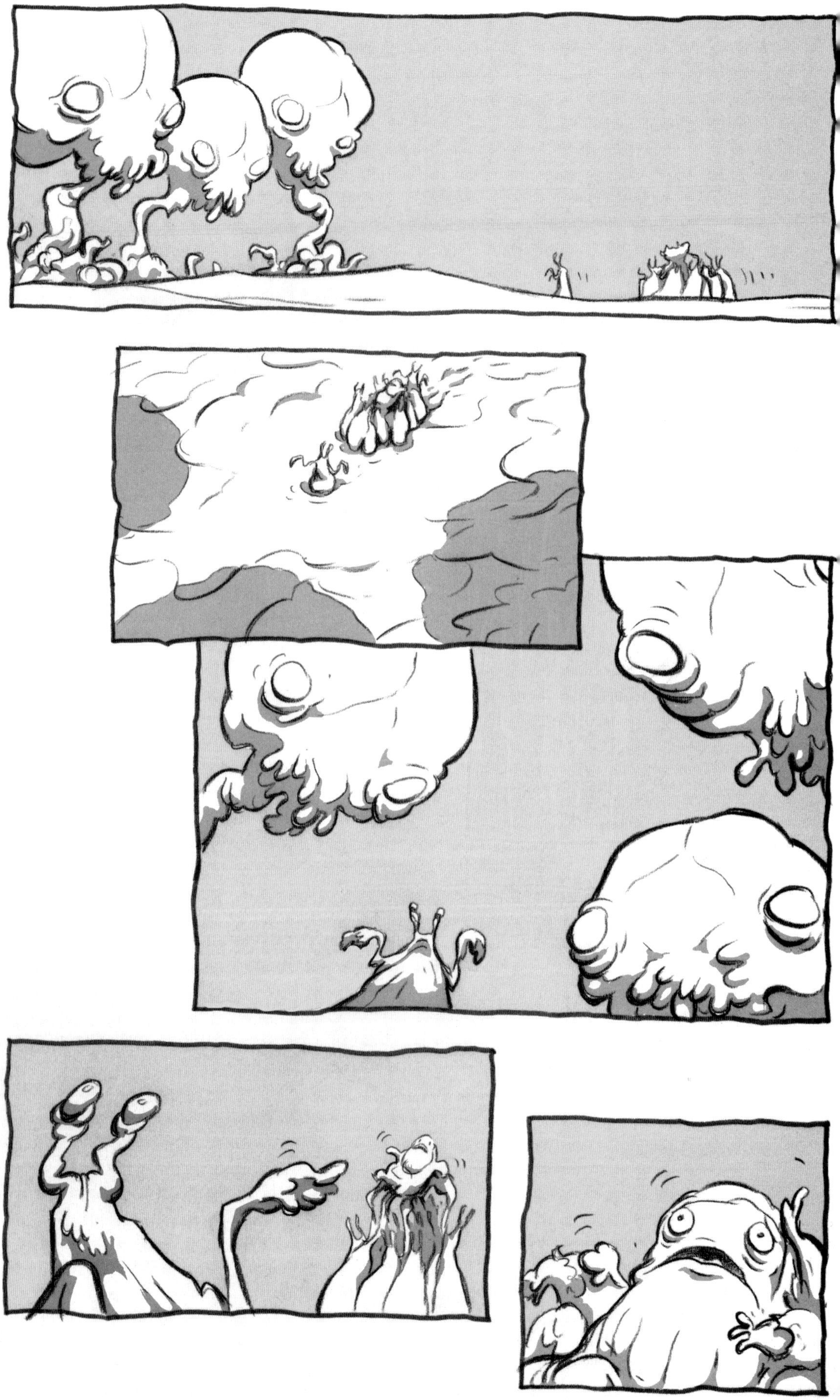

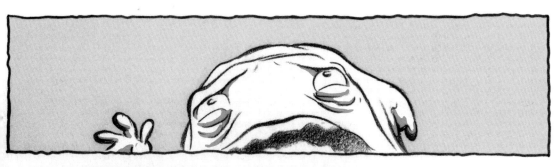

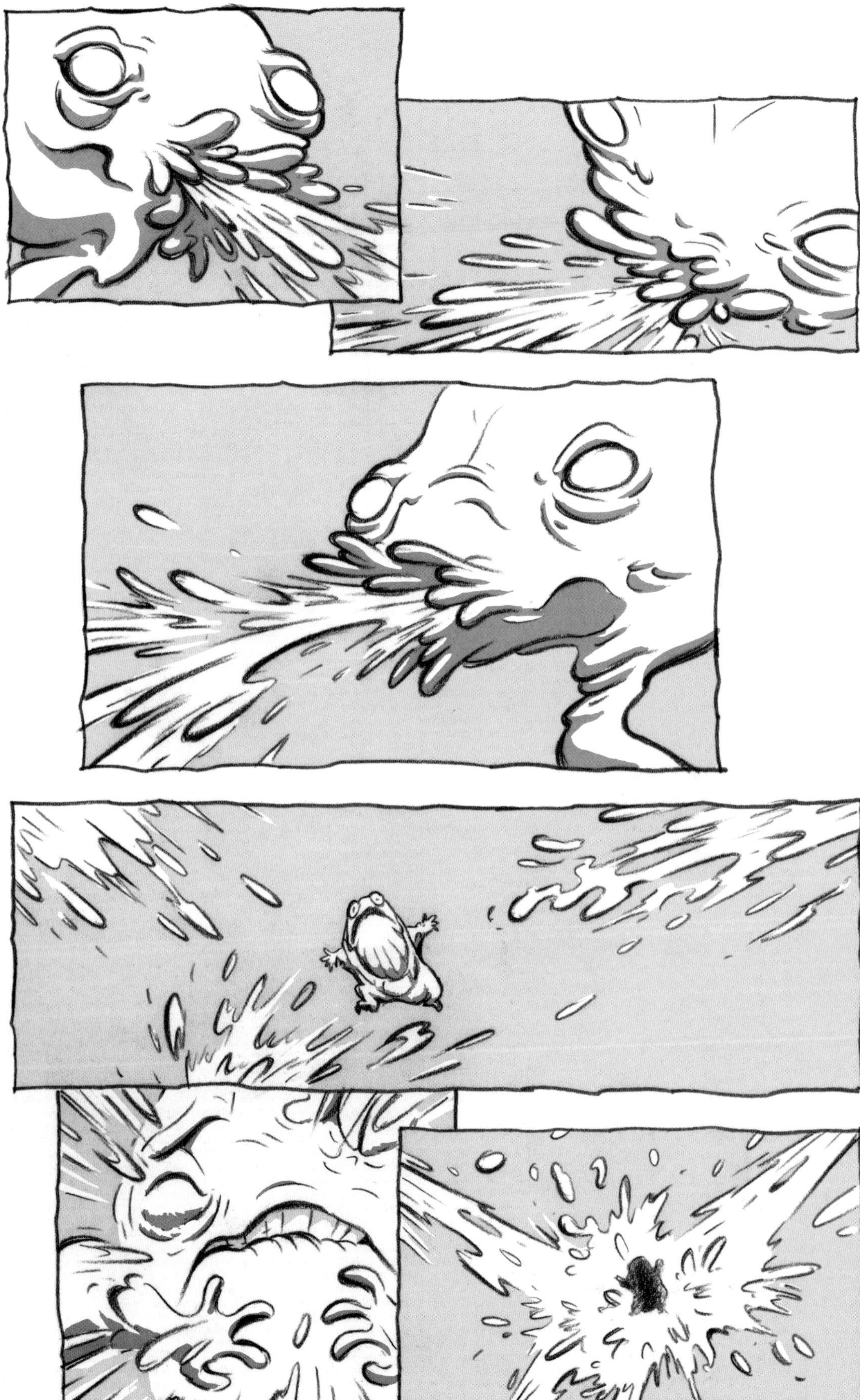

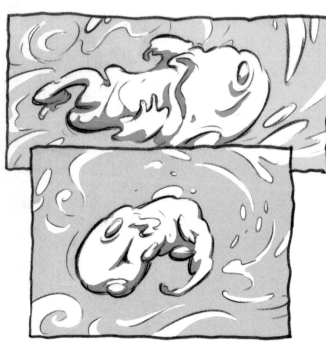

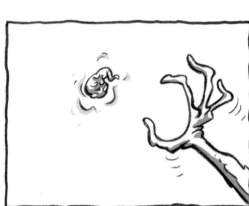

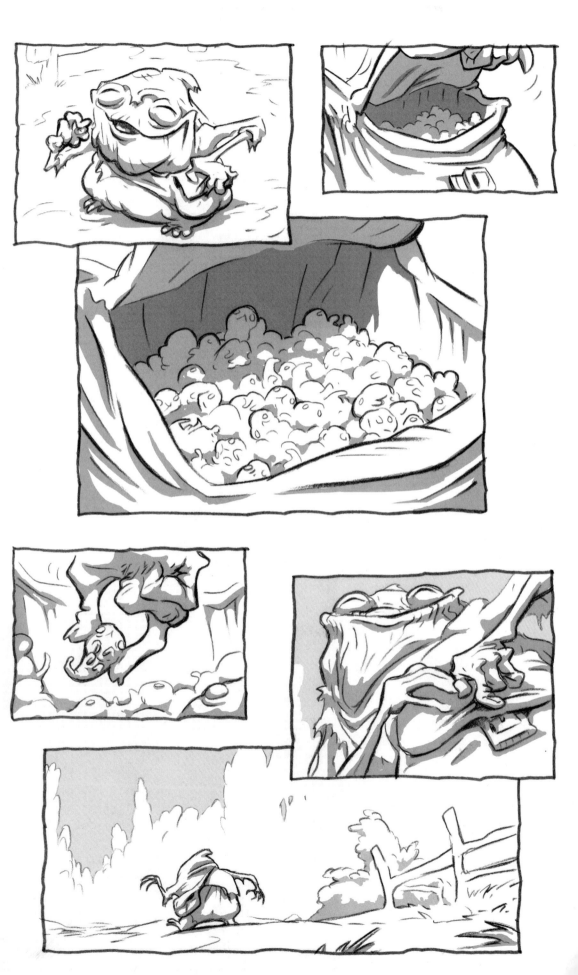

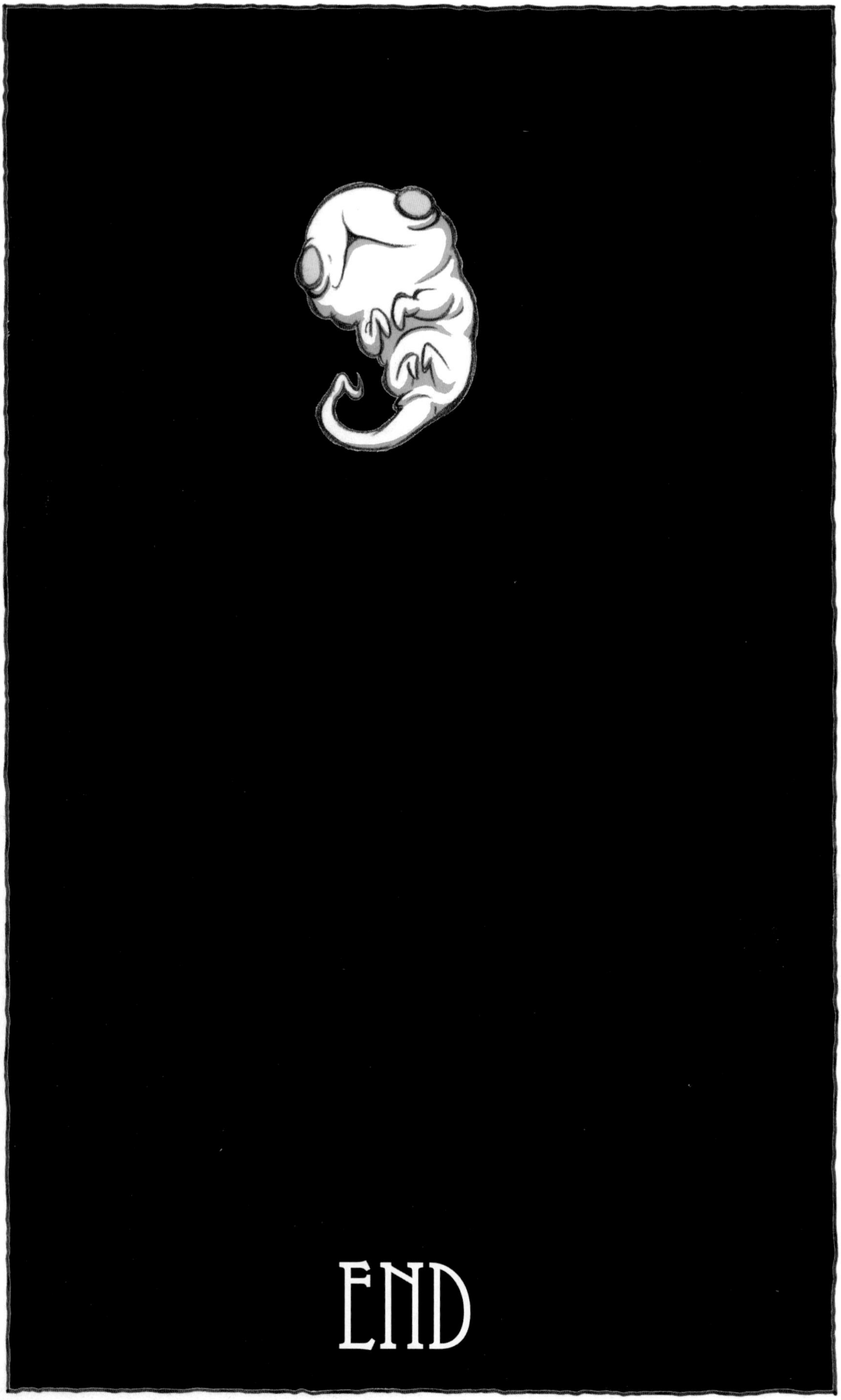
END

sanjay patel

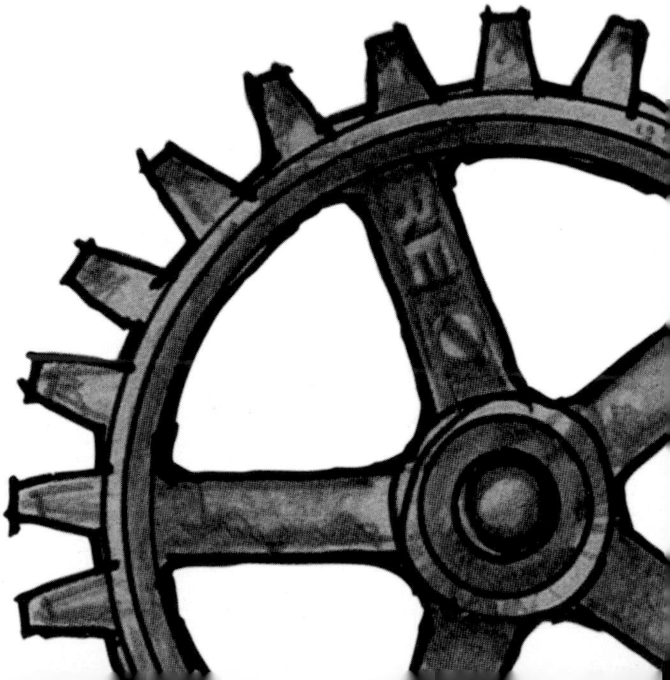
RE

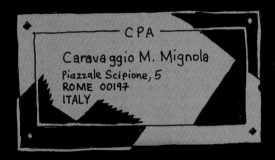

CPA
Caravaggio M. Mignola
Piazzale Scipione, 5
ROME 00197
ITALY

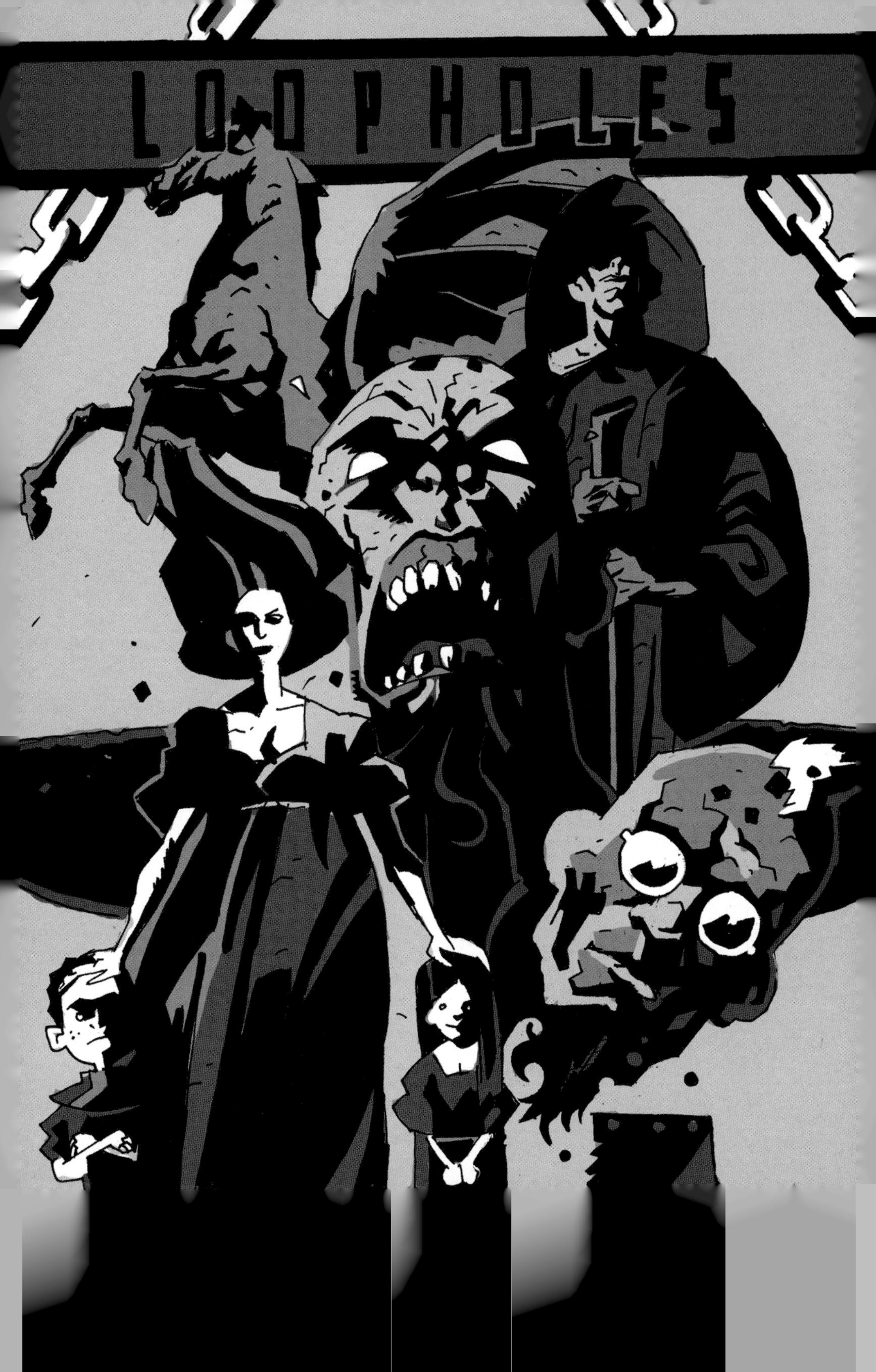
LOOPHOLES

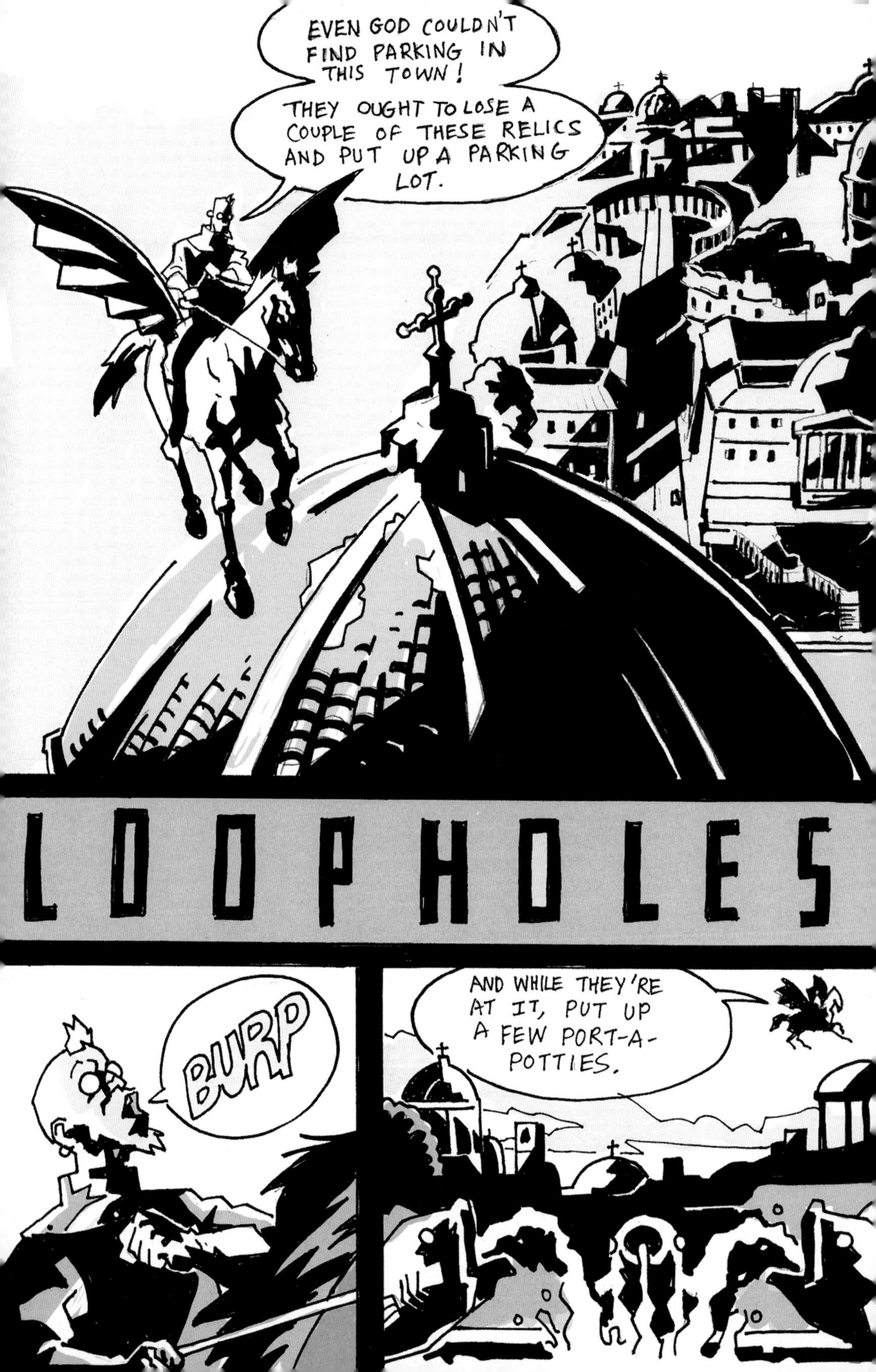
EVEN GOD COULDN'T FIND PARKING IN THIS TOWN!
THEY OUGHT TO LOSE A COUPLE OF THESE RELICS AND PUT UP A PARKING LOT.
LOOPHOLES
BURP
AND WHILE THEY'RE AT IT, PUT UP A FEW PORT-A-POTTIES.

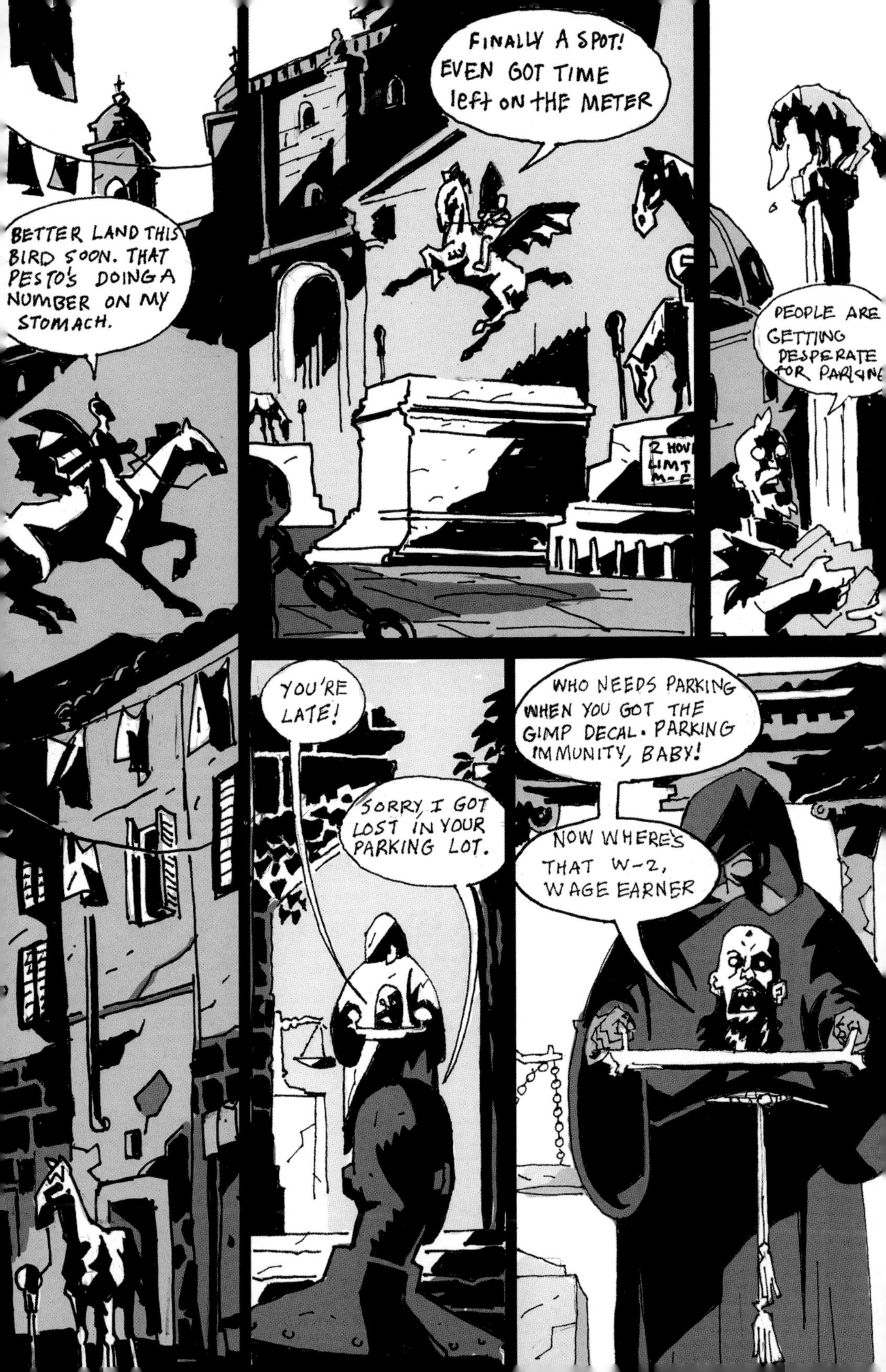
BETTER LAND THIS BIRD SOON. THAT PESTO'S DOING A NUMBER ON MY STOMACH.
FINALLY A SPOT! EVEN GOT TIME left on THE METER
2 HOU LIMT M-F
PEOPLE ARE GETTING DESPERATE FOR PARKING
YOU'RE LATE!
SORRY I GOT LOST IN YOUR PARKING LOT.
WHO NEEDS PARKING WHEN YOU GOT THE GIMP DECAL. PARKING IMMUNITY, BABY!
NOW WHERE'S THAT W-2, WAGE EARNER

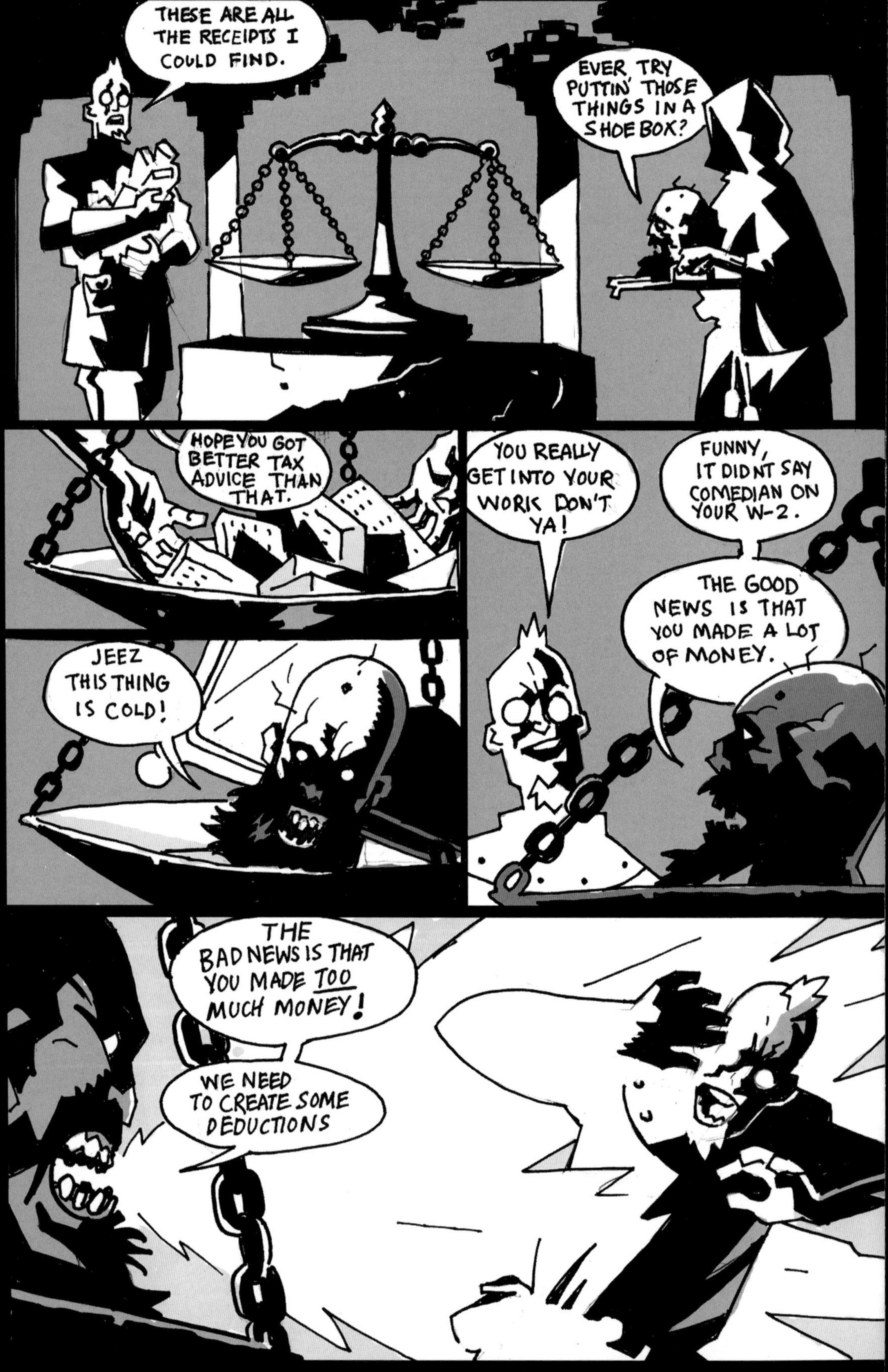
THESE ARE ALL THE RECEIPTS I COULD FIND.
EVER TRY PUTTIN' THOSE THINGS IN A SHOE BOX?
HOPE YOU GOT BETTER TAX ADVICE THAN THAT.
YOU REALLY GET INTO YOUR WORK DON'T YA!
FUNNY, IT DIDNT SAY COMEDIAN ON YOUR W-2.
THE GOOD NEWS IS THAT YOU MADE A LOT OF MONEY.
JEEZ THIS THING IS COLD!
THE BAD NEWS IS THAT YOU MADE TOO MUCH MONEY!
WE NEED TO CREATE SOME DEDUCTIONS

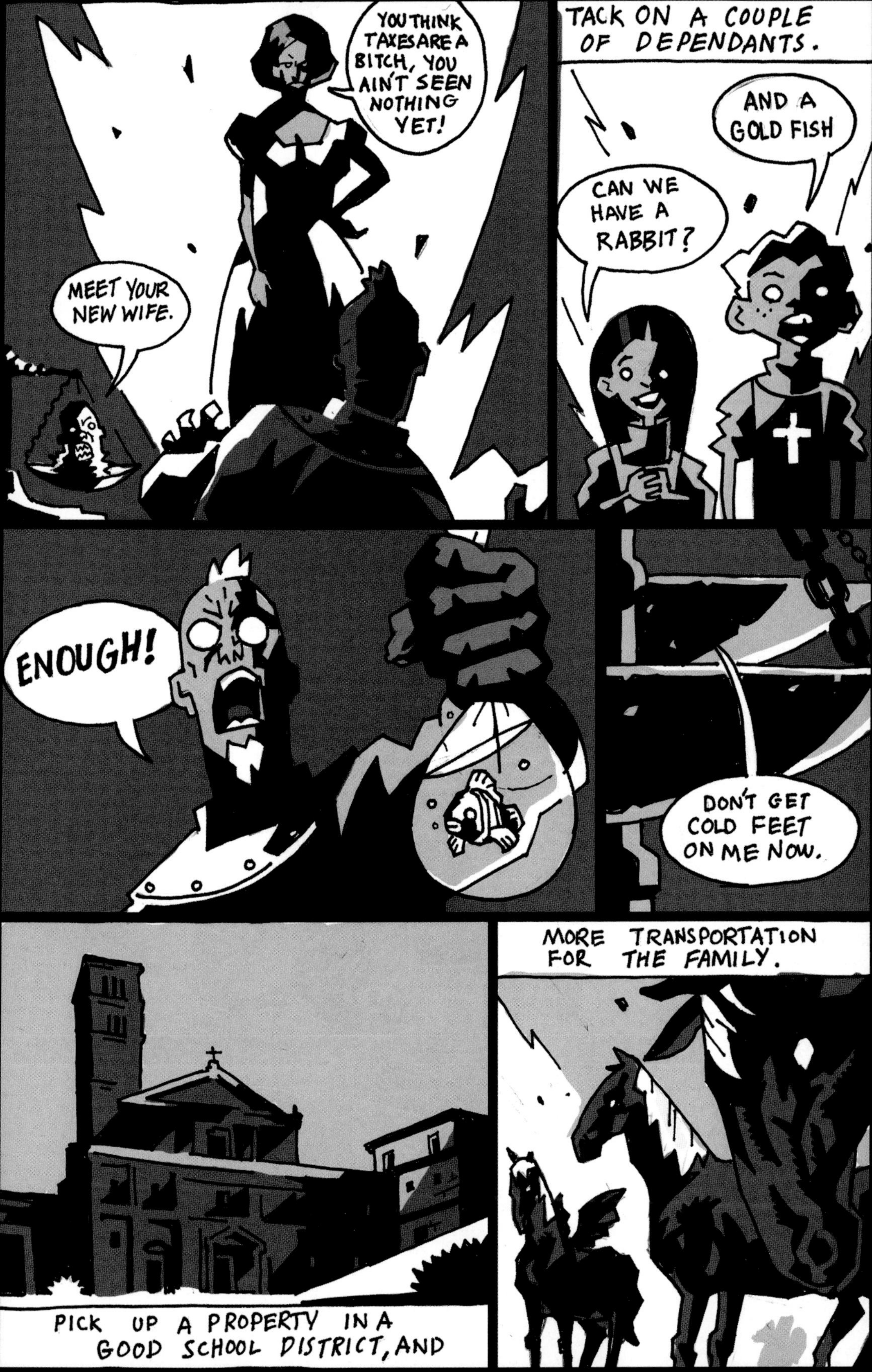
YOU THINK TAXES ARE A BITCH, YOU AIN'T SEEN NOTHING YET!
MEET YOUR NEW WIFE.
TACK ON A COUPLE OF DEPENDANTS.
AND A GOLD FISH
CAN WE HAVE A RABBIT?
ENOUGH!
DON'T GET COLD FEET ON ME NOW.
PICK UP A PROPERTY IN A GOOD SCHOOL DISTRICT, AND
MORE TRANSPORTATION FOR THE FAMILY.

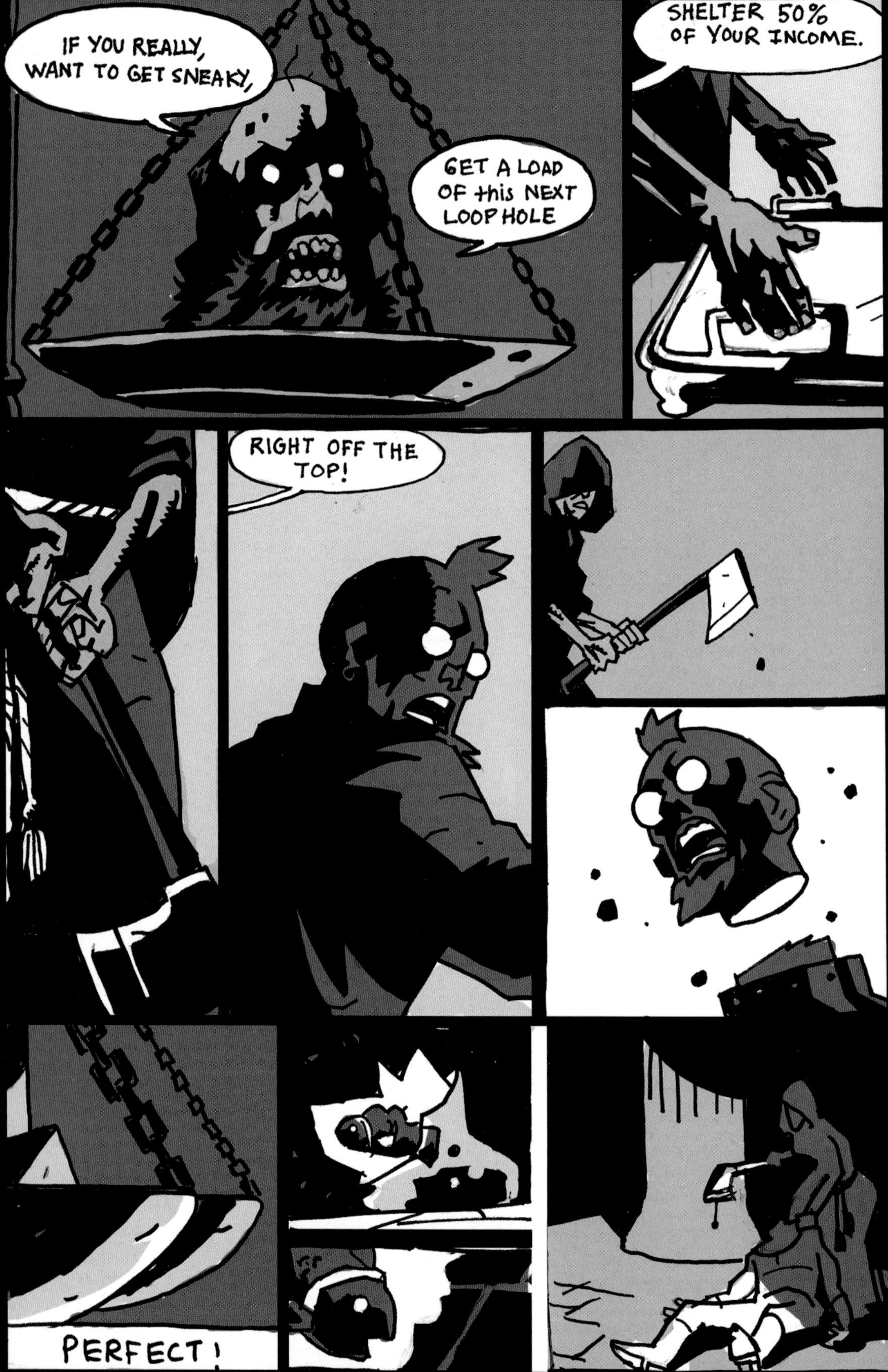
IF YOU REALLY, WANT TO GET SNEAKY,
GET A LOAD OF this NEXT LOOPHOLE
SHELTER 50% OF YOUR INCOME.
RIGHT OFF THE TOP!
PERFECT!

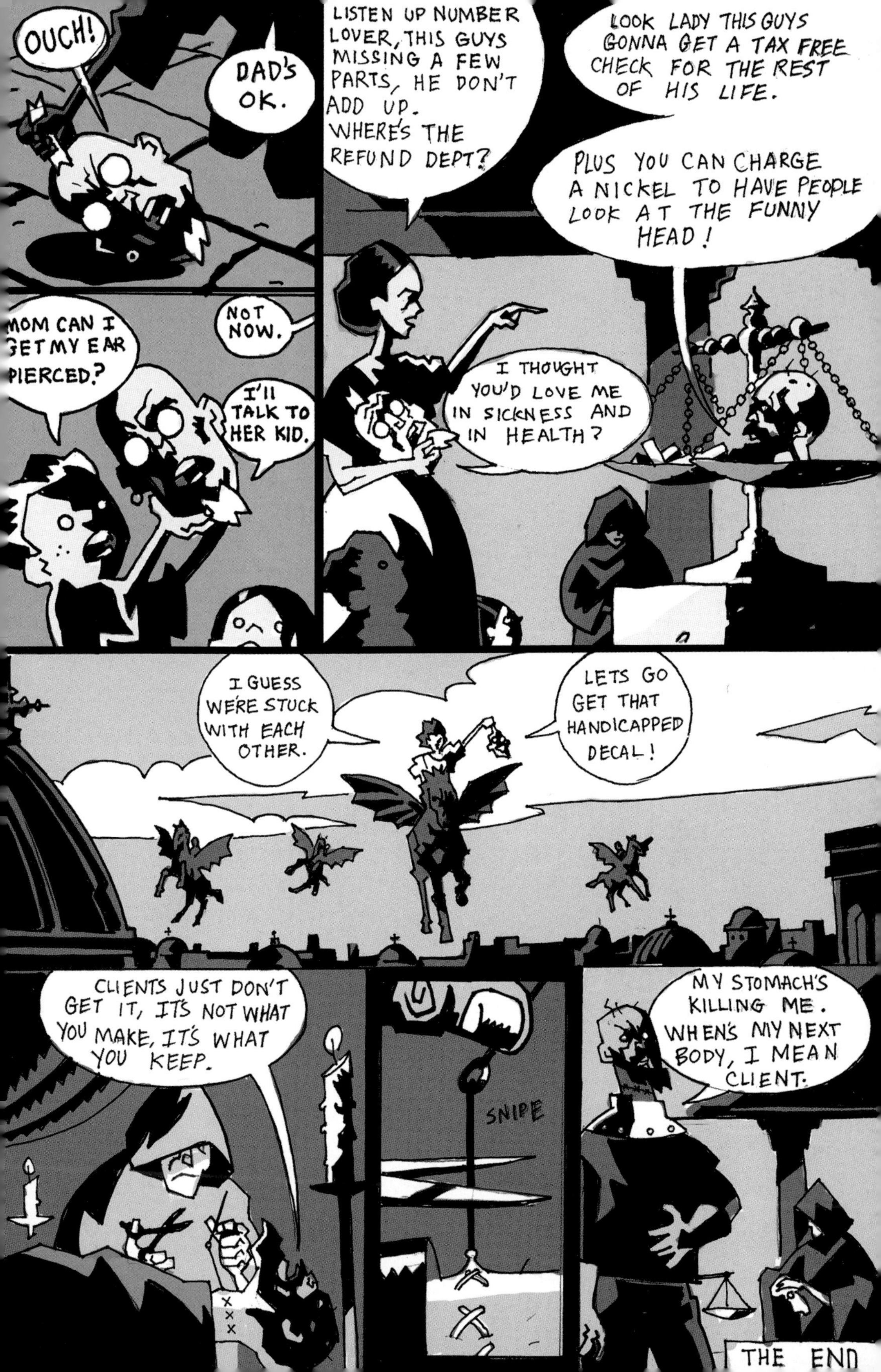
OUCH!
DAD'S OK.
LISTEN UP NUMBER LOVER, THIS GUYS MISSING A FEW PARTS, HE DON'T ADD UP. WHERE'S THE REFUND DEPT?
LOOK LADY THIS GUYS GONNA GET A TAX FREE CHECK FOR THE REST OF HIS LIFE.
PLUS YOU CAN CHARGE A NICKEL TO HAVE PEOPLE LOOK AT THE FUNNY HEAD!
MOM CAN I GET MY EAR PIERCED?
NOT NOW.
I'll TALK TO HER KID.
I THOUGHT YOU'D LOVE ME IN SICKNESS AND IN HEALTH?
I GUESS WE'RE STUCK WITH EACH OTHER.
LETS GO GET THAT HANDICAPPED DECAL!
CLIENTS JUST DON'T GET IT, IT'S NOT WHAT YOU MAKE, IT'S WHAT YOU KEEP.
SNIPE
MY STOMACH'S KILLING ME. WHEN'S MY NEXT BODY, I MEAN CLIENT.
THE END

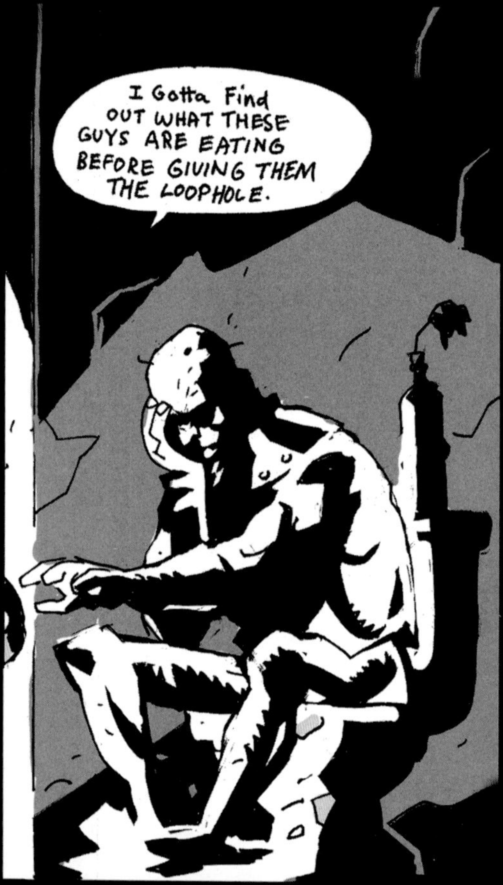
I Gotta Find OUT WHAT THESE GUYS ARE EATING BEFORE GIVING THEM THE LOOPHOLE.

max brace

MAX BRACE in:

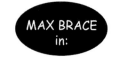

SUDDEN CHOLECYSTECTOMY!!

(A.K.A. SUDDEN GALLBLADDER SURGERY!!)

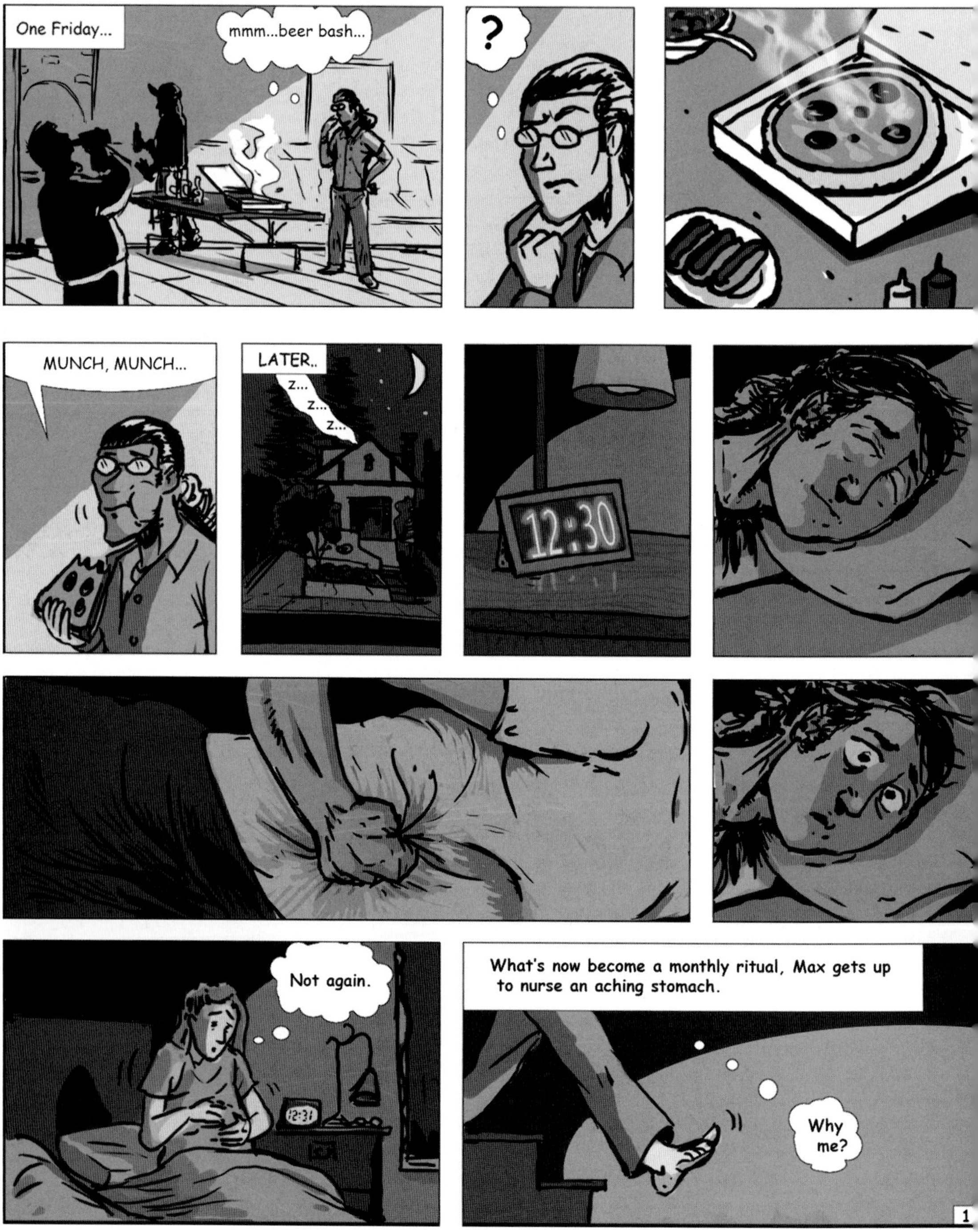
One Friday...
mmm...beer bash...
?
MUNCH, MUNCH...
LATER..
z...
z...
z...
12:30
Not again.
12:31
What's now become a monthly ritual, Max gets up to nurse an aching stomach.
Why me?

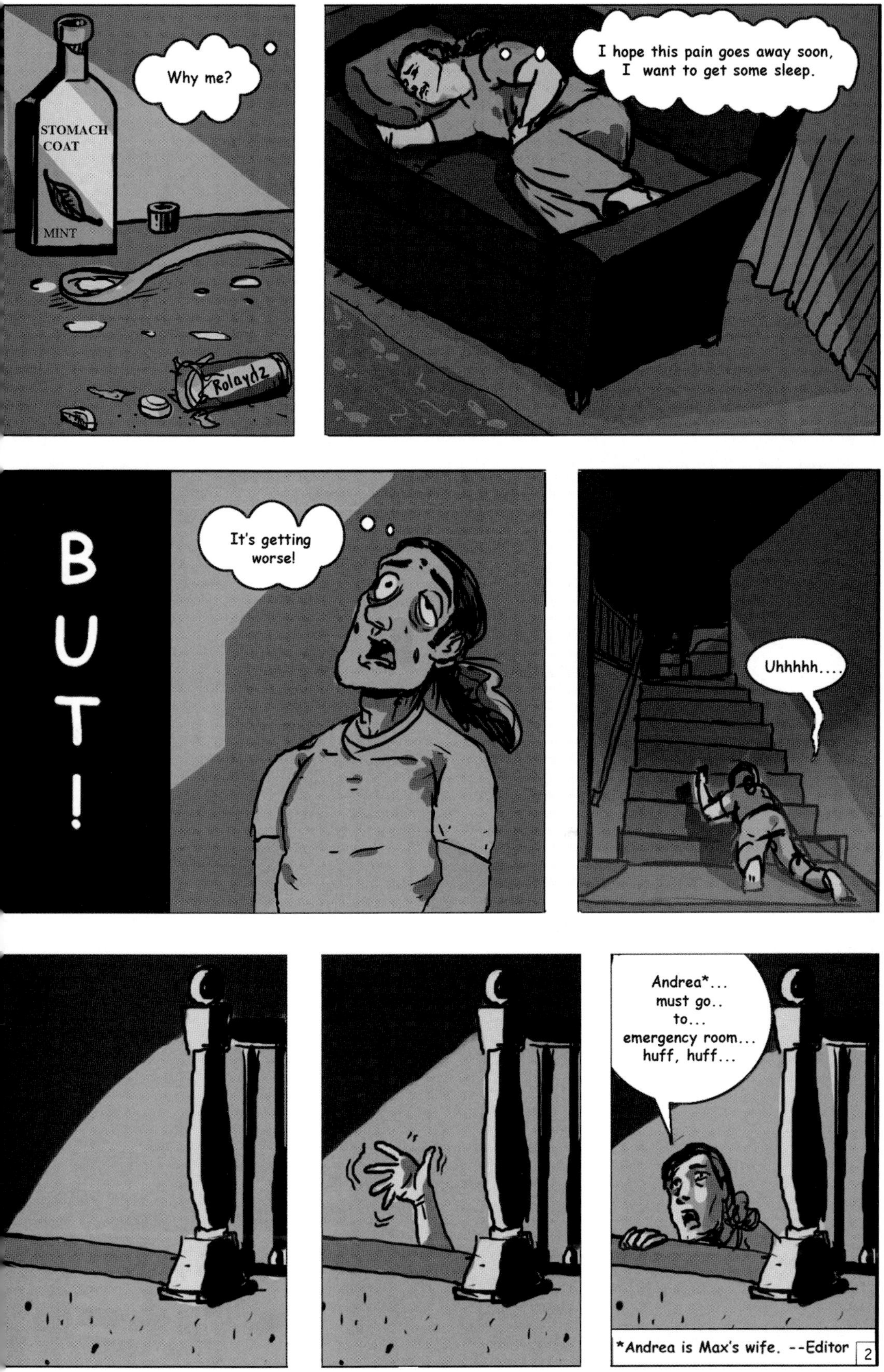
STOMACH COAT
MINT
Why me?
Rolaydz
I hope this pain goes away soon, I want to get some sleep.
BUT!
It's getting worse!
Uhhhhh....
Andrea*... must go.. to... emergency room... huff, huff...
*Andrea is Max's wife. --Editor

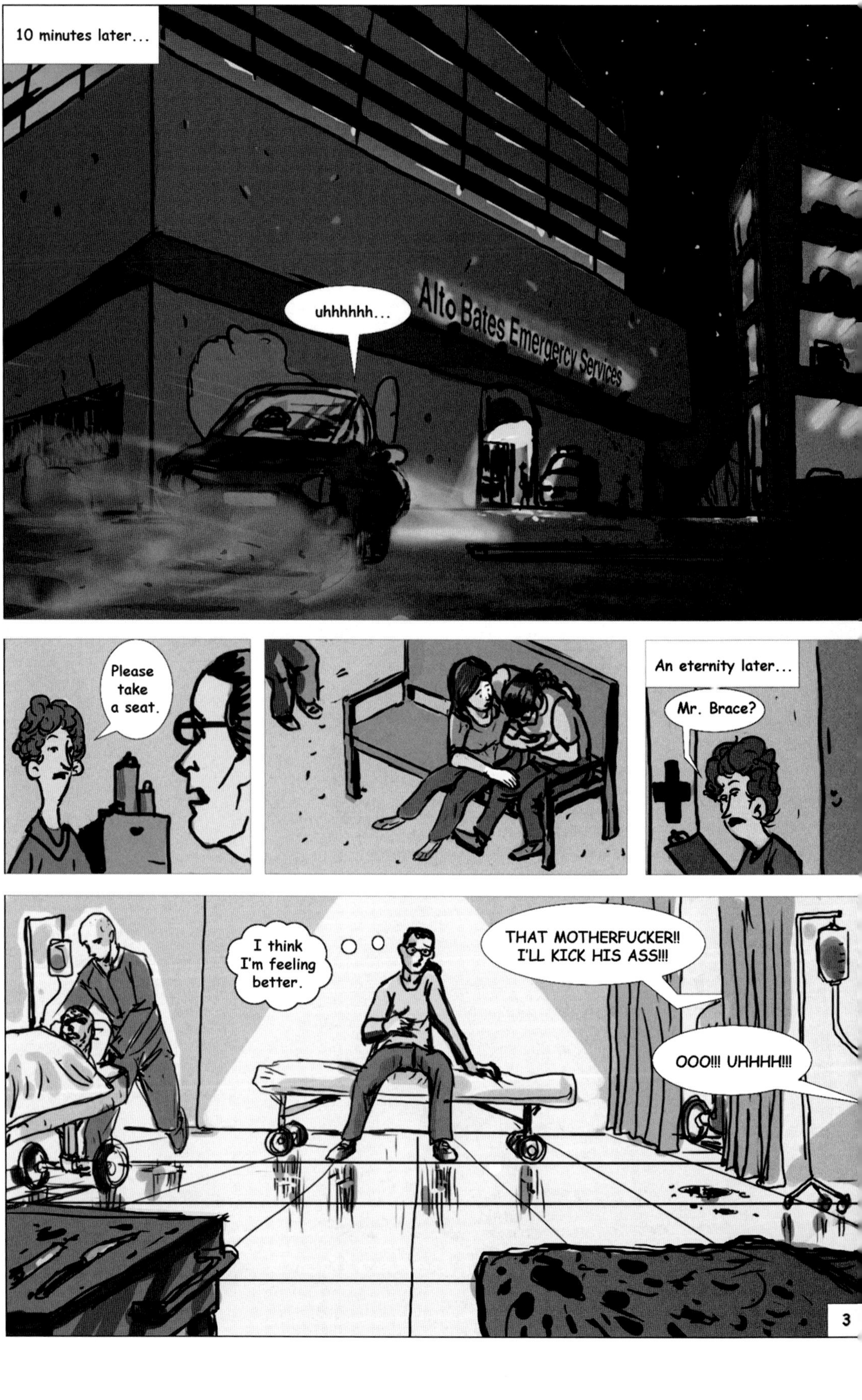
10 minutes later...
uhhhhhh...
Alto Bates Emergency Services
Please take a seat.
An eternity later...
Mr. Brace?
I think I'm feeling better.
THAT MOTHERFUCKER!! I'LL KICK HIS ASS!!!
OOO!!! UHHHH!!!

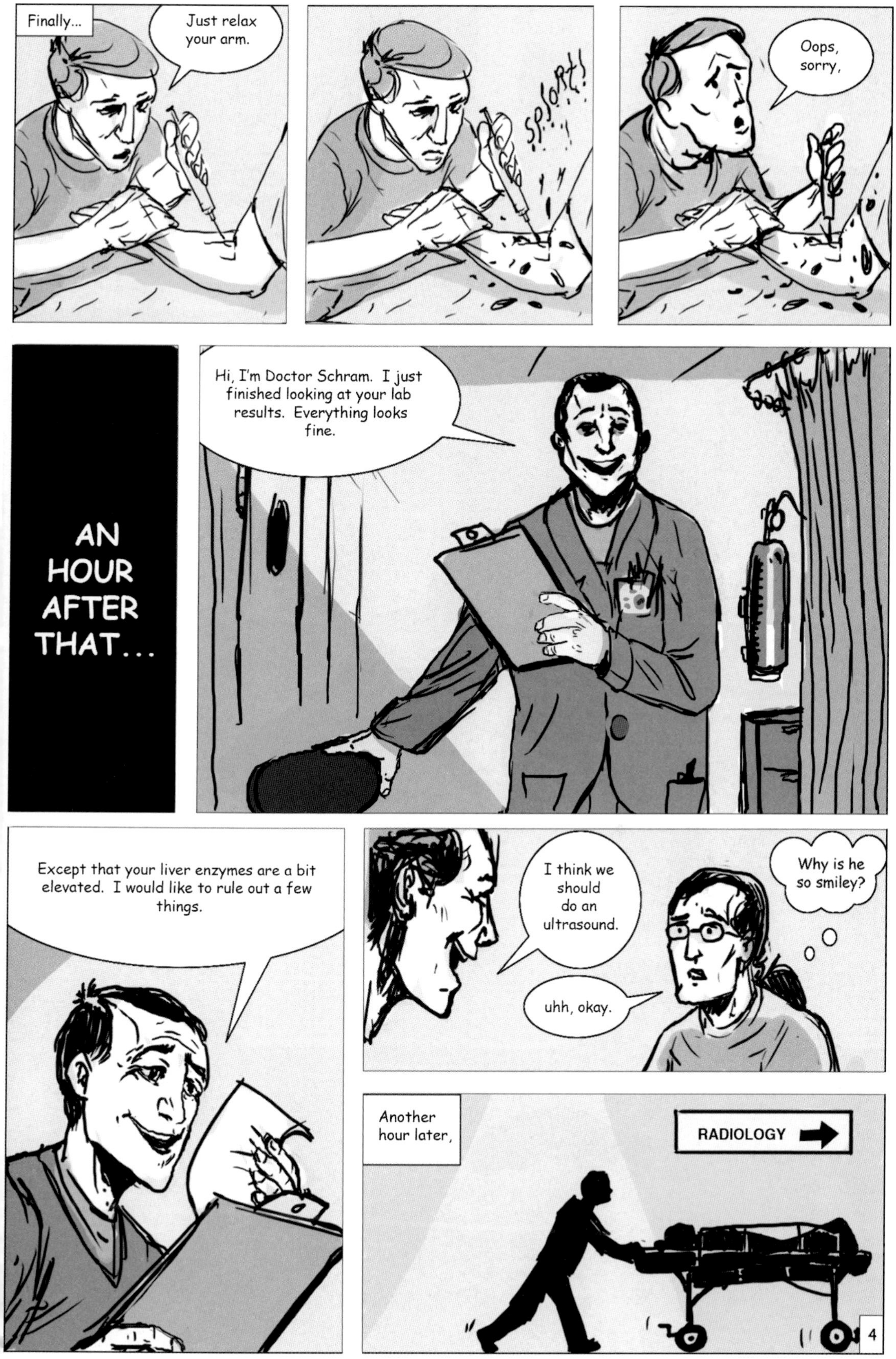

Finally...
Just relax your arm.
SPSORT!
Oops, sorry,
AN HOUR AFTER THAT...
Hi, I'm Doctor Schram. I just finished looking at your lab results. Everything looks fine.
Except that your liver enzymes are a bit elevated. I would like to rule out a few things.
I think we should do an ultrasound.
Why is he so smiley?
uhh, okay.
Another hour later,
RADIOLOGY

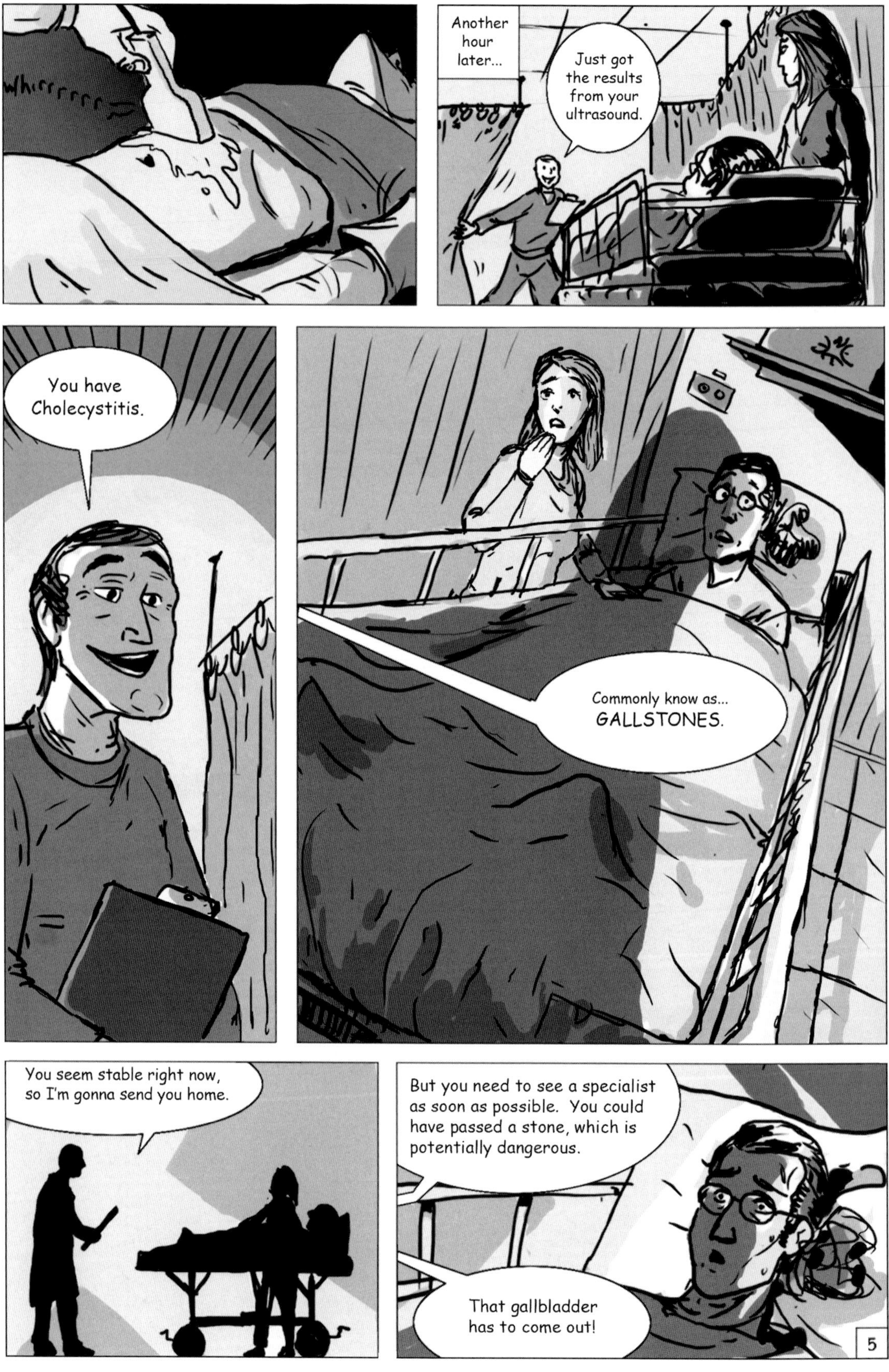
whirrrrrr
Another hour later...
Just got the results from your ultrasound.
You have Cholecystitis.
Commonly know as... GALLSTONES.
You seem stable right now, so I'm gonna send you home.
But you need to see a specialist as soon as possible. You could have passed a stone, which is potentially dangerous.
That gallbladder has to come out!

Two days later...

My eyes are all yellow!

That's because you have a blockage in your bile duct.

At the surgeon's office...

You probably passed a stone when you went to the emergency room, hence the incredible pain you were in. The bile you are now secreting is now going into your bloodstream. This is why you have yellow eyes.

I don't understand.

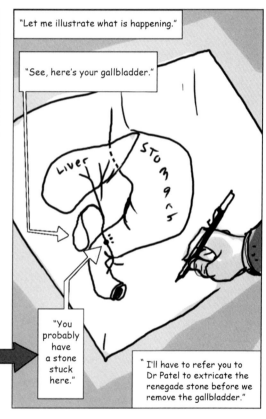

"Let me illustrate what is happening."

"See, here's your gallbladder."

Liver STOmach

"You probably have a stone stuck here."

" I'll have to refer you to Dr Patel to extricate the renegade stone before we remove the gallbladder."

So this is a pretty routine procedure, right?

Son, there's nothing routine about gallbladder surgery...

ever.

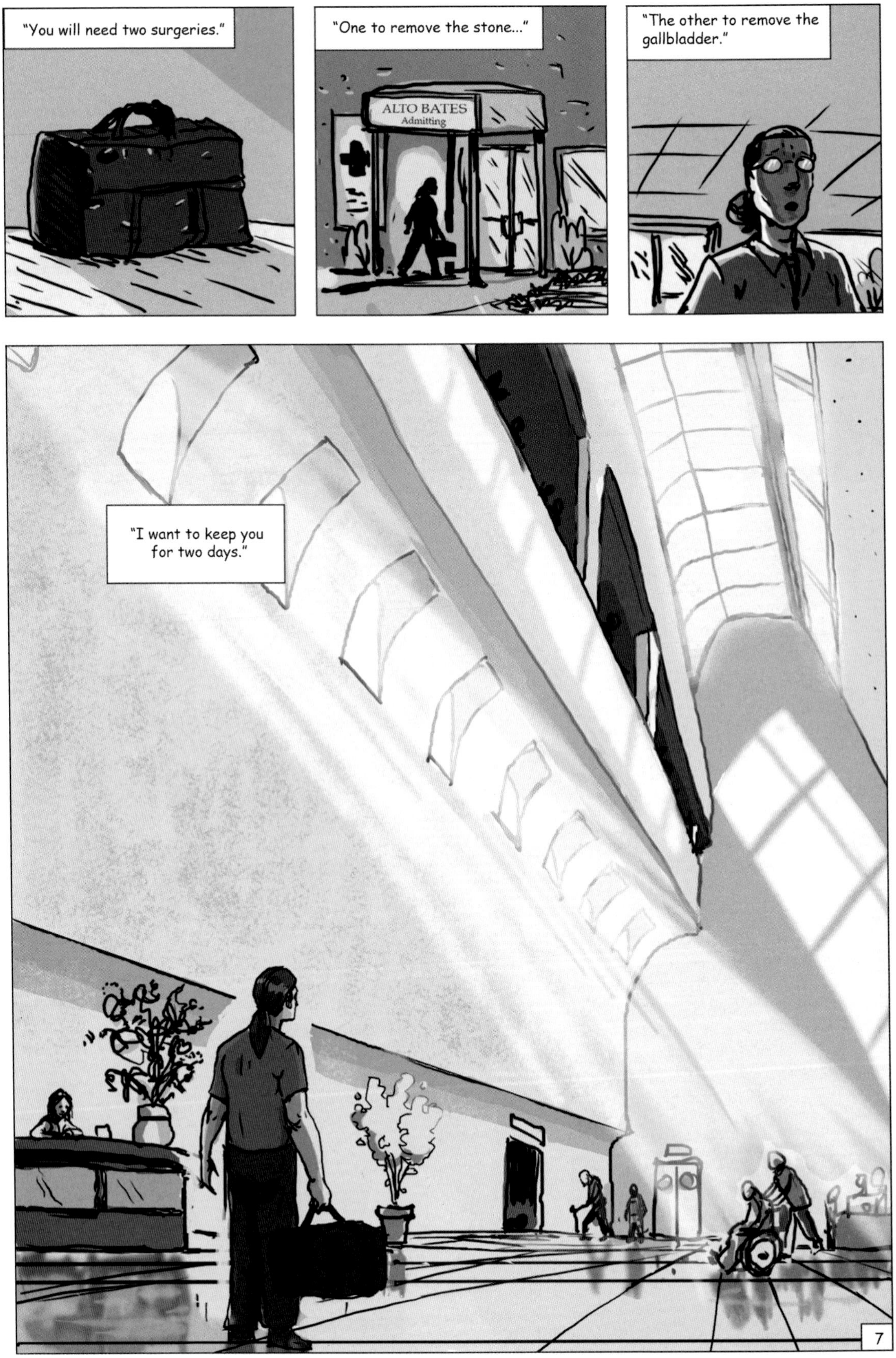
"You will need two surgeries."
"One to remove the stone..."
ALTO BATES
Admitting
"The other to remove the gallbladder."
"I want to keep you for two days."

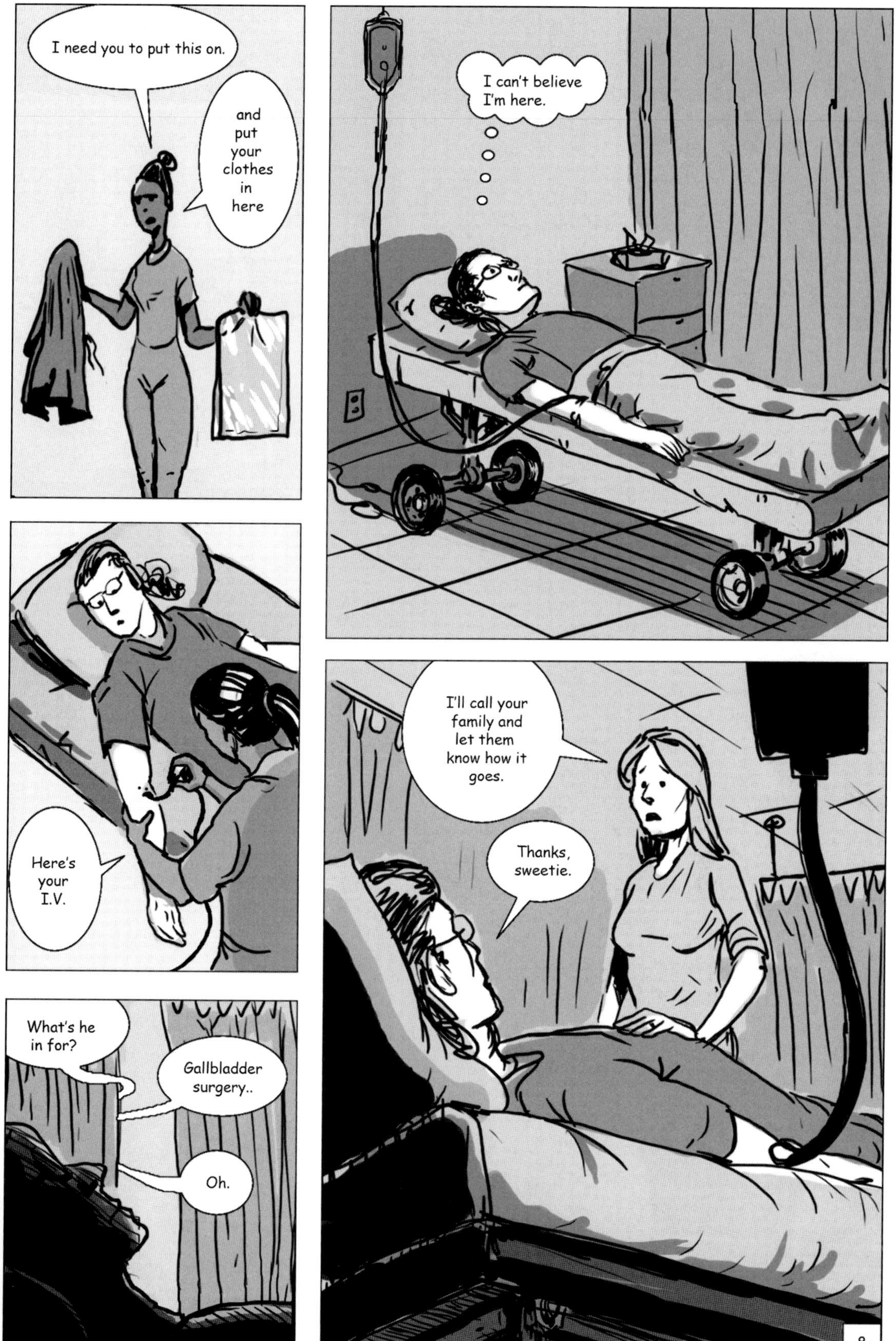
I need you to put this on.
and put your clothes in here
I can't believe I'm here.
Here's your I.V.
I'll call your family and let them know how it goes.
Thanks, sweetie.
What's he in for?
Gallbladder surgery..
Oh.

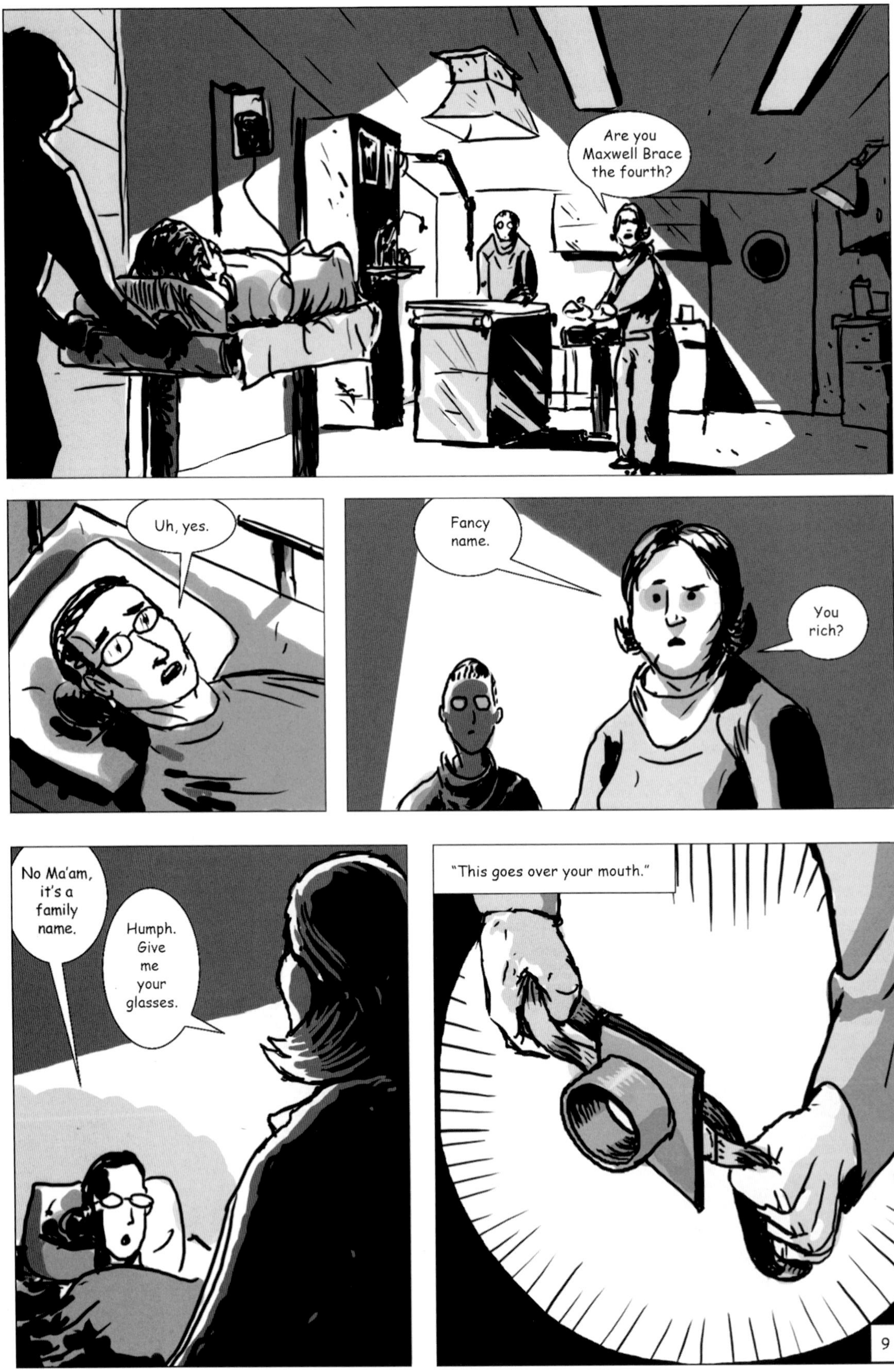
Are you Maxwell Brace the fourth?
Uh, yes.
Fancy name.
You rich?
No Ma'am, it's a family name.
Humph. Give me your glasses.
"This goes over your mouth."

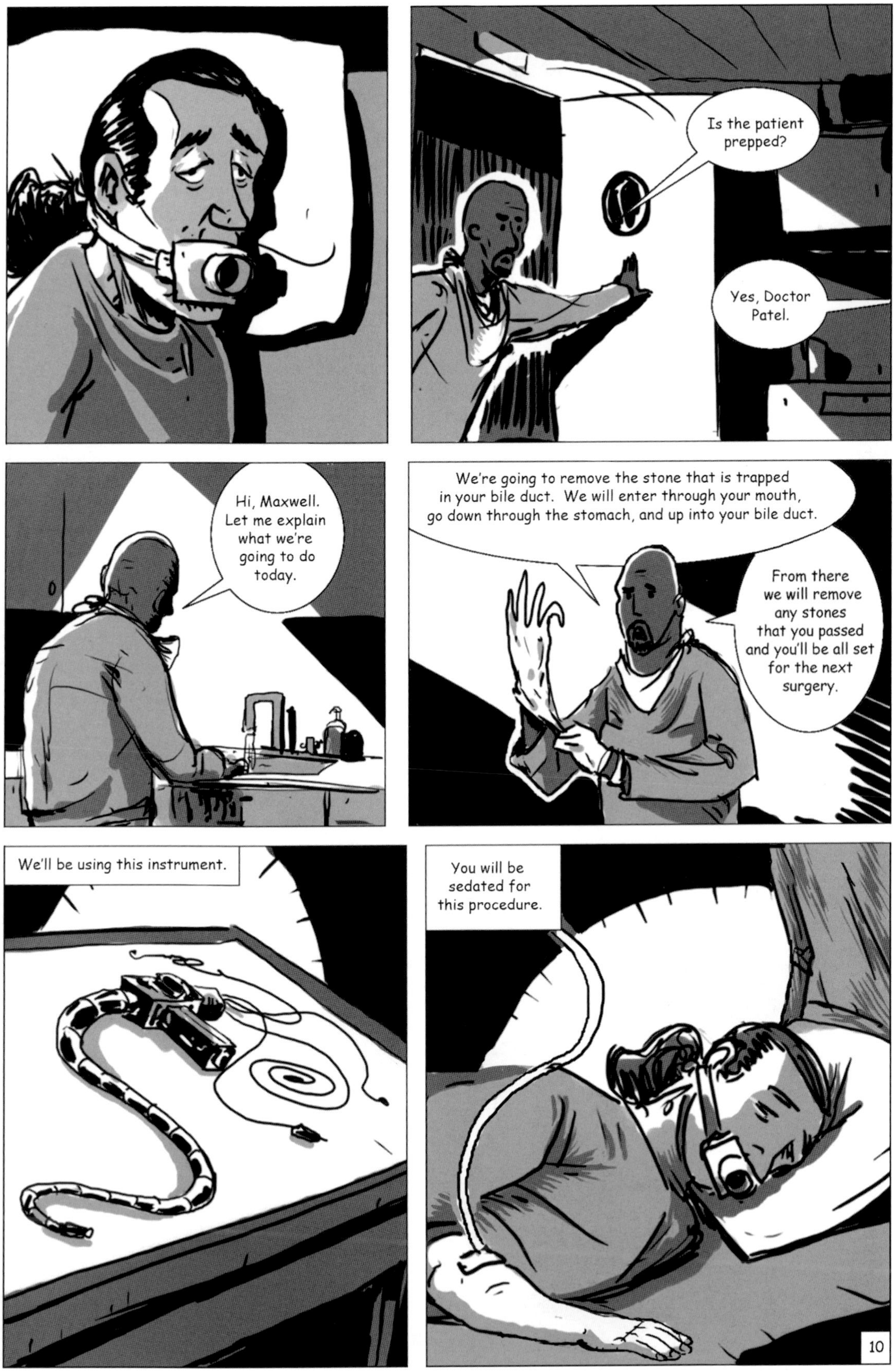
Is the patient prepped?
Yes, Doctor Patel.
Hi, Maxwell. Let me explain what we're going to do today.
We're going to remove the stone that is trapped in your bile duct. We will enter through your mouth, go down through the stomach, and up into your bile duct.
From there we will remove any stones that you passed and you'll be all set for the next surgery.
We'll be using this instrument.
You will be sedated for this procedure.
10

But unfortunately...

GAG!

Breathe slowly, Max!

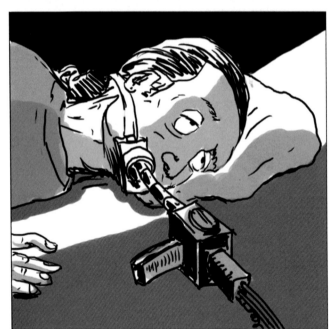

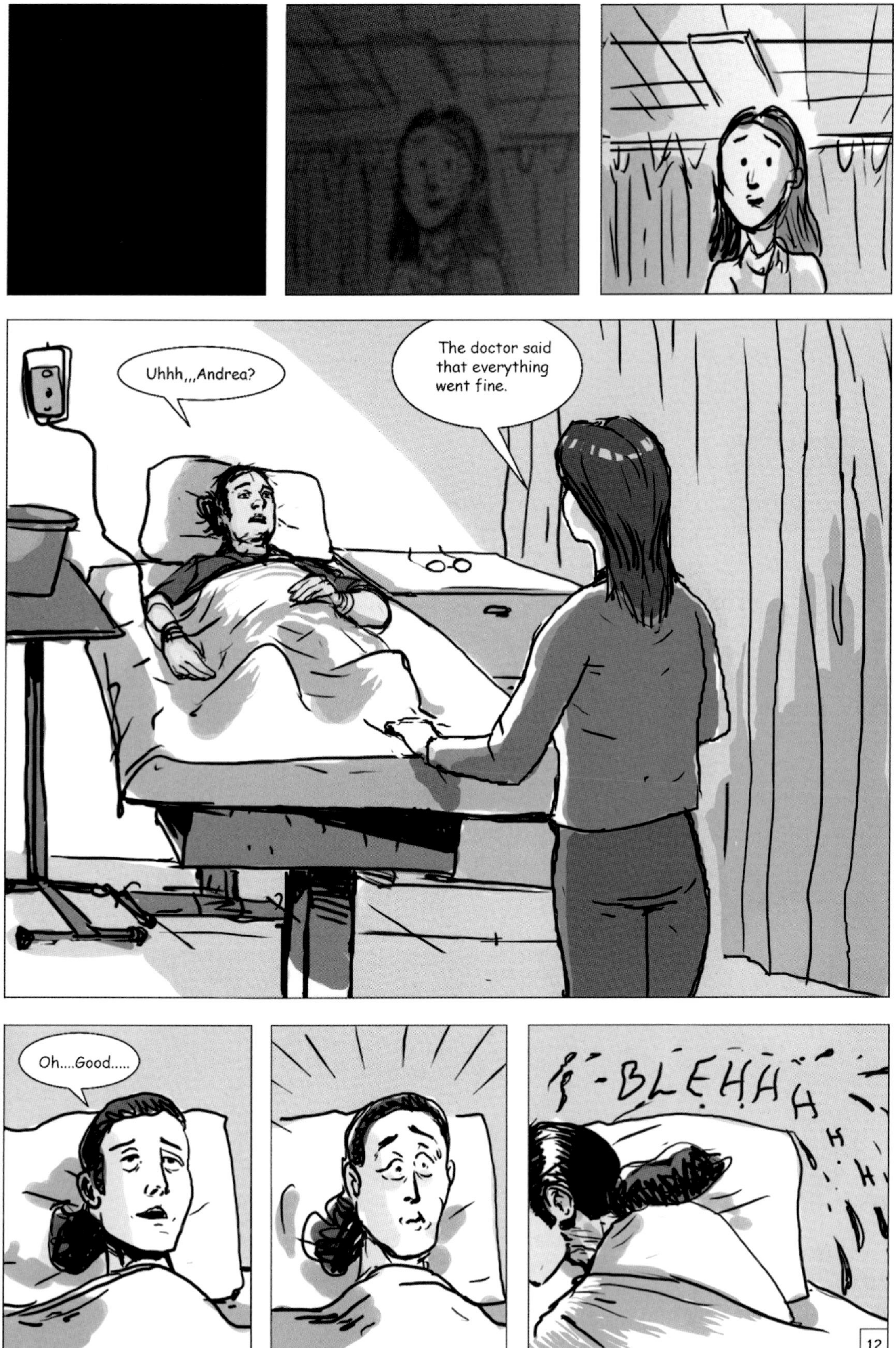

Uhhh,,,Andrea?
The doctor said that everything went fine.
Oh....Good.....
BLEHHH

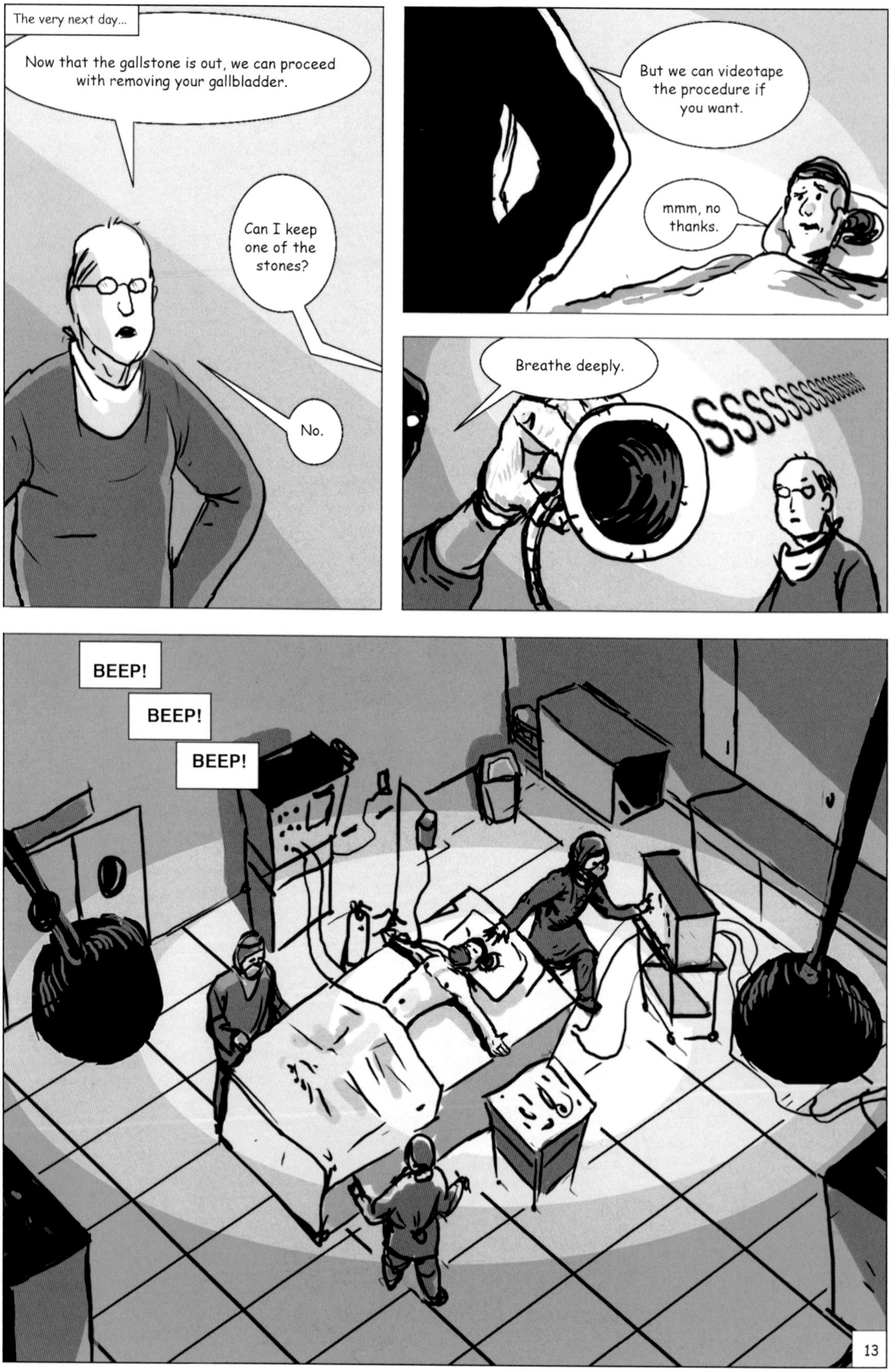
The very next day...
Now that the gallstone is out, we can proceed with removing your gallbladder.
Can I keep one of the stones?
No.
But we can videotape the procedure if you want.
mmm, no thanks.
Breathe deeply.
SSSSSSSSSSSSSSS
BEEP!
BEEP!
BEEP!

BEEP...

BEEP...

BEEP...

BEEP

Oh good,
you're awake.

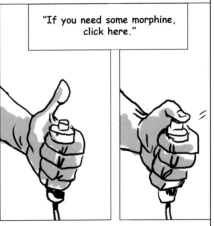

"If you need some morphine,
click here."

Ahhhhh...relief.

ZZZZZZZZZZZZZZZZ.....

14

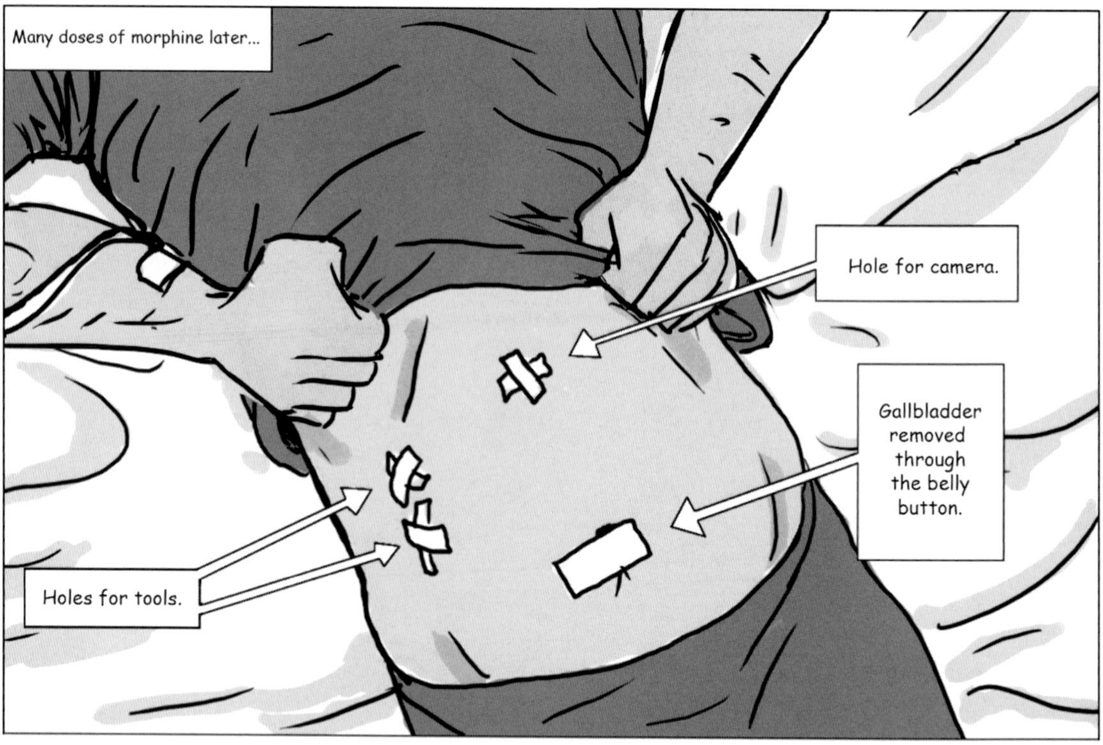
Many doses of morphine later...
Hole for camera.
Gallbladder removed through the belly button.
Holes for tools.

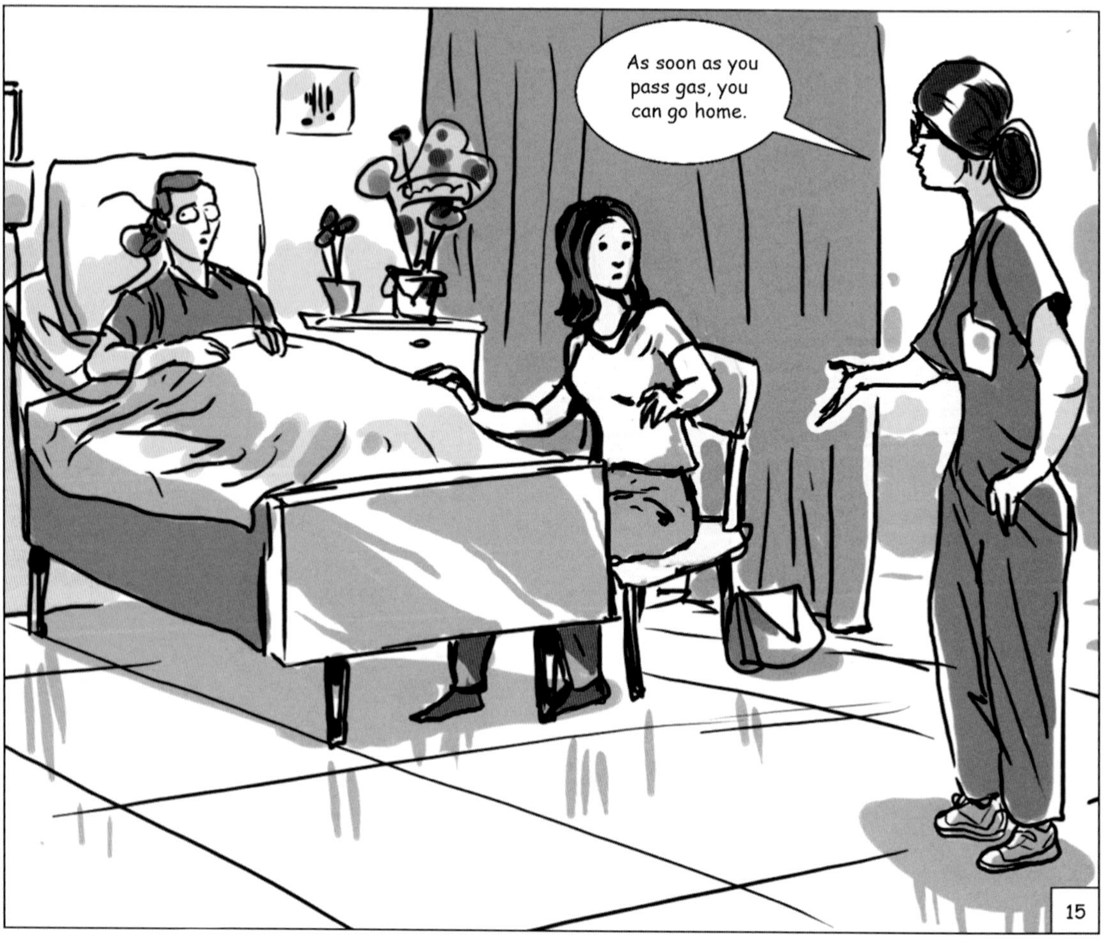
As soon as you pass gas, you can go home.

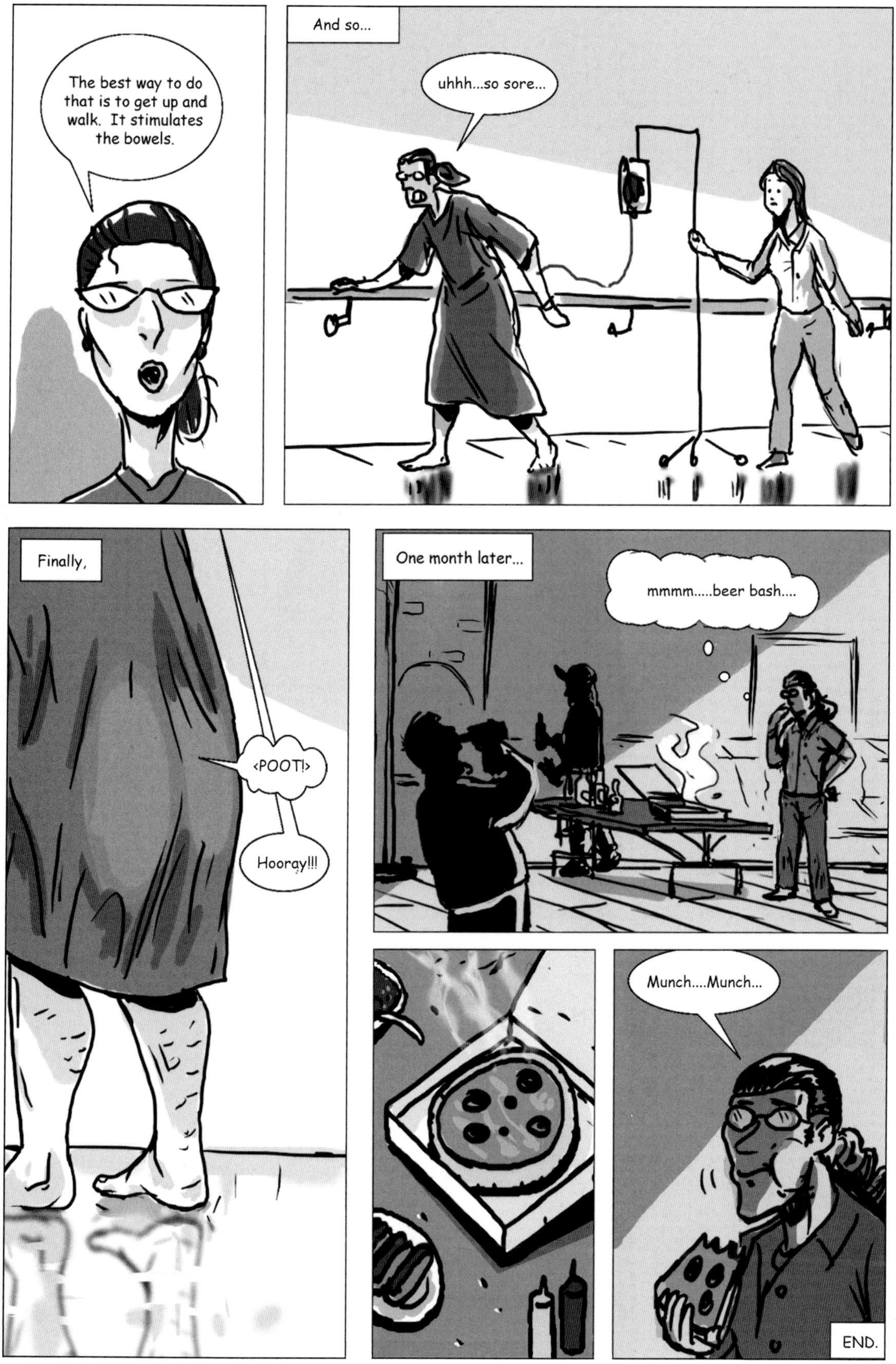
The best way to do that is to get up and walk. It stimulates the bowels.
And so...
uhhh...so sore...
Finally,
<POOT!>
Hooray!!!
One month later...
mmmm.....beer bash....
Munch....Munch...
END.

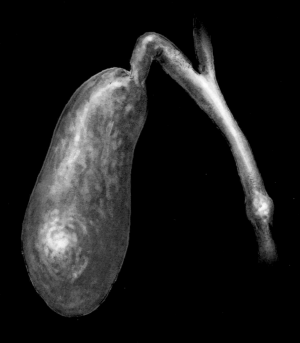

Dedicated to AVP

When not under the knife, **Max Brace** works at Pixar Animation Studios as a storyboard artist. He has a story credit on every film the studio has released since "A Bug's Life". In his spare time, Max is an avid landscape painter and enjoys spending time with his wife and newborn son. Max lives in Oakland, California and now enjoys eating whatever he wants. For more info, please visit www.MaxBrace.com

Simon Dunsdon completed a traditional UK Art School education, gained his Degree in Theatre Design and Pubs, then spent a few sticky years as a model-maker for Film and TV. Tired of smelling of fiberglass, he rekindled an old romance with Computers and was soon producing CG Design and VFX for 'proper movies'. Some of which even had proper money. After escaping rainy London for a spell at childhood nirvana Skywalker Ranch, a door opened at Pixar where he currently resides under the deceptively fancy sounding catch-all title of a "Technical Director". He enjoys working, drinking tea and writing in the third person.

Born and Raised in the San Fernando Valley, **Louis Gonzales** stumbled into the animation industry and has managed to stay employed there for 8+ years by looking extremely busy. He recently entered the self publishing world with his debut sketchbook "Dumping Gounds vol.1". With other self-published projects in the works he now tries to find time drink Southern Comfort. To see more, visit his website www.louisgonzales.com

Robert Kondo went to school at the Art Center in Pasadena and luckily found a job in the animation industry designing. He enjoys foosball and eating, and loves when he can do both at the same time. A website is in the works, but for now, visit: www.homepage.mac.com/rkkondo

Kevin O'Brien was born and bred in suburban New Jersey. He went to art school at Pratt Institute in Brooklyn. In 1990 a tornado picked up his Bedford-Stuyvesant apartment and dropped it on a witch in Hollywood, CA. There, he became a storyboard artist on "The Simpsons", "Futurama", "Iron Giant", "Ice Age", "The Incredibles", and others. He likes reading about science, history, and anything to do with the space program. He enjoys long walks on the beach and Burning Man. He lives with his lovely wife, Mercelle, and two cats: Cornelius and Dr. Zaius.

Sanjay Patel "Loopholes" is my first comic. The idea of doing a story about taxes stems from the fact that my wife was studying to become an accountant. My problem was trying to make the subject matter fun to draw. While drawing locations from travel books on Italy, I found a wonderful Caravaggio painting depicting a woman carrying a severed head on a silver platter. This gruesome image seemed to contrast perfectly with the mundane world of taxes. The head on a silver platter seemed to suggest a character that was bitter from being decapitated and a perfect antagonist for the average Joe getting their taxes prepared. This also became a really fun character to draw. From there, the rest just fell into place.
Currently, I am working at Pixar as an animator and story board artist.
To see more work, visit www.gheehappy.com/

Nathan Stanton was born and raised in Rockport, Massachusetts where he spent most of his scholastic years drawing in the back of the classroom. In 1992 he graduated from the California Institute of the Arts in lovely Valencia, California and promptly made his way to Northern California. He got his first job in 1993 on "Nightmare Before Christmas" as an Assistant 2D Animator. He then worked all over San Francisco as an Assistant Animator for Danger Productions, Skellington Productions, Wild Brain and Colossal Pictures. In 1996 he settled down as a Storyboard Artist at Pixar Animation Studios, where he continues to work today. This is Nathan's first comic book, but certainly not his last.

A collective thank you from the artists of Afterworks to Pixar Animation Studios.

Visit us online at evillepress.com